THE BIBLE, JUSTICE AND PUBLIC THEOLOGY

The Bible in the Modern World, 63

Series Editors
J. Cheryl Exum, Jorunn Økland, Stephen D. Moore

Editorial Board
Alastair G. Hunter, Alison Jasper, Tat-siong Benny Liew,
Hugh Pyper, Caroline Vander Stichele

The Bible, Justice and Public Theology

Edited by
David J. Neville

WIPF & STOCK · Eugene, Oregon

Wipf and Stock Publishers
199 W 8th Ave, Suite 3
Eugene, OR 97401

The Bible, Justice and Public Theology
By Neville, David J.
Copyright©2014 Sheffield Phoenix Press
ISBN 13: 978-1-4982-0775-1
Publication date 9/23/2014
Previously published by Sheffield Phoenix Press, 2014

Contents

Preface and Acknowledgments	vii
Abbreviations	ix
Contributors	xiii

THE BIBLE, JUSTICE AND PUBLIC THEOLOGY:
AN INTRODUCTORY ESSAY
   David J. Neville   1

PARABLES AS PARADIGMS FOR PUBLIC THEOLOGY
   Christopher D. Marshall   23

LUKE'S GOSPEL ECONOMICS OF RESTORATIVE JUSTICE
   Merrill Kitchen   45

STOP, TAKE, CARE: READING LUKE 10.25-37 WITH ISLANDERS
IN PRISON
   Jione Havea   59

MAKING PUBLIC THEOLOGY MORE BIBLICAL OR BIBLICAL
THEOLOGY MORE PUBLIC? CHRISTOPHER MARSHALL'S
INTERPRETATION OF THE PARABLE OF THE PRODIGAL SON
IN LUKE 15
   Geoff Broughton   72

'BEYOND REASONABLE DOUBT'? AN EXPLORATION OF
THE HERMENEUTICS OF ENGAGEMENT FOR JUSTICE
   Helen-Ann Hartley   88

PROPHETS PERFORMING AS PUBLIC THEOLOGIANS
   Jeanette Mathews   101

RESURRECTION AND JUSTICE
   Thorwald Lorenzen   114

JUSTICE AND GENDER: ON FEMINIST THEOLOGY AND
RESTORATIVE JUSTICE
    Heather Thomson   133

PARABLE AS PARADIGM FOR PUBLIC THEOLOGY:
RELATING THEOLOGICAL VISION TO SOCIAL LIFE
    David J. Neville   145

JUSTICE: THIN PRAGMATISM BETWEEN THICK PRACTICES
    Philip J. Matthews   161

PUBLIC THEOLOGY THROUGH POPULAR CULTURE
    Stephen Garner   175

Bibliography   191
Index of References   205
Index of Authors   210

PREFACE AND ACKNOWLEDGMENTS

This collection of studies came together in response to a landmark work by Christopher Marshall entitled *Compassionate Justice: An Interdisciplinary Dialogue with Two Gospel Parables on Law, Crime, and Restorative Justice* (Cascade Books, 2012). Marshall, a New Testament scholar with both theoretical expertise and practical experience in restorative justice, had earlier published *Beyond Retribution: A New Testament Vision for Justice, Crime, and Punishment* (Eerdmans, 2001), in which he appraised biblical texts relating to crime and punishment in light of restorative justice theory. With these two books and other related studies, Marshall has established himself as a leading authority on biblical resources for restorative justice theory and practice—or, as he might prefer to put it, a facilitator of dialogue between biblical texts and current legal and criminal justice theory. He now holds a sponsored research chair in Restorative Justice at Victoria University of Wellington in Aotearoa New Zealand.

Upon learning of the publication of *Compassionate Justice*, the idea soon formed that it would be a valuable exercise to gather together a group of scholars from a variety of theological subdisciplines to discuss pertinent issues arising from this book. From the outset, Marshall expressed interest in the project and duly set aside time to participate in a seminar on the Bible, justice and public theology to be held in Canberra over a weekend at the end of May and beginning of June 2013. My first thanks, then, go to Chris Marshall, who wears his learning lightly and participated in the seminar as if he had as much to learn from everyone else as they from him.

The seminar was held under the auspices of two Canberra-based focus groups within Charles Sturt University's Public and Contextual Theology Research Centre, principally the Scripture and Public Theology focus group in tandem with the focus group concerned with Christianity and Australian Society. University funding through its Public and Contextual Theology Research Centre covered Marshall's travel and accommodation costs, accommodation for other presenters from Aotearoa New Zealand and elsewhere in Australia, and also meals for all seminar participants, which included scholars from several universities, postgraduate, postdoctoral and independent researchers, as well as clergy and mission agents.

The seminar program began on the afternoon of Friday, 31 May, and concluded after lunch on Sunday, 2 June 2013. During that time draft versions of most of the essays contained in this volume were presented and discussed. The seminar opened with Chris Marshall's paper and ended with his reflections on all the other presentations. On the Friday evening he also gave a public lecture entitled 'Violence, Victimhood and Recovery: On "Doing" Eternal Life', with a response by Terry O'Connell.

Crucial to the success of the seminar were both the hospitality and assistance of the staff of the Australian Centre for Christianity and Culture: the then Executive Director, Professor James Haire, the incomparable Centre Manager, Margaret Roberts, and also Lyndon Mayfield (for technical assistance). I should also like to thank several other people for their support and assistance: Heather Thomson and Geoff Broughton, teaching colleagues who not only participated in the seminar but also served as my informal advisors; Jeanette Mathews and Steve Bevis for leading worship; Hazel Francis and Julia Bell of St Mark's National Theological Centre for administrative assistance; and Miriam Bruning for catering arrangements. Finally, to all who contributed directly to the seminar, whether as presenters or as engaged participants, I here record my gratitude.

David Neville
February 2014

ABBREVIATIONS

Bible

Gen.	Genesis
Exod.	Exodus
Lev.	Leviticus
Num.	Numbers
Deut.	Deuteronomy
Josh.	Joshua
Judg.	Judges
1 or 2 Sam.	1 or 2 Samuel
1 or 2 Kgs	1 or 2 Kings
1 or 2 Chron.	1 or 2 Chronicles
Neh.	Nehemiah
Est.	Esther
Ps(s).	Psalm(s)
Prov.	Proverbs
Eccl.	Ecclesiastes
Song	Song of Songs
Isa.	Isaiah
Jer.	Jeremiah
Lam.	Lamentations
Ezek.	Ezekiel
Dan.	Daniel
Hos.	Hosea
Obad.	Obadiah
Jon.	Jonah
Mic.	Micah
Nah.	Nahum
Hab.	Habakkuk
Zeph.	Zephaniah
Hag.	Haggai
Zech.	Zechariah
Mal.	Malachi
Mt.	Matthew
Mk	Mark
Lk.	Luke
Jn	John
Rom.	Romans
1 or 2 Cor.	1 or 2 Corinthians
Gal.	Galatians

Eph.	Ephesians
Phil.	Philippians
Col.	Colossians
1 or 2 Thess.	1 or 2 Thessalonians
1 or 2 Tim.	1 or 2 Timothy
Tit.	Titus
Phlm.	Philemon
Heb.	Hebrews
Jas	James
1 or 2 Pet.	1 or 2 Peter
1 or 2 or 3 Jn	1 or 2 or 3 John
Rev.	Revelation

Apocrypha and Pseudepigrapha

Wis.	Wisdom
Sir.	Sirach
1 or 2 Macc.	1 or 2 Maccabees
Pss. Sol.	*Psalms of Solomon*
T. Ash.	*Testament of Asher*
T. Jud.	*Testament of Judah*
T. Levi	*Testament of Levi*

Other Ancient Literature

Ant.	Josephus, *Antiquities of the Jews*
War	Josephus, *The Jewish War*

Periodicals and Reference Works

AusBR	*Australian Biblical Review*
BBR	*Bulletin for Biblical Research*
BibInt	*Biblical Interpretation: A Journal of Contemporary Approaches*
BTB	*Biblical Theology Bulletin*
CBQ	*Catholic Biblical Quarterly*
EJT	*European Journal of Theology*
ExpTim	*The Expository Times*
FemTh	*Feminist Theology*
IJPT	*International Journal of Public Theology*
IJST	*International Journal of Systematic Theology*
Interpretation	*Interpretation: A Journal of Bible and Theology*
JBL	*Journal of Biblical Literature*
JR	*Journal of Religion*
JRE	*Journal of Religious Ethics*
JSCE	*Journal of the Society of Christian Ethics*
JSNT	*Journal for the Study of the New Testament*
JSNTSup	*Journal for the Study of the New Testament*, Supplement Series
KJV	King James Version

LCC	Library of Christian Classics
MQR	*Mennonite Quarterly Review*
NEB	New English Bible
NIV	New International Version
NJPS	New Jewish Publication Society
NovT	*Novum Testamentum*
NRSV	New Revised Standard Version
PT	*Political Theology*
RevExp	*Review and Expositor*
RSV	Revised Standard Version
SBL	Society of Biblical Literature
SCE	*Studies in Christian Ethics*
TynBul	*Tyndale Bulletin*
WW	*Word & World: Theology for Christian Ministry*
ZAW	*Zeitschrift für die alttestamentliche Wissenschaft*

CONTRIBUTORS

Geoff Broughton is an Anglican priest in the inner city of Sydney, the Deputy Director of St Mark's National Theological Centre in Canberra and lecturer in practical theology within the School of Theology of Charles Sturt University. His doctoral research explored resources within Luke–Acts for developing an integrated Christology for restorative justice theory and practice. He has authored articles on Luke's Gospel, restorative justice and Christian engagement in inner-city contexts. His first book, *Restorative Christ: Jesus, Justice, and Discipleship*, is forthcoming from Pickwick Publications.

Stephen Garner is Head of the School of Theology, Mission and Ministry at Laidlaw College in Auckland, Aotearoa New Zealand. Prior to this he was Lecturer in Theology at the University of Auckland. He holds an MSc in computer science and a PhD in theology, and he teaches primarily in the area of practical theology, including theological ethics, spirituality, public and contextual theology, and religion and popular culture. His research interests include religion and popular culture, theology and the new media, and theological anthropology in dialogue with new technologies.

Helen-Ann Hartley is the Bishop of Waikato, Diocese of Waikato and Taranaki, Aotearoa New Zealand. At the time of writing, Helen-Ann was the Dean of the New Zealand Dioceses at the College of St John the Evangelist in Auckland, Aotearoa New Zealand. Prior to moving to Auckland in February 2012, she was Lecturer in New Testament and Director of Biblical Studies at Ripon College Cuddesdon and an associate member of the Theology Faculty of Oxford University. Helen-Ann has also been a member of the 'Theological Education in the Anglican Communion' group. She is the author of *Making Sense of the Bible* (SPCK, 2011).

Jione Havea is a native of Tonga who teaches biblical studies at United Theological College and School of Theology, Charles Sturt University. Jione studies biblical texts with islanders at Parklea Prison (NSW) and has presented some of their insights in 'Lazarus troubles', in *Bible Trouble: Queer Reading at the Boundaries of Biblical Scholarship* (ed. Ken Stone and Holly Toensing; Atlanta: SBL, 2011), pp. 157-73, and also in

'The bible on postmodern surfaces', in *Ecumenical Directions in the United States Today: Churches on a Theological Journey* (ed. Antonios Kireopoulos with Juliana Mecera; New York: Paulist Press, 2012), pp. 172-89.

Merrill Kitchen OAM is an ordained minister of Churches of Christ in Australia. She was initially trained as a Medical Scientist and worked in hospitals in Melbourne and Israel/Palestine. On her return to Australia she engaged in theological studies while teaching tertiary students in the health sciences. Her postgraduate theological studies have been in the areas of social, political and cultural readings of the New Testament. At the end of 2009 she retired after ten years as Dean of the Evangelical Theological Association and a further ten years as Principal of the Churches of Christ Theological College in Melbourne. During that time she participated in the governing body of the Melbourne College of Divinity, serving as its President in 2004–2005. In 2011 she was appointed a Fellow of The University of Divinity (Melbourne). She is the author of several studies on the Gospels, discipleship and social justice, some of which have been published in Arabic.

Thorwald Lorenzen was the Senior Minister of the Canberra Baptist Church. Before that, for over twenty years, he was Professor of Systematic Theology and Social Ethics at the International Baptist Theological Seminary in Rüschlikon, Switzerland. He has been a member and the chair of the Human Rights Commission of the Baptist World Alliance for twenty years. He is now retired but is engaged as Professor of Theology and Principal Researcher with St Mark's National Theological Centre and Charles Sturt University, and he teaches regularly at Whitley College, University of Melbourne. His publications include *Resurrection and Discipleship: Interpretive Models, Biblical Reflections, Theological Consequences* (Orbis Books, 1995; reprinted in 2004 by Wipf and Stock); *Resurrection – Discipleship – Justice: Affirming the Resurrection of Jesus Christ Today* (Smyth & Helwys, 2003); and *Toward a Culture of Freedom: Reflections on the Ten Commandments Today* (Cascade Books, 2008).

Christopher Marshall is Professor of Restorative Justice at Victoria University of Wellington, Aotearoa New Zealand. He is the author of many articles and several books, including *Beyond Retribution: A New Testament Vision for Justice, Crime, and Punishment* (Eerdmans, 2001), *The Little Book of Biblical Justice* (Good Books, 2005), and, most recently, *Compassionate Justice: An Interdisciplinary Dialogue with Two Gospel Parables on Law, Crime, and Restorative Justice* (Cascade Books, 2012).

Jeanette Mathews is a lecturer in Old Testament and Biblical Hebrew at the School of Theology of Charles Sturt University, based at St Mark's National Theological Centre in Canberra. She is an ordained Baptist minister and researches in the area of Biblical Performance Criticism. The author of *Performing Habakkuk: Faithful Re-enactment in the Midst of Crisis* (Pickwick Publications, 2012), she is committed to upholding, transmitting and improvising the biblical traditions in all their wondrous diversity for new settings in our own times and places.

Philip Matthews is Associate Dean in the School of Philosophy and Theology at the Fremantle campus of the University of Notre Dame Australia. His doctoral work focused on moral enquiry in a pluralist context, and he is the author of various essays relating to ethics and law. He is also co-editor of *Faith and Freedom: Christian Ethics in a Pluralist Context* (ATF Press, 2003).

David Neville teaches biblical studies at St Mark's National Theological Centre, the Canberra campus of the School of Theology of Charles Sturt University (CSU). He also convenes a focus group on scripture and public theology within CSU's Public and Contextual Theology Research Centre. Alongside journal articles on the Bible, justice and public theology, he has written two books on the synoptic problem and has edited or co-edited six interdisciplinary collections of essays concerned with biblical interpretation, theology and ethics. His most recent book is *A Peaceable Hope: Contesting Violent Eschatology in New Testament Narratives* (Baker Academic, 2013).

Heather Thomson is the Associate Head of the School of Theology, Charles Sturt University (CSU), and Senior Lecturer in Theology at St Mark's National Theological Centre in Canberra. Her research interests include hermeneutics, feminist theology, liberation theology and peace studies. She also convenes a focus group on Christianity and Australian Society within CSU's Public and Contextual Theology Research Centre. She is author of *The Things that Make for Peace* (Barton Books, 2009), editor or coeditor of three collections of theological essays and the author of various essays, journal articles and book chapters.

The Bible, Justice and Public Theology:
An Introductory Essay

David J. Neville

Most of the essays in this volume may be read on their own terms, but many are best read in dialogue with Christopher Marshall's central concerns in *Compassionate Justice*.[1] In response to the publication of Marshall's book, contributors were invited to participate in a seminar on the Bible, justice and public theology by addressing either some aspect(s) of Marshall's work or an issue broached by his book. Most of the essays contained in this collection were therefore written for this seminar after their authors had first read and reflected on *Compassionate Justice*. Since Marshall's book is not only the stimulus for this set of studies as a whole but also a point of reference for several within it, it seems fitting to provide an overview for readers unacquainted with Marshall's most recent work.[2]

Marshall characterizes his book as 'an interdisciplinary dialogue with two Gospel parables on law, crime, and restorative justice'. The two parables are the parable of the Compassionate Samaritan and the parable of the Prodigal Son in Lk. 10.25-37 and 15.11-32, respectively. These are two of Jesus' best-known parables, which have had profound influences on both the Christian church and Western culture. One of Marshall's concerns is to examine these parables afresh in light of developments inspired by them, whether in social psychology, ethics or legal theory. In so doing, however, he is equally (if not more) concerned to hear these parables afresh so as to enable them to continue to make their mark in contexts characterized by biblical amnesia. For Marshall, the parables of Jesus continue to have public pertinence, and *Compassionate Justice* gives renewed voice to two parables with enduring potency and appeal.

After a brief introduction, Marshall's book comprises eleven chapters subdivided into three unequal parts. Part 1, which takes up roughly half of the book, addresses the theme of 'Restoration and the Victim' by

---

1. Christopher D. Marshall, *Compassionate Justice: An Interdisciplinary Dialogue with Two Gospel Parables on Law, Crime, and Restorative Justice* (Eugene, OR: Cascade Books, 2012).
2. For the author's own overview, see Marshall, *Compassionate Justice*, pp. 8-11.

focusing on the parable of the Compassionate Samaritan. In his opening chapter, Marshall draws attention to the way in which Martin Luther King Jr appealed to this parable both to critique injustice and to call for social transformation. This leads into a discussion of various dimensions of this parable's cultural legacy, especially in societies shaped by the Western tradition. Within this chapter Marshall also offers criteria for credible interpretations of Jesus' parables.

In his second chapter Marshall addresses both the authenticity of the parable of the Compassionate Samaritan and its literary setting before setting out four reasons why the parable may legitimately be read as concerned with restorative justice: its focus on victimization; its attention to aspects of duty of concern for victims; its legal orientation, especially with respect to interpretation of Jewish Law; and its challenge to reconsider conventional binary categorizations of people as either good or bad, guilty or innocent, victim or offender.

In chapter 3 Marshall explores the preamble to the parable in Lk. 10.25-29, in which a lawyer asks Jesus what he must do to inherit eternal life. Distinctively within the synoptic tradition, Luke has the lawyer proffer the double commandment of love as a distillation of the Jewish Law, which Jesus affirms by saying, 'Do this and you will live'. In his discussion of the exchange between the lawyer and Jesus, Marshall probes the complex, indeed, paradoxical relation between love and the Law. As he summarizes,

> the story denies that Jesus championed love instead of law, or that he considered love and law to be mutually exclusive regimes. Love belongs to the law, it takes the form of a legal requirement, and it satisfies the deepest intent of the law. At the same time love, being what love is, necessarily transcends the law. It transcends it both in the sense that the law cannot exhaustively describe or prescribe what love requires and it cannot empower or energize the love it enjoins.[3]

In chapter 4 Marshall focuses both on the unnamed victim in the parable and on possible reasons why a priest and a Levite, both legal experts as well as temple functionaries, fail to provide assistance to one violently victimized. In so doing, he draws on recent research into criminal victimization, altruism and the 'bystander effect' to explore various social dynamics within the parable. Marshall's 'interdisciplinary dialogue' brings many details of the parable to life and also rounds out the characters in the story.

Marshall's fifth chapter concentrates on the compassionate response of the Samaritan. After describing what can be known of the reasons for hostility between Jews and Samaritans, he attends to details within the parable regarding the Samaritan's actions and motivation. As in the previous chapter, Marshall adds texture to his discussion by comparing interpersonal

---

3. Marshall, *Compassionate Justice*, pp. 79-80.

dynamics within the parable to social-science investigations into altruism and prosocial behaviour. Beyond the Samaritan's compassionate example at an individual level, moreover, Marshall detects hints within the parable of the need for transformation at the systemic and structural levels if justice is to be realized.

In chapter 6, the final chapter of Part 1, Marshall considers the potential of this parable to inform present-day public policy. Since he characterizes the parable of the Compassionate Samaritan as a parable of law, crime and justice, he brings insights derived from his study of the parable into dialogue with legal theory in today's world. This is not done naively, as if applying parabolic biblical insights to complex contemporary concerns were a straightforward exercise. Rather, Marshall's model is 'to envisage a dialectical relationship between biblical perspectives and current practice, a dialogue in which current political and policy options are weighed against the values and priorities evident in relevant biblical analogies, with the aim of sharpening moral judgment today and clarifying the ethical commitments on which all sound public policy finally must rest'.[4] As part of his interdisciplinary dialogue in this chapter, Marshall devotes considerable space to appraising the value of 'Samaritan laws' in certain Western legal systems.

The next three chapters of Marshall's book compose Part 2, 'Restoration and the Offender', which focuses on the parable of the Prodigal Son. Whereas the first part of the book explores restorative justice in relation to victims, this part addresses restorative justice with respect to offenders. Chapter 7, the first on the parable of the Prodigal Son, reviews the significant impact of what has been described as the 'most beautiful story ever told'. Marshall helpfully surveys the principal reasons why this parable has captured the imagination of so many, including scholars: 'its superb literary qualities, its emotional intensity and psychological acuity, and its theological depth'.[5] He also offers two reasons why this parable may profitably be interpreted from a criminal justice perspective.

After providing a rationale for reading the parable of the Prodigal Son as a narrative of restorative justice, focusing not only on the nature and impact of offending but also on how best to respond to such wrongdoing, Marshall addresses, in chapter 8, 'offending as relational rupture'. Here he shows how a restorative justice framework facilitates understanding of what lies at the heart of criminal offending as well as of interpersonal obligations that must be met for a sense of justice to be attained in the wake of serious wrongdoing. Marshall's discussion of the parable highlights both the prodigal son's rupture of relationship through socially shameful disrespect toward his father and also four dimensions of the son's repentant

---

4. Marshall, *Compassionate Justice*, pp. 150-51.
5. Marshall, *Compassionate Justice*, p. 191.

accountability that made relational restoration possible: genuine contrition; confession and apology; correction of life, displayed by a willingness, where possible, to rectify wrongs; and openness to reconciliation.

Chapter 9 focuses on the restorative response of the compassionate father as a signpost to 'a better justice'. In contrast to the reflex social notion that the default meaning of justice is retribution, Marshall argues for a thicker, more textured conception of justice whose goal is relational restoration. In such a view of justice, compassion and mercy are not alien but rather integral dimensions of justice. In this chapter, attention is also given to the stance of the elder son, who resents his father's generosity toward his brother and thereby contests his father's compassionate justice.

In both parables of the Compassionate Samaritan and the Prodigal Son, the decisive turning point occurs when an exemplary character feels compassion. Since Marshall reads both parables as paradigmatic accounts of restorative justice, the role of compassion in the process of restoring justice is seen as central. The third and final part of the book is therefore devoted to elaborating and defending 'Just Compassion'. Chapter 10 explores the meaning of compassion and its role in moral reasoning. It also examines the place of compassion in public life, together with the potential influence of biblical stories in fostering a public spirit of compassion.

The final chapter of Marshall's book is devoted to the question of the proper role of compassion in the criminal justice system. In the first half of the chapter, Marshall undertakes what he describes as the 'calculus of compassion', on the basis of which he advocates making greater room for reciprocal compassion (empathetic engagement between victims and offenders) in legal processes. Both the chapter and the book end with Marshall's defence of restorative justice processes in response to the critique of restorative justice theory and practice by Annalise Acorn. Although critical of her conclusions, Marshall nevertheless credits Acorn with providing a profoundly perceptive account of the role of compassion within justice conceived as—and aimed at—relational restoration. Although Acorn eschews a vision of restorative justice, in which the notion of right relation facilitates a conceptual reconciliation between justice and love, Marshall concurs with her analysis of its central features and dynamics:

> Restorative justice does strive for a uniquely compassionate or loving style of doing justice. It not only affirms the principle that compassion is integral to the work of justice; it also provides the procedural mechanisms by which such compassion can be engaged and enlarged in the process. Most significantly, it conceives of compassion as a horizontal or bilateral reality that flows in both directions between victims and offenders, between the guilty and the innocent, between the hurters and the hurting.[6]

---

6. Marshall, *Compassionate Justice*, p. 319.

As a number of scholarly endorsements attest, *Compassionate Justice* is a profound contribution to restorative justice discourse. It also models a dialogical approach to parable interpretation that stretches more familiar social-scientific approaches to biblical texts. In this respect, Marshall's book is not only hermeneutically adept but also methodologically innovative. In recognition of Marshall's achievement, William Cavanaugh proffers this endorsement (printed on the book's back cover): 'This is how political theology ought to be done. Marshall takes the fundamentally local problem of how communities restore relationships broken by criminal behavior and applies the insights of Jesus' best-known parables. Marshall shuttles back and forth between the biblical narratives and the best of social science to enhance both...' Marshall might well disavow the claim that his interpretive labours actually enhance Jesus' parables, but many will find that his dialogical approach to Jesus' parables enhances their understanding of them. In the introduction to his feature essay in this volume, Marshall's own appraisal of his work in *Compassionate Justice* includes the sense that at least certain parables of Jesus might well serve as paradigms for conceptualizing the task of public theology. Hence the title of his essay and the interrelated themes of this essay collection.

Perhaps because Marshall is a biblical scholar with longstanding interest and involvement in the restorative justice movement, he is well versed in the challenge of relating biblical imperatives (both explicit and implicit) to public concerns within a pluralist social context.[7] Thus, in addressing interrelations between the Bible, justice and public theology,[8] this collection of studies explores a set of relations of particular interest to Marshall and to which he has made signature contributions.

The Bible and Justice

In the opening chapter of *Justice—The Biblical Challenge*, Walter Houston charts a course for exploring the relevance of the Bible to understanding and

---

7. See Christopher D. Marshall, *Beyond Retribution: A New Testament Vision for Justice, Crime, and Punishment* (Grand Rapids: Eerdmans, 2001), pp. 17-31, and 'What Language Shall I Borrow? The Bilingual Dilemma of Public Theology', *Stimulus* 13.3 (August 2005), pp. 11-18, in which Marshall integrates in a nuanced manner what he describes as 'common-currency' and 'distinctive-discourse' approaches to public theology. Also relevant is Marshall's article, 'A Prophet of God's Justice: Reclaiming the Political Jesus', *Stimulus* 14.3 (August 2006), pp. 28-41.

8. In what follows I draw from some of my earlier studies on the Bible, justice and public theology, although such content is recontextualized and further supplemented: 'The Bible as a Public Document: A Perspective on the Contribution of Anglicanism', *St Mark's Review*, No. 203 (November 2007), pp. 35-45; 'Justice and Divine Judgement: Scriptural Perspectives for Public Theology', *IJPT* 3 (2009), pp. 339-56; and 'Christian Scripture and Public Theology: Ruminations on their Ambiguous Relationship', *IJPT* 7 (2013), pp. 5-23.

implementing justice that avoids two extremes: first, the sceptical perspective that the Bible is irrelevant to justice today because of its antiquity and hence antiquated view of reality; and second, the confessional perspective that because the Bible is the Word of God its every statement remains inherently authoritative.⁹ For Houston, who has reflected deeply both on justice in the Bible and on how biblical perspectives on justice pertain to present-day challenges,¹⁰ much contextual work is needed to facilitate an honest and worthwhile 'merging of horizons' between ancient texts and current readers. In the process, discernment, critical reflection and imagination are essential to the task of relating biblical perspectives (and even ideologies) regarding justice to present-day contexts.¹¹

An important feature of Houston's work is his demonstration that there are different and, indeed, dissonant conceptions of justice in the Bible.¹² This has an important bearing on whether and how one appeals to the Bible (or any part thereof) in relation to thinking about and acting for justice today. Lest the realization that there are different biblical conceptions of justice should lead anyone to the conclusion that it is futile to look to the Bible either for insight on the meaning of justice or for inspiration on its implementation, two related observations warrant careful and continuing consideration.

First, despite dissonant descriptions and depictions of justice in the Bible, biblical understandings of justice are inextricably associated with the God of Israel. As Houston affirms, 'The God of Israel is consistently seen as a god of justice, though we must realize that even in the Bible that

---

9. Walter J. Houston, *Justice—The Biblical Challenge* (London: Equinox, 2010), pp. 1-19.

10. See Walter J. Houston, *Contending for Justice: Ideologies and Theologies of Social Justice in the Old Testament* (London: T. & T. Clark, 2nd edn, 2008). Another important volume that addresses complex challenges associated with relating biblical texts to present-day concerns is *Bible and Justice: Ancient Texts, Modern Challenges* (ed. Matthew J.M. Coomber; London: Equinox, 2011).

11. Only a brief discussion of this critical topic is possible here. For further resources on the Bible and justice, see the following annotated bibliographies: 'Annotated Bibliography on Justice', compiled and annotated by Nathanael Putnam, *Ex Auditu* 22 (2006), pp. 222-32; 'The Top One Hundred Books on the Bible and Social Justice', compiled and annotated by Laurel Dykstra, in *Liberating Biblical Study: Scholarship, Art, and Action in Honor of the Center and Library for the Bible and Social Justice* (ed. Laurel Dykstra and Ched Myers; Eugene, OR: Cascade Books, 2011), pp. 223-45.

12. For a sharp statement about discordant biblical conceptions of justice, see John Dominic Crossan, 'Divine Violence in the Christian Bible', in *The Bible and the American Future* (ed. Robert L. Jewett with Wayne L. Alloway Jr and John G. Lacey; Eugene, OR: Cascade Books, 2009), pp. 208-236 (210-18). This collection contains other noteworthy studies on relating biblical justice to present-day contexts.

word has many different connotations'.[13] Because God is just, whatever that might mean, God's people ought to be just. Moreover, certain prophetic traditions reveal justice to constitute what might be described as an *ultimate theological* concern, not only a *penultimate moral* concern. In this respect, the canonical record of the prophet Jeremiah is especially instructive. Echoing a trajectory from within the Deuteronomistic tradition, Jeremiah affirms an understanding of justice centred on concern for society's most needy such as orphans, widows and resident aliens. More than this, however, Jeremiah not only reiterates that acting justly complies with the divine will but also contends that acting justly within a covenantal context constitutes *knowing God* (Jer. 9.23-24; 22.3, 15-16; cf. Deut. 24.19-22).[14] In other words, not only does Jeremiah retrieve a notion of justice that surpasses and in certain respects relativizes another prominent trajectory within the Deuteronomistic tradition—strict 'payback' or recompense—but he also renovates by associating justice with knowing and relating rightly to God. Acting justly and rightly thus belongs to the sphere of the ultimate, not merely the morally penultimate, by virtue of participating in God's own concern for those who are vulnerable. Or, as John Donahue remarks in relation to Jeremiah 22, 'The doing of justice is not the application of religious faith, but its substance; without it, God remains unknown.'[15] Thus, to wrestle with issues of justice is to step into a sphere of pressing concern to the God of biblical tradition such that this wrestling transcends the merely moral plane.

Second, beyond Jeremiah's coupling of justice for the vulnerable with knowing God, Isa. 28.17 signals that justice is the criterion of divine judgment: 'I will make justice the rule, right-dealing the plumbline' (my translation). This announcement echoes through decisive prophetic traditions, especially Amos 5.24 and Mic. 6.8.[16] Moreover, certain Gospel traditions reveal that a central dimension of Jesus' proclamation and enactment of divine reign was indebted to prophetic pronouncements pertaining to justice. This indebtedness on the part of Jesus did not preclude interpretive innovation, however. As passages such as Mt. 11.2-6 and Lk. 4.16-21 indicate, especially when compared with biblical intertexts in the book of Isaiah, Jesus may be understood to have re(de)fined judgment according to divine justice such that judgment is just *insofar as it brings about*

---

13. Houston, *Justice*, p. 12.

14. Cf. Chris Marshall, *The Little Book of Biblical Justice: A Fresh Approach to the Bible's Teachings on Justice* (Intercourse, PA: Good Books, 2005), pp. 22-28.

15. John R. Donahue, 'Biblical Perspectives on Justice', in *The Faith that Does Justice: Examining the Christian Sources for Social Change* (ed. John C. Haughey; New York: Paulist Press, 1977), pp. 68-112 (76).

16. See James L. Mays, 'Justice: Perspectives from the Prophetic Tradition', *Interpretation* 37.1 (1983), pp. 5-17.

restoration and wholeness. In these passages, the words of Jesus invite readers to envisage his mission of restoration as but the *form* of divine judgment. Even if divine judgment retains a retributive dimension, the critical point is that God's judgment, as Jesus reconstructed it in his own mission, is neither purely nor even primarily retributive. So, although more restrictive ('to each his or her due') and retributive notions of justice are represented in the Bible, reflection on biblical justice in light of the story of Jesus arguably leads to the conclusion that scriptural justice in its truest and deepest sense may be said to be restorative, rectifying or transformative, reflecting God's commitment to, concern for and intent toward the created order as a whole.[17]

For both Marshall and Houston, biblical justice is a *relational* reality. 'Biblical justice is comprehensively relational', as Marshall states succinctly.[18] Or as Houston remarks, 'The touchstone of justice in the Bible is relationship.'[19] Within a relational framework, justice is not a stand-alone reality. Whether in sustaining wholesome relationships or in repairing broken relationships, justice has dimensions that people are often inclined to hold in opposition to justice, for example, love, grace, mercy and compassion. As Willard Swartley observes, however, 'Compassion and mercy are inherent to justice in the biblical understanding.'[20] Even if one is inclined to nuance such an assertion by affirming that compassion and mercy are inherent to *determinative* biblical understandings of justice, the point remains that to speak truly about biblical justice one must utilize qualifiers such as 'loving', 'gracious', 'merciful' or 'compassionate', as indeed Marshall does in *Compassionate Justice*.

The Bible and Public Theology

The status and role of the Bible in public theology is an important but relatively neglected topic.[21] Perhaps this is because the Bible is no longer

---

17. See also James K. Bruckner, 'Justice in Scripture', *Ex Auditu* 22 (2006), pp. 1-9.
18. Marshall, *Biblical Justice*, p. 35.
19. Houston, *Justice*, p. 16.
20. Willard M. Swartley, 'The Relation of Justice/Righteousness to *Shalom/Eirēnē*', *Ex Auditu* 22 (2006), pp. 29-53 (30). A similar perspective is articulated by Carol J. Dempsey, *Justice: A Biblical Perspective* (St Louis: Chalice Press, 2008). For a complementary philosophical appraisal, see Richard H. Bell, *Rethinking Justice: Restoring Our Humanity* (Lanham, MD: Lexington Books, 2007).
21. Note, however, the recent publication of *The Bible: Culture, Community, Society* (ed. Angus Paddison and Neil Messer; London: Bloomsbury T. & T. Clark, 2013), which contains several essays pertaining to this topic, especially Andrew Bradstock, 'The Bible and Public Theology' (pp. 171-88). Unfortunately, I was unable to inspect this valuable collection of studies until the final stages of editing this volume.

recognized as a source of authority in Western public consciousness.[22] As Paul Joyce observes, 'There stands...a big question mark against the role in our time of the Bible, no longer a shared point of reference in our society as a whole, and in many ways not even functioning as Scripture within the modern Church.'[23] Similarly, according to Philip Knight, 'In our contemporary pluralistic age any reading of the Bible can be privately inspiring and good for just that reason. However, the institutions and ideologies through which we shape our common life no longer defer to the Bible as a source of meaning.'[24] Yet the Bible remains a quintessentially public document that has profoundly shaped Western institutions and social values. A collection of publicly accessible texts that begins with the creation of the cosmos and ends with its renewal centred on a city (the New Jerusalem) can hardly be said to focus on the private, rather than public, sphere. The Bible addresses matters of concern to a broad public, not only those pertaining to private spirituality or individual morality. It is as concerned with power politics as with prayer, with social structures as with spirituality, with money matters as with mercy and with jubilee justice as with 'justification'.

For the church, however, the Bible is not simply a public document (or collection of publicly accessible documents) that has had profound historical and cultural influence. It is, rather, something identified as 'Scripture', with all that such an appellation implies. For those who consider that the Bible has a role to play in public theological discourse, it is important to keep in mind that Scripture retains an authoritative status for the church that is not shared generally, even if scriptural authority is qualified with reference to tradition, reason, experience or communal discernment over time, especially in relation to the critical or normative content (*die Sache*) of Scripture.[25] For some, Scripture was shaped by the church and is there-

---

22. In global terms, the Bible remains a public book in Africa, Asia and Latin America. See Philip Jenkins, *The New Faces of Christianity: Believing the Bible in the Global South* (New York: Oxford University Press, 2006), which expands upon his observations in *The Next Christendom: The Coming of Global Christianity* (New York: Oxford University Press, 2002). See also Sebastian C.H. Kim, *Theology in the Public Sphere* (London: SCM Press, 2011), pp. 27-56.

23. Paul Joyce, 'Reading the Bible within the Public Domain', in *Dare We Speak of God in Public?* (ed. Frances Young; London: Mowbray, 1995), pp. 67-79 (69).

24. Philip Knight, 'Pragmatism, Postmodernism and the Bible as a Meaningful Public Resource in a Pluralistic Age', in *Biblical Interpretation: The Meanings of Scripture—Past and Present* (ed. John M. Court; London: T. & T. Clark International, 2003), pp. 310-25 (311).

25. On the role of *Sachkritik* in twentieth-century biblical interpretation, see Robert Morgan, '*Sachkritik* in Reception History', *JSNT* 33.2 (2010), pp. 175-90. Since holding to biblical authority inevitably implies interpretive nuance, perhaps it is time to acknowledge public pertinence, accountability and benefit as yet another dimension of the church's necessary qualification of biblical authority. In other words, perhaps the

fore secondary to the church's teaching office; for others, Scripture is the touchstone of truth on matters of faith and practice; and for others still, Scripture is primary and is therefore a necessary, if not sufficient, source of doctrinal and moral authority. Whether one perceives the church as a biblical people, perhaps the more compelling perspective theologically, or the Bible as the church's book, perhaps the more compelling perspective historically,[26] the reality is that those whose worldview, moral vision and communal ethos have been shaped by Christian faith relate to the Bible not only as a religious and cultural 'classic' but also as a norm for faith and practice.[27]

The special status of Scripture for the church and therefore for a good many Christian public theologians implies the need for interpretive care when appealing to the Bible in discourse that goes by the name of public theology. Marshall is one biblical scholar who has reflected carefully on this challenge, as already noted. In view of the relative rarity of studies directly concerned with the role of the Bible (and biblical scholarship) in public theology, however, I have sought to encourage further reflection and dialogue on this issue by setting out, in an earlier study, a taxonomy of approaches to the relation between the Bible and public theology.[28] Much of what follows in this subsection is an abbreviated overview of that attempt at classification.

First, there is the effort on the part of some to retrieve the Bible as a public resource. In a post-Enlightenment context within the industrialized West, perhaps the most important mode of relating the Bible to public theology

authority of Scripture is also contingent on whether and how appeal to the Bible can be shown to contribute to the public or common good.

26. On this contested question regarding the status of Scripture, see Francis Watson, 'Hermeneutics and the Doctrine of Scripture: Why They Need Each Other', *IJST* 12.2 (2010), pp. 118-43 (131-37).

27. On the Bible as a 'classic', see David Tracy, *The Analogical Imagination: Christian Theology and the Culture of Pluralism* (New York: Crossroad, 1981); Krister Stendahl, 'The Bible as a Classic and the Bible as Holy Scripture', *JBL* 103 (1984), pp. 3-10. Among the various implications of the notion of 'Scripture' for engagement with publics other than the church, one must, at a minimum, think dialectically. This is undoubtedly so when appealing to the Bible in public discourse because publics other than communities positively oriented to the Bible do not share fundamental biblical and theological premises. The relation between Scripture and other potential sources of theological, moral and interpretive guidance such as tradition, reason and communally tested experience over time is also dialectical, as is the relation between Scripture and the normative content (*die Sache*) of Scripture, since the Bible is not univocal. For suggestions about the value of dialectic as a methodological resource for public theology, see my 'Dialectic as Method in Public Theology: Recalling Jacques Ellul', *IJPT* 2 (2008), pp. 163-81.

28. See Neville, 'Christian Scripture and Public Theology', pp. 8-13.

is to retrieve the capacity to perceive the public character of the Bible.[29] As observed above, the Bible is a document that addresses issues pertaining to public life and has had profound historical and cultural effects. Thus, there is 'scriptural warrant for public theology', as Heather Thomson has remarked to me in person. She also notes the Bible's role in nurturing the kind of spirituality that supports public theology, whether in the lives of individual theologians or in the ecclesial communities within which they are shaped and sustained.[30] In this respect, she echoes Bruce Birch on the Bible's essential role in shaping Christian individuals and communities capable of engaging with the wider world in an edifying way:

> The church, as those persons who claim to be the covenant people of God and the body of Christ, is shaped continuously by Scripture and its influence in worship, preaching, study, and life together in the community of faith... Here is where Christians receive nourishment in a biblical identity that allows them to stand as an alternative to the world and its values while at the same time living their lives for the sake of that world and its brokenness.[31]

Second, perhaps the most readily recognizable mode of relating the Bible to public theology is to identify biblical exemplars for public theology. An example is the study by Howard Marshall entitled 'Biblical Patterns for Public Theology', in which he explores biblical texts with a view to extrapolating principles for Christian social responsibility.[32] Searching the Scriptures for ways in which they might inform Christian participation in public life has a long history and is likely to continue to bear fruit.

A third approach is to grapple with various challenges arising from the task(s) of public theology for Christian conceptions of the Bible. The purposes and foci of public theology pose perplexing questions regarding the role, status and value of the Bible. For example, is the Bible a normative source for public theology and, if so, is it normative in the same way as for traditional dogmatic or systematic theology? Or do the concerns of public theology imply a different conception of the Bible's role in relation to it? Such questions surely deserve critical responses.

29. On the pietistic privatization of biblical interpretation, see Tim Gorringe, 'Political Readings of Scripture', in *The Cambridge Companion to Biblical Interpretation* (ed. John Barton; Cambridge: Cambridge University Press, 1998), pp. 67-80 (67).

30. For her own contributions to public theology, see Heather Thomson, 'Stars and Compasses: Hermeneutical Guidelines for Public Theology', *IJPT* 2 (2008), pp. 258-76, and *The Things that Make for Peace* (Canberra: Barton Books, 2009). See also her essay in this volume.

31. Bruch C. Birch, 'The Role of Scripture in Public Theology', *WW* 4.3 (1984), pp. 260-68 (264).

32. I. Howard Marshall, 'Biblical Patterns for Public Theology', *EJT* 14.1 (2005), pp. 73-86.

A fourth approach to the relation between the Bible and public theology focuses on making biblical texts and either scholarly study of, or confessional attachment to, such texts more accessible and therefore more comprehensible to a public broader than the community of faith. Exemplifying this approach in two different ways are the well publicized Jesus Seminar, which has deliberately made available to a broad public the processes and results of academic biblical scholarship, and the dialogical 'scriptural reasoning' project formed in 1995 to facilitate meeting in interfaith groups so as to learn from each others' interpretations of Jewish, Christian and Islamic scriptures.[33]

A fifth approach might be described as relating the Bible to public discourse within a pluralist context so as to contribute to such discourse in an edifying way.[34] One version of such an approach is to explore key biblical passages or themes as points of contact with issues under discussion in broader public discourse. Justice is undoubtedly one such concern; others include violence, poverty and ecological responsibility. Finding points of contact between the Bible and public discourse is relatively straightforward, but the way in which biblical perspectives are brought to bear in the context of public discourse is vital. All too often, 'biblical' perspectives simplistically proffered in public simply confirm the public's prejudice against turning to the Bible for insight or edification. A variation on this approach is to explain the public pertinence of distinctive or 'publicly suspicious' biblical themes such as creation, covenant, salvation, divine Spirit active in the world or moral accountability to a transcendent 'Other', and to do so in ways that do not presuppose either a religious worldview or a privileged access to truth.

A sixth approach to relating the Bible to public theology emerges from developments in biblical hermeneutics. According to Birch, 'The emergence and continued importance of liberation theologies is one of the most significant developments of our time for the impact of theology on public life.'[35] In view of the importance of biblical interpretation for theologies of liberation, liberationist interpretive approaches to the Bible are inevitably a mode of public theology by virtue of their advocacy stance on behalf of a significant proportion of the world's population. Liberation readings of biblical texts have proliferated into various modes of ideological critique of

---

33. For two collections of studies on 'scriptural reasoning', see David F. Ford and C.C. Pecknold (eds.), *The Promise of Scriptural Reasoning* (Oxford: Blackwell, 2006), and the *Journal of Anglican Studies* 11.2 (November 2013).

34. See, e.g., Gerd Theissen, *The Bible and Contemporary Culture* (trans. David E. Green; Minneapolis: Fortress Press, 2007). For further discussion of this book by Theissen, see Neville, 'Christian Scripture and Public Theology', pp. 13-17.

35. Birch, 'The Role of Scripture in Public Theology', p. 261.

the Bible in response to the historically damaging impact of biblical texts in relation to the politics of wealth distribution, gender, class, race relations and ecology. Such critique was theoretically possible from within, so to speak, but it seems that a standpoint of suspicion was necessary to demonstrate how damaging and demeaning the Bible could be—or could be used.

Ideological critique of biblical texts is a necessary and important mode of public engagement with the Bible. Unless due diligence is given to such ideological critique, in which biblical texts are contested and deconstructed, biblical scholarship will be represented naively and/or counterproductively in the public domain. Apart from reactionary responses to such critique, however, one wonders whether enough has been done to foster a seventh approach to the relation between the Bible and public theology, namely, to enable the Bible to 'speak back' to critical theory in a meaningful and edifying way. The Bible does not speak with one voice only, and many who find it necessary to engage in ideological critique of biblical texts nevertheless find the Bible indispensable to their faith, spirituality and moral vision.

Within this admittedly provisional taxonomy of approaches to relating the Bible to public theology, the final approach concerns the development of a 'public hermeneutic' of the Bible.[36] Although this has yet to be done for public theology, Paul Hanson has developed a five-faceted hermeneutic for a biblically informed political theology.[37] While a public hermeneutic of the Bible might well turn out to differ in certain respects from Hanson's proposed interpretive process, it will likely be similar in certain key respects. For Tim Gorringe, for example, Christian political theology takes its bearings from Scripture, understood as an extended 'argument' or tradition, as defined by Alasdair MacIntyre.[38] Much the same might also be said of Christian public theology.

Marshall's 'interdisciplinary dialogue with two Gospel parables on law, crime, and restorative justice' might well transcend or transgress certain distinctions within this taxonomy, but the important point is that

---

36. One who has signalled the need for a public hermeneutic of the Bible is Clive Pearson, who has been a member of the executive of the Global Network for Public Theology since its inception.

37. Paul D. Hanson, *Political Engagement as Biblical Mandate* (Eugene, OR: Cascade Books, 2010), pp. 35-41. Hanson describes his interpretive proposal as 'a five-step hermeneutic for a biblical based political theology', but the steps are not necessarily sequential. The key point is that his proposed hermeneutic is a process entered into within a community of faith concerned to be politically responsible in a pluralist context.

38. Tim Gorringe, 'Political Theology', *ExpTim* 122.9 (2011), pp. 417-24. From the biblical tradition, Gorringe focuses on 'three key themes for a Christian political theology': freedom, *shalom* and justice. For a comparison between public and political (as well as liberation) theology, see Kim, *Theology in the Public Sphere*, pp. 20-25.

Compassionate Justice is a major contribution to public theology and one in which biblical resources are indispensable. Building on ideas developed in *Compassionate Justice*, Marshall's essay in this volume takes the discussion further by proposing that certain parables of Jesus may be perceived as paradigmatic for public theology.

Justice and Public Theology

Insofar as public theology is understood in big-picture terms as being broader than the direct impact of either theology or the church on national, state or institutional public policy initiatives,[39] the theme of justice would seem to be a central concern for public theology. Justice is a daunting topic, however, not only because it looms large in Western intellectual history and culture but also because it is so momentous in moral and practical terms. Yet justice weighs heavily on the moral scales not so much because it has exercised great minds but because it relates directly to pressing social, cultural, political, economic and ecological concerns. It is difficult to conceive of an issue that exercises our collective conscience that is not also related to justice.

In an evidently unjust world, perhaps there is no issue more pressing for public theology than that of justice. Despite its recognized importance, however, justice is neither easily defined nor readily realized. Both the meaning and implementation of justice are critical, but both are also elusive. After exploring and critiquing six significant theories of justice,[40] Karen Lebacqz observes that 'there is no single agreed standard for justice in our contemporary world. All the talk about justice today may not bring us any nearer to making justice a lived reality'.[41] Here Lebacqz makes two crucial observations, each pertinent for public theology: first, there are competing conceptions of justice, which conflict because theorists cannot concur on what constitutes justice; and second, even if agreement could be

---

39. One who views public theology as theological discourse aimed at shaping public policy is Robin Gill. See, e.g., Robin Gill, 'Public Theology and Health Care Ethics', *St Mark's Review*, No. 203 (November 2007), pp. 9-22. By contrast, I envisage public theology as non-insular Christian theology that addresses pressing public concerns by sharing the resources of its heritage with the wider world in an accessible, non-coercive way.

40. Karen Lebacqz, *Six Theories of Justice: Perspectives from Philosophical and Theological Ethics* (Minneapolis: Augsburg Publishing House, 1986). The six theories investigated by Lebacqz are those of John Stuart Mill, John Rawls, Robert Nozick, the National Conference of Catholic Bishops, Reinhold Niebuhr and Jose Porfirio Miranda.

41. Karen Lebacqz, *Justice in an Unjust World: Foundations for a Christian Approach to Justice* (Minneapolis: Augsburg Publishing House, 1987), p. 7.

reached concerning that which comprises justice, reaching consensus on that which makes for justice does not necessarily lead to the implementation of justice.

With respect to public theology, Lebacqz's first observation can be taken as given in current pluralist contexts. Today's public theologians generally appreciate that although their deliberations about justice may—but also might not—gain a hearing, their pronouncements necessarily compete with conflicting perspectives. This is both a challenge and an opportunity. In a pluralist context, to be heard and heeded is a significant challenge for the Christian theologian, but it is also an opportunity to contribute something distinctive to public conversation. Even more challenging for public theology, however, is Lebacqz's second observation. If, as public theologians generally agree, Christian theology no longer holds a privileged position in the public sphere, what is likely to gain theology a hearing in public is not whether it addresses matters of justice (and other issues of public import) but whether what it has to say about such matters effects change for good, especially with respect to decisive social, political, economic and, perhaps most importantly, ecclesiastical structures. In this connection, careful discernment is critical because in order to gain a hearing public theology might well be tempted to say what serves the status quo. Gaining a hearing for this reason would not serve the public good, however. Rather, a measure of the value of public theology might well be the extent to which its voice unsettles entrenched social structures that make injustice systemic and thereby endemic.

In certain respects, Lebacqz anticipated Alasdair MacIntyre's interrelated questions, *Whose Justice? Which Rationality?*,[42] by reminding readers that traditional tools of ethical enquiry such as logic, rationality and consistency were developed within privileged contexts and sustained by those with education, wealth and power, thereby largely excluding perspectives of the poor and powerless. In other words, within the Western tradition(s) of ethical enquiry, theories of justice have done little to disturb the advantaged because they have been constructed according to the rationality of the advantaged. Whose justice? The 'justice' of those with power and wealth who thereby determine what counts as justice concerns. Which rationality? That particular form of rationality developed by the educated élite, without regard for the perspectives of the poor and the powerless. As a result, Lebacqz argues for alternative forms of rationality attuned to the inherent bias and value-ladenness of so-called objective ethical analysis and also sensitive to the pain and passion of those whose lives are both

---

42. Alasdair MacIntyre, *Whose Justice? Which Rationality?* (Notre Dame: University of Notre Dame Press, 1988); also his 'Précis of *Whose Justice? Which Rationality?*', *Philosophy and Phenomenological Research* 51.1 (March 1991), pp. 149-52.

overwhelmed and undermined by injustice. 'Instead of taking reason as the starting point or as an adequate tool for ethics', she writes, 'a new kind of logic is required...a historical logic that attends to the history out of which current patterns of distribution and current decisions about action are taken.'[43]

Not long after the publication of Lebacqz's two books on justice, Stanley Hauerwas voiced the view that justice is a 'bad idea' for Christians.[44] Writing in the wake of various forms of liberation theology, Hauerwas observes that Christians generally agree that justice is integral to Christian faith. In his view, however, Christian commitment to justice frequently buys into the presuppositions and thought forms of post-Enlightenment liberalism, especially when justice is understood largely in terms of individual rights. His basic critique of Christian advocacy for justice is that it often lacks biblical and theological integrity because of its detachment from specifically Christian sources. There is no universally accepted understanding of justice, so Christians delude themselves if they consider that by advocating for justice they are necessarily acting out the inherent implications of their faith and thereby witnessing to it. Indeed, according to Hauerwas, glib Christian concern for justice may well disclose an eliding of specifically Christian conviction and deliberation. As he writes,

> There are no doubt many reasons why justice is so appealing to Christians; not the least of which is our increasing sense that the salvation wrought in Jesus is social and political in its very form. Jesus' salvation does not have social and political implications, but it is a politics that is meant as an alternative to all social life that does not reflect God's glory. Yet why should that politics be expressed in the language of justice? Part of the reason has to do with the church's attempt to remain a societal actor in societies that we feel are slipping away from our control. The current emphasis on justice among Christians springs not so much from an effort to locate the Christian contribution to wider society as it does from Christians' attempt to find a way to be societal actors without that action being colored by Christian presupposition.[45]

The challenge (or chastisement) articulated by Hauerwas is important, especially for Christian public theology. Although public good can come from Christian involvement in justice advocacy on the basis of 'thin' agreement with others who do not hold Christian convictions, something Hauerwas concedes elsewhere, Hauerwas nevertheless identifies something crucial in relation to Christian motivation to work for justice: if Christians

---

43. Lebacqz, *Justice in an Unjust World*, pp. 55-56.
44. Stanley Hauerwas, *After Christendom? How the Church Is to Behave if Freedom, Justice, and a Christian Nation Are Bad Ideas* (Nashville: Abingdon Press, 1991), chapter 2: 'The Politics of Justice: Why Justice Is a Bad Idea for Christians'.
45. Hauerwas, *After Christendom?*, p. 58.

fail to advocate for justice on the basis of resources at the wellsprings of Christian faith, we will probably fail to proffer what only Christians are able to contribute with respect to the *meaning* of justice and the *means* to agitate for it.

Notwithstanding the clarity and coherence of Hauerwas's critique of Christian 'enthusiasm' for justice, which is nevertheless probably overstated, it is somewhat surprising that he has devoted *comparatively* little effort to articulating a distinctively Christian conception of justice and the practices that sustain such a conception, especially in view of his long-standing defence of Christian pacifism. One might have thought that a commitment to Christian pacifism would go hand in hand with a Christian understanding of justice.[46] My own sense is that although justice per se has not been a major theme in Hauerwas's writings, it has nevertheless been a significant practical concern for him at an existential level. In this respect, how Hauerwas has lived in relation to others and what he has done with his time and money are more important than how much he has written on justice.[47] Moreover, various Hauerwasian themes other than peace (for example, character and the virtues, truthfulness, care for and friendship toward those disabled in body or mind, anti-liberalism) bespeak an implicit concern for, and commitment to, justice.[48] In any case, during the past decade Hauerwas has clarified his views on justice in response to criticisms by Jeffrey Stout and Nicholas Wolterstorff.[49]

---

46. As a Christian pacifist or, perhaps better, a theologian who has renounced violence and coercion in line with his Christian convictions and discipleship, Hauerwas has necessarily wrestled with considerations of justice in relation to the moral theory of just war.

47. See, for example, Stanley Hauerwas, *Hannah's Child: A Theologian's Memoir* (Grand Rapids: Eerdmans, 2010), p. 4: 'Toward the end of his life, Samuel asked the people he had led to testify against him if he had defrauded or oppressed anyone, or taken a bribe. They responded that Samuel had not defrauded or oppressed anyone, nor taken anything "from the hand of anyone". If I have any similarity to Samuel, I hope people might cast it in terms like these.' Even more important in this connection, however, are dimensions of his life he does not divulge.

48. Hauerwas has written much and continues to write prolifically, but for a bibliography of his writings up until 2010, see Angus Paddison and Darren Sarisky, 'A Comprehensive Bibliography of the Writings of Stanley Hauerwas', *MQR* 84.3 (July 2010), pp. 311-55.

49. This is not the place for a critical appraisal of Hauerwas on justice, important as that may be in relation to the rest of his oeuvre. My remarks here are simply to signal that one cannot appeal to Hauerwas to justify lack of *theological* concern for justice. For a fair-minded assessment, see Michael S. Northcott, 'Reading Hauerwas in the Cornbelt: The Demise of the American Dream and the Return of Liturgical Politics', *JRE* 40.2 (2012), pp. 262-80. Cf. Stanley Hauerwas, 'Remembering How and What I Think: A Response to the *JRE* Articles on Hauerwas', *JRE* 40.2 (2012), pp. 296-306.

In a postscript to his *Performing the Faith: Bonhoeffer and the Practice of Nonviolence*,[50] Hauerwas responds to Jeffrey Stout's criticism of his apparent denigration or, perhaps better, belittlement of justice as a result of the influence on his thought of John Howard Yoder's pacifism and Alasdair MacIntyre's anti-liberalism.[51] Here one learns that despite the (false) impression one might gain from the subtitle of chapter 2 of *After Christendom?*, Hauerwas's critique targets general conceptions of justice dissociated from narrative accounts of Jesus' mission and message in the Gospels—including especially his crucifixion and resurrection—and also from specific ecclesial practices faithful to Jesus' vision of God's fair reign. For the Christian, according to Hauerwas, to speak of 'justice' implies that the meaning or content of this term is dependent on and determined by Christological convictions. In other words, Hauerwas's reticence to appeal to justice in general or abstract terms is in certain respects theologically grounded. As he explains,

> After Reinhold Niebuhr, liberal Protestants thought the way to be 'politically responsible' was to leave talk about Jesus behind and instead talk about love and justice. So, the problem of something called 'social ethics' became how to understand the relation between love, that is, disinterested regard for each person, and justice, dealing fairly with conditions of scarcity. Justice named the arrangements necessary to secure more equitable forms of life when love could not be achieved. At least one of the problems with the issue that way is that love and justice become abstractions divorced from concrete practices necessary for Christians and non-Christians alike to know what we mean when we say 'justice'. We should not be surprised such abstractions began to dominate ethical theory because that is exactly the result Niebuhr wanted. Good Barthian (and Yoderian) that I am, I had to resist those who thought that justice qua justice was more important than the justice God has shown us in the cross and resurrection of Jesus.[52]

Hauerwas's resistance to the notion 'that justice qua justice [is] more important than the justice God has shown us in the cross and resurrection of Jesus' is further elaborated in 'Jesus, the Justice of God', originally presented at a conference on Bible and Justice at the University of Sheffield in 2008 and subsequently published in two essay collections.[53] In this essay,

---

50. Stanley Hauerwas, *Performing the Faith: Bonhoeffer and the Practice of Nonviolence* (Grand Rapids: Brazos Press, 2004), pp. 215-41. That same year he published another justice-related essay. See Stanley Hauerwas, 'Punishing Christians', in *Public Theology for the 21st Century: Essays in Honour of Duncan B. Forrester* (ed. William F. Storrar and Andrew R. Morton; London: T. & T. Clark, 2004), pp. 285-301.

51. See Jeffrey Stout, *Democracy and Tradition* (Princeton, NJ: Princeton University Press, 2004), pp. 61-179.

52. Hauerwas, *Performing the Faith*, p. 230.

53. Stanley Hauerwas, 'Jesus: The Justice of God', in *Bible and Justice: Ancient*

Hauerwas largely adopts the theological account of justice developed by his former student, Daniel Bell,[54] which he then brings into critical conversation with the more philosophical and rights-oriented conception of justice developed by Nicholas Wolterstorff in *Justice: Rights and Wrongs*.[55] Hauerwas highlights Bell's critique of the assumption (by Christians) that justice is comprehensible without reference to specifically Christian convictions and practices. Against views characterized as 'social justice advocacy' and 'justice as justification', each of which effectively displaces Jesus as God's justice, Hauerwas endorses Bell's christocentric conception of justice: 'For Bell, Jesus does not exemplify a justice that can be known apart from his life, nor does he provide a motivation for us to underwrite some secular version of justice. "Rather, Jesus in his person *is* the justice of God."'[56] Such an understanding of justice enables Bell (followed by Hauerwas) to develop an account of justice thickly textured by biblical and theological precedents such that love, mercy and forgiveness are not conceived as alien to justice but rather as integral to it.

Turning to Wolterstorff's account of justice, Hauerwas acknowledges that he provides biblical and theological grounding for his philosophical proposal. Even so, Hauerwas finds unsustainable Wolterstorff's use of biblical and theological resources in the service of a 'theory of primary justice as inherent rights', not only because Hauerwas shares with others a philosophical distrust in inherent rights but also because he considers the distinction Wolterstorff makes between primary and rectifying justice to be 'scripturally problematic'. Moreover, despite Wolterstorff's appeal to both testaments of the Bible, 'he does not seem to think the [scriptural and historical] narrative he has provided is necessary for the justification of a natural-rights view of justice'.[57] In effect, Hauerwas considers that Wolterstorff appeals to Scripture in support of a (non-biblically derived) theory of justice rather than developing an understanding of justice from

---

Texts, Modern Challenges (ed. Matthew J.M. Coomber; London: Equinox, 2011), pp. 70-90; also published as 'Jesus, the Justice of God', in Stanley Hauerwas, *War and the American Difference: Theological Reflections on Violence and National Identity* (Grand Rapids: Baker Academic, 2011), pp. 99-116. The latter version is cited below.

54. See Daniel M. Bell, Jr, 'Deliberating: Justice and Liberation', in *The Blackwell Companion to Christian Ethics* (ed. Stanley Hauerwas and Samuel Wells; Oxford: Blackwell, 2004), pp. 182-95, and 'Jesus, the Jews, and the Politics of God's Justice', *Ex Auditu* 22 (2006), pp. 87-111.

55. Nicholas Wolterstorff, *Justice: Rights and Wrongs* (Princeton, NJ: Princeton University Press, 2008). See also his follow-up volume, *Justice in Love* (Grand Rapids: Eerdmans, 2011).

56. Hauerwas, *War and the American Difference*, p. 104. (The internal citation is to Bell, 'Jesus, the Jews', p. 97.)

57. Hauerwas, *War and the American Difference*, p. 112.

the particularities of the biblical witness itself. For Hauerwas, this makes the Bible as a whole and Jesus in particular incidental or accidental in relation to the meaning and significance of justice. As a result, despite his evident regard for Wolterstorff, he finds Bell's biblical-theological proposal for understanding justice more compelling.

Hauerwas concludes his essay on 'Jesus, the Justice of God' by voicing his admiration for, and solidarity with, Wolterstorff's 'passion for justice',[58] yet not on the basis of a natural-rights theory of justice to which anyone might assent but rather by the recovery of peculiar practices evoked in the people of God by what might be described as biblical recollection. By way of illustration, he points to Bell's appeal to Mt. 25.31-46 in support of envisaging justice as inclusive of works of mercy, indeed, 'justice shaped by the works of mercy'.[59] Justice conceived and construed in relation to the Gospel accounts of the life story of Jesus cannot but be understood and practised in ways that conform justice to the contour of Jesus' mission and message.[60] In other words, Christian public discourse regarding justice is inseparable from careful reflection on the Bible and justice.

As adamant as Hauerwas is about the decisive significance of the Bible for a Christian account of justice, it is noteworthy that one finds far greater engagement with biblical sources on the part of Wolterstorff than by Hauerwas, even though Hauerwas's essay was specifically written for a conference on the Bible and justice. One might have thought that the author of a commentary on the Gospel according to Matthew would have found in Matthew's narrative of Jesus' mission and message sufficient biblical resources for setting out a distinctively Christian account of justice, especially in view of the significance of justice/righteousness (*dikaiosunē*) for Matthew.[61] In any case, Hauerwas's ruminations on justice would seem to call for further research of the kind one finds in Christopher Marshall's *Compassionate Justice*.

---

58. Hauerwas, *War and the American Difference*, pp. 114-16.

59. Hauerwas, *War and the American Difference*, pp. 115-16. Another phrase used by Hauerwas in this concluding section to describe a Christian understanding *and practice* of justice is 'charity-formed justice'.

60. In this connection, it is telling that Hauerwas's title for this essay on justice, 'Jesus, the Justice of God', matches the title of the central chapter in his *Peaceable Kingdom*, 'Jesus: The Presence of the Peaceable Kingdom'. See Stanley Hauerwas, *The Peaceable Kingdom: A Primer in Christian Ethics* (Notre Dame: University of Notre Dame Press, 1983), pp. 72-95. The Christian understanding of justice or peace derives from the particularities and peculiarities of the mission and message, death and resurrection of Jesus.

61. See Stanley Hauerwas, *Matthew* (Brazos Theological Commentary on the Bible; Grand Rapids: Brazos Press, 2006).

Or do they? Marshall has devoted much of his energies, both scholarly and practical, to the exposition and implementation of restorative justice. In 'Jesus, the Justice of God', however, Hauerwas targets 'restorative' no less than 'social' justice as deeply problematic:

> You know something has gone wrong when the phrase 'social justice' is used. What kind of justice would not be 'social'? The very description 'social justice' reproduces the public/private distinction characteristic of liberal political regimes. I also think the phrase 'restorative justice' has the same problems as the locution 'social justice'. Justice is or must be restorative if it is to be justice.[62]

Hauerwas has a point, but in ordinary parlance 'justice' so often simply means retribution or vengeance. Although not an entirely novel development, the present-day restorative justice movement can be traced to Mennonite-influenced initiatives during the 1970s. As such, restorative justice does not necessarily reflect liberal rather than Christian presumptions. And in Marshall's work, it is precisely the qualifier 'restorative' or 'compassionate' that signals that the justice with which he is concerned is the justice of God present in the life story of Jesus and hence replete with transforming potential still.

---

62. Hauerwas, *War and the American Difference*, p. 101 n. 6.

PARABLES AS PARADIGMS FOR PUBLIC THEOLOGY

Christopher D. Marshall

In the preface to *Compassionate Justice*,[1] I explain how the book evolved from an initial hunch that the parable of the Prodigal Son might have something valuable to say to me as the father of two grown sons, the younger of whom was proving a bit of a challenge at the time. I never set out to read the parable from a restorative justice perspective. That happened fortuitously, though also, I hope, productively. As my grappling with the parable grew beyond purely private, domestic concerns, I began to sense certain resemblances between the nature of parabolic communication and the task of public theology. I started to ponder whether the parables, or at least certain key parables, could serve as helpful paradigms for understanding public theology, that is, as tools for helping the church conceptualize its vocation in society as the bearer of a message—the 'gospel of the kingdom'—that is both intelligible and unintelligible to the world, both ethically feasible and eschatologically radical, both relevant to secular society and yet particular and distinctive to the community of faith. It is a message dependent on theological presuppositions that general society does not share or begin to comprehend, yet equally a message that promotes the common good by suggesting pragmatically achievable policy solutions to commonly experienced social and political problems.

Despite its pleasing (or perhaps irritating) alliteration, the designation of parables as paradigms for public theology could still prove to be a misleading or confusing one. I am certainly not meaning to imply that Christian contributions to public debate should typically take the form of telling enigmatic little tales which leave their hearers utterly perplexed about their intended meaning, even if this might sometimes be worth trying in place of the more sterile position papers usually offered, particularly in view of the significant role imagination plays in ethical reflection.[2] Nor am I suggesting

---

1. Christopher D. Marshall, *Compassionate Justice: An Interdisciplinary Dialogue with Two Gospel Parables on Law, Crime, and Restorative Justice* (Eugene, OR: Cascade Books, 2012), pp. ix-x.

2. See, for example, Kieran Cronin, *Rights and Christian Ethics* (Cambridge: Cambridge University Press, 1992), p. 116: 'The important role of imagination in

that all policy proposals made by Christians should invariably engage with the parables of Jesus, even if in my book I show the fruitfulness of doing so with respect to at least a couple of well known parables.

It is not the use of parables as a communication device or as a source of specialist information that I principally have in mind. Rather, it is the parables as the articulation or encapsulation of a particular perspective on reality, parables as a way of conceiving how God's redemptive initiative in the person and proclamation of Jesus of Nazareth comes to bear on present reality, including on the systems and institutions of public life. And this, surely, is what public theology should aim to do. It should endeavour to show how God's saving intervention in Jesus Christ has concrete implications, not only for the community of faith but also for how we manage 'the commons'—the natural, cultural and political resources of life we share in common in society.

Public Theology

The phrase 'public theology' is of quite recent coinage. It was first used, evidently, by the American historian of religion, Martin E. Marty, in an article published in 1974.[3] The term soon caught on however and is now commonplace, despite its considerable ambiguity. As we will see, both the words 'public' and 'theology' can be construed in diverse ways, and the collocation of the two terms, as well as being imprecise, can have unintended consequences for how the larger theological endeavour is envisaged. This means that any attempt to define public theology and its objectives is to open a rather large can of worms.

In one sense, there is no need to lift the lid and spill the worms here, because the issue under consideration—the relevance of parables to the undertaking—is common to all the ways public or political theology might be construed. For present purposes, it is enough to adopt a broad definition of public theology as *the attempt to address matters of common or public concern in society in light of the special truth-claims, insights and moral convictions of Christian faith, in the pursuit of peace and justice for all.*[4]

---

human knowing and being in the world has at last been widely recognized across the boundaries of various disciplines. Where once the value of the imagination was largely restricted to the category of art and literature, it has now escaped such limits, and finds a home in philosophy, science and theology. Imagination has come of age. Like the language of rights, it has become respectable, even indispensable.'

3. Martin E. Marty, 'Reinhold Niebuhr: Public Theology and the American Experience', *JR* 54 (1974), pp. 332-59.

4. On the need for the definition to include the intention of fostering peace and justice for all, see Heather Thomson, 'Stars and Compasses: Hermeneutical Guidelines for Public Theology', *IJPT* 2 (2008), pp. 258-76 (259).

In the words of Duncan Forrester, public theology is the attempt 'to offer distinctive and constructive insights from the treasury of faith to help in the building of a decent society...to offer something that is distinctive, and that is gospel, rather than simply adding the voice of theology to what everyone is saying already'.[5] Simply put, public theology is theology employed for public ends, the conscious effort to construct a 'theologically sound', 'publicly accessible' and 'practically viable social ethic'.[6]

With this inclusive definition in mind, we could now move directly to consider the role of Jesus' parables in executing this task. But the distinctive value of *parables* to this end will emerge all the more clearly if we first pause to open our can of worms and have at least a peek inside.

As noted, the label 'public theology' is not an altogether perspicuous one, since the component parts can be taken to mean different things, both on their own and in combination. The adjective 'public' in the label is sometimes understood in a spatial or sociological sense, to denote the institutional dimensions of society or distinct solidarities within society, such as the 'general public' or the 'voting public', and sometimes in an epistemological sense, to designate norms and forms of language that are accessible to or comprehensible by all reasonable people. The implied referent of the adjective is also equivocal. Is public theology 'public' because it enables the Christian public to better understand the social and political issues of its day so as to better discharge its mission in the world? Or is it public because it is addressed to the general public or to the public authorities, on behalf of the church? If it is the latter, then in what sense is it truly 'theology', especially if the distinctive grammar and vocabulary of theological discourse is first filtered out for the sake of public intelligibility, as is often the case?

The noun 'theology' is also understood in different ways. It is sometimes used generically to mean all talk that involves God or, even more broadly, religion, and sometimes in a more technical sense to designate one disciplinary branch of Christian scholarship, the branch concerned with systematic reflection on Christian doctrine or dogma. Which sense is intended in the label 'public theology'?[7]

---

5. Duncan B. Forrester, 'The Scope of Public Theology', *SCE* 17.2 (2004), pp. 5-19 (16).

6. This set of phrases is drawn from Max L. Stackhouse, 'Public Theology and Political Economy in a Globalizing Era', *SCE* 14.2 (2001), pp. 63-86 (80). See also John W. de Gruchy, 'Public Theology as Christian Witness: Exploring the Genre', *IJPT* 1 (2007), pp. 26-41.

7. In his plea for a genuine public *theology* in place of noise about 'Christian values', 'Christian principles' or a 'Christian nation', Charles Marsh comments: 'At its best, theology has a way of slowing down language, interrupting easy formulas, unsettling partisan confidences, and disciplining thought. Can anyone doubt that the churches in the United States could use a little more theology and a lot less religious

The amalgamation of the two words creates a further difficulty too. It could imply that only one part of Christian theology is public in nature and that the rest is somehow private, with the distinction between the two realms being self-evident. But this is plainly untrue, since all theology, of its very nature as a human response to the self-revelation of the one true God, is inescapably public in character. That is to say, its subject matter encompasses all created reality and deals in statements that claim universal validity, irrespective of whether particular persons or communities subscribe to them. As Jürgen Moltmann rightly states, 'From the perspective of its origins and its goal, Christian theology is *public* theology, for it is the theology of the *kingdom of God*.'[8] As such, it *must* engage with the public as well as the private spheres of life. As Jim Wallis is fond of saying, Christian faith may be personal, but it is never strictly private.

To muddy the waters still further, there is also the question of whether public theology is the same thing as *political* theology or *public religion*. These terms are often used interchangeably and there are obvious areas of overlap between them. But in the view of Max Stackhouse, each category has 'a distinct pedigree and entails a particular set of assumptions and implications'.[9] It is worth taking time to spell out these differences, partly because Stackhouse's characterization of public theology provides a helpful vantage point for thinking afresh about the socio-ethical value of the parables and partly because it affords those of us who subscribe to Anabaptist convictions a helpful way of thinking about the nature of Anabaptist witness in the public domain, in light of that tradition's acute sensitivity to the dangers of the church's political capture.[10]

Public Theology, Political Theology and Civil Religion

The term 'public religion' or 'civil religion' usually refers to the overt use of religious beliefs, practices and symbols to unify and sacralise a national or ethnic community. Stackhouse describes civil religion as 'a projection by a civic order of its experiences and values onto the cosmic order for the sake of social solidarity. It is, so to speak, society worshipping the image

---

talk?' See Charles Marsh, *Wayward Christian Soldiers: Freeing the Gospel from Political Captivity* (Oxford: Oxford University Press, 2007), pp. 98-99.

8. Jürgen Moltmann, with Nicholas Wolterstorff and Ellen T. Charry, *A Passion for God's Reign: Theology, Christian Learning, and the Christian Self* (ed. Miroslav Volf; Grand Rapids: Eerdmans, 1998), p. 24 (Moltmann's emphasis); cf. pp. 51-52.

9. Max L. Stackhouse, 'Civil Religion, Political Theology and Public Theology: What's the Difference?', *PT* 5.3 (2004), pp. 275-93 (276-77).

10. I say this notwithstanding Stackhouse's characterization of neo-Anabaptist perspectives, as popularized by Stanley Hauerwas, as a kind of 'sectarian pietism'. See Stackhouse, 'Civil Religion', pp. 278-79.

of itself, from the bottom up'.[11] Stackhouse traces its roots back to Cicero's delineation of the civic virtues and religious beliefs which a political authority should encourage or forbid in order to ensure the sacred solidarity and loyalty of its citizenry (*De legibus*, Book II). Rousseau adapted this notion shortly before the French Revolution. He distinguished between the universal, 'spiritual' religion of Christianity, which people accept or reject as a matter of private conviction, and the distinctive religious ideas and practices that should govern the life of the nation as a whole and express its unique character.

In the United States of America, this unifying civil religion could be called 'Americanism', sometimes characterized as the 'Shinto of the United States'. For historical and cultural reasons, American civil religion has been baptized by Christianity, though a baptism by sprinkling rather than by immersion, Stackhouse wryly notes. It is currently a Christianity of a distinctly evangelical or fundamentalist kind, one wholly bereft of any social or political theory, except for a generalized patriotism.[12] It is also, we might add, bereft of much theological sophistication.

'Political theology', by comparison, has its deepest philosophical roots in Aristotle's understanding of the political order as something that comprehends and structures all of society and of human beings as constitutionally political animals. Its Christian roots go back at least to Eusebius's eulogizing of Constantine and, subsequently, to the profound influence of Aristotle on Catholic, Anglican and Lutheran higher education. The Aristotelian view of the primacy of political institutions to society became the dominant understanding in most post-feudal European states. It found expression, amongst other ways, in the emergence of established and liturgically distinctive national churches, both Protestant and Catholic, each subordinate to their respective political regimes and, in many cases, explicitly legitimating them.

In the modern era, in response to the totalitarianisms of the twentieth century, political theology has become more reformist or progressive in character, even at times revolutionary, often challenging political oppression and championing democratic principles and human rights. Still, undergirding most political theology, Stackhouse argues, is the assumption that the political order has primacy in society and that governmental power should be exercised in the interests of justice to shape the policies of all subordinate organisations:

> [Political theology] tends to see politics, focused on a centralized government, as the comprehending institution of society and the primary manifestation and guarantor of public justice. Politics, in this view, is dedicated to

---

11. Stackhouse, 'Civil Religion', p. 291.
12. Stackhouse, 'Civil Religion', pp. 278-79.

the accumulation, organization and exercise of the kind of power that sees itself as responsible for the control and guidance of all the social institutions within it. It may be more or less benevolent, authoritarian or totalitarian; but it is always deeply concerned with the power to guide, limit, empower or command every subject or citizen and every other institution in a geographical territory, and the threat of the use of force stands behind its actions.[13]

In this sense, political theology is 'top-down'. It is also top-down in the sense that it considers the existence and norms of the political order to be of divine origin, not simply a human construction. For that reason, theologians, pastors and parishioners have a positive duty to address the political as well as the personal sphere in light of God's will, 'since the policies of every political order need direct guidance and transformation at the hands of theological-ethical insight'.[14]

'Public theology' shares this top-down conviction that the source of normative thought and life for society resides in divine revelation rather than in the bottom-up religious sentiments and experiences of particular human communities (as in civil religion). Such revelation addresses the whole of life and has implications not only for the church but also for the social, political, cultural and economic arrangements of wider society. The term 'public theology' itself may be of recent American origin, but its underlying orientation and convictions are not new. Stackhouse traces its philosophical roots to 'those streams of thought deriving from the Platonic tradition that appeared not only in Augustinian motifs, but in certain branches of the Renaissance, Reformation and Enlightenment'.[15] This stream of tradition emphasizes that, notwithstanding the radical impact of sin, all human beings retain a capacity to recognize and respond to the norms of faith, hope, love and justice (cf. Rom. 2.15).

Drawing on both philosophical reason (sometimes employing the concept of natural law) and the biblical heritage, public theology affirms the idea that Christian faith 'can and should not only address believers in the church in ways that touch their souls, but empower the faithful to address the world in its wider structures and dynamics by developing the kind of reasonable moral theology that is able to assess and reform the institutions of civil society'.[16] Such a conviction is well established in certain strands of Roman Catholic theology, where official documents routinely affirm that several Christian doctrines can and should address all people of good will. It is also consistent with the Protestant reformational emphasis on the

---

13. Stackhouse, 'Civil Religion', p. 288.
14. Stackhouse, 'Civil Religion', p. 282.
15. Stackhouse, 'Civil Religion', p. 283.
16. Stackhouse, 'Civil Religion', p. 286.

sovereignty of God and lordship of Christ, which similarly leads to the conviction that all spheres of life are finally accountable to God's Word.

The way in which public theology *differs* from political theology, Stackhouse proposes, is that public theology does not assume the primacy and dominance of the political order in working out the implications of revelation. God's revelation is intended 'first of all for inner personal convictions, the communities of faith and the associations they generate in an open society…'.[17] This does not mean that the principles and purposes of Christian revelation are limited to the religious community or private sphere alone, for they are meant to shape society by working their way out through 'the people and policies of the multiple institutions of civil society where people live and work and play, that make up the primary public realm'.[18]

In other words, in place of the top-down model of political theology, where theological witness presupposes the primacy and predominance of the state, and the bottom-up model of civil religion, where religious unity is secured by the cosmic projection of cultural self-celebration, public theology envisages a 'centre-out' process, where theological insight is mediated through the believing community to the multiple associations that make up pluralist society. Such a process acknowledges the legitimacy of a limited constitutional political order that serves people, protects human rights and allows all the manifold institutions and spheres of civil society to flourish to the glory of God. It also affirms the value of co-operation across cultural, religious and confessional lines because all people, regardless of their particular beliefs, have the capacity to discern the basic principles of right and wrong.

Put simply, we might say that public theology *includes* a theology of politics and government, but it *is* essentially a theology of society, a society in which the state is one institution among many, not the all-comprehending and society-constituting reality it is often assumed to be. It is also not the principal addressee of the church's public witness. As Stackhouse conceives it, public theology is 'based on the conviction that the public is prior to the republic, that the fabric of civil society, of which religious faith and organisation are inevitably the core, is more determinative of, and normatively more important for, politics than politics is for society and religion'.[19]

Whereas political theology inclines toward a *political view of society*, public theology tends to adopt a *social theory of politics*. According to this understanding, every political order is itself the product of, and subject to, more primary powers and authorities in society: 'those spheres of life that embody those moral and spiritual orientations that become embodied in

---

17. Stackhouse, 'Civil Religion', p. 291.
18. Stackhouse, 'Civil Religion', p. 291.
19. Stackhouse, 'Civil Religion', p. 285.

social and ethical tissues and associations of the common life and that are prior to the formation of political orders'.[20] Political structures are not primary; they are generated by 'religious, cultural, familial, economic and social traditions that are prior to government, and every government is, sooner or later, accountable to them'.[21] Public theology accepts the legitimate role of political and judicial institutions in society; it simply wants politics to be the limited servant of other institutions of society, not its master.[22]

Stackhouse's way of distinguishing between 'political' and 'public' theology, and his tying the latter to a particular kind of social theory, will not be universally shared by all political theologians, many of whom presume a more generic view of the discipline.[23] But his depiction of public theology as addressing civil society more than the role of the political state is significant and should be especially attractive to Anabaptists and other peace church traditions. The Anabaptist tradition has always been wary of the danger of theology serving to divinize the state and its claim to monopolize legitimate violence, and of the church being captured by political or provincial allegiances. To the extent that public theology cuts political sovereignty down to size,[24] emphasizes the crucial role of the church in working out God's will for civil society in general, not only for government, and recognizes the foundational significance of the religious, cultural and moral traditions that give rise to society and its institutions, it provides a valuable space for Anabaptist witness to find expression (even if much Anabaptist writing on social ethics remains curiously state-centred).[25]

Understood in these terms, Anabaptist pacifism can be seen as a legitimate expression of public theology rather than the 'moral perfectionism' and 'sectarian withdrawal' it is often cast as by its magisterial critics. Non-participation in the violence of the state may indeed represent a *partial* withdrawal from the political arena, but it is not a withdrawal from the *polis* as a

---

20. Stackhouse, 'Civil Religion', p. 289.
21. Stackhouse, 'Civil Religion', p. 289.
22. Stackhouse, 'Civil Religion', p. 286.
23. For a useful survey of recent political theology, see William T. Cavanaugh, Jeffrey W. Bailey and Craig Hovey (eds.), *An Eerdmans Reader in Contemporary Political Theology* (Grand Rapids: Eerdmans, 2012).
24. For a fascinating analysis of the way in which the nation-state has usurped all other forms of political community and 'colonized' the Christian imagination, see William T. Cavanaugh, *Migrations of the Holy: God, State, and the Political Meaning of the Church* (Grand Rapids: Eerdmans, 2011).
25. The premier Mennonite social ethicist of the twentieth century, John Howard Yoder, focused almost entirely on the Christian witness to the state and had little to say in detail about Christian witness to civil society or the wider cultural realm. For a discussion of how state-centrism has over-determined neo-Anabaptist political thought, see Jamie Pitts, *Principalities and Powers: Revising John Howard Yoder's Sociological Theology* (Eugene, OR: Pickwick Publications, 2013).

whole or from social responsibility as such. In fact, it need not even be seen as a withdrawal from *state* politics. A principled refusal by the church to be assimilated to the state's monopoly of lethal violence actually performs a valuable *political* service *to* the state: it acts as a check on the state's proclivity to tyranny and absolute power. In that sense, it remains politically, as well as publicly, engaged, not disengaged.

Shaping Public Theology

Public theology aims to make a plausible and principled Christian contribution to matters of public life and debate. In doing so, as I have discussed elsewhere, it faces two main challenges: the challenge of constructing a *credible* Christian perspective on the matter under discussion, and the challenge of expressing this perspective in an *intelligible* way to the diverse audiences that comprise secular society.[26] The latter issue has attracted most attention in recent scholarship, for it raises the thorny question of whether 'public reason' requires the use of exclusively secular language and categories by every citizen, including by religious actors, or whether such a normative requirement is indefensible in terms of the liberal premises and democratic constitutional arrangements it claims to uphold.[27] I will not say any more about that matter here, but it may be helpful to the analysis of parables that follows to reiterate my comments on the first issue of how public theologians go about determining what constitutes a credible and distinctively Christian position on the topic at issue.

This is by no means easy, for several reasons. To begin with, there is the *problem of sources*. There is more to public theology than the exegesis of relevant biblical texts or the application of so-called 'biblical principles' to current issues. It entails, rather, a wide-ranging conversation between the full range of Christian sources (Scripture, tradition, reason and experience) and the insights of moral philosophy, history, political theory and the social sciences. In other words, public theology is necessarily an interdisciplinary enterprise, and interdisciplinary work is always enormously difficult. The challenge is to weigh all the available evidence within a self-consciously

---

26. See my essay, 'What Language Shall I Borrow? The Bilingual Dilemma of Public Theology', *Stimulus* 13.3 (2005), pp. 11-18.

27. Particularly insightful here are the writings of Jonathan Chaplin, such as 'Beyond Liberal Restraint: Defending Religiously-based Arguments in Law and Public Policy', *UBC Law Review* 33 (2000), pp. 617-46; 'The Future of Theological Ethics: A Response to Robin Lovin and Nigel Biggar', *SCE* 25.2 (2012), pp. 148-52; and 'Law, Religion and Public Reasoning', *Oxford Journal of Law and Religion* 1.2 (2013), pp. 1-21. Also interesting is Brett T. Wilmot, 'Defending Democracy Against its "Cultured Despisers": A Critical Consideration of Some Recent Approaches', *JSCE* 26.1 (2006), pp. 37-59.

Christian worldview, conditioned by the witness of Scripture, the history of doctrine and the lived experience of the church down through the ages and across cultures, all of which are amenable to sundry interpretations.

For most Christians, the canonical Scriptures play an indispensable and primary role in formulating their views. Pride of place here belongs to the New Testament, for without it we would know virtually nothing about Jesus and the origins of Christian theology. But in turning to the New Testament, public theology encounters what could be called the *problem of focus*. The New Testament has very little to say about the role of the state and the functioning of civil institutions. Instead, it has a faith focus, an ecclesial focus and an eschatological focus.[28]

It has a faith focus inasmuch as it addresses committed Christian believers, not unbelievers. It has an ecclesial focus in that it is concerned primarily with the internal life of tiny, voluntary Christian communities rather than with the affairs of wider Jewish or Greco-Roman society. And it has an eschatological focus in that it views moral life from the perspective of the eschatological transformations that have occurred with the dawning of God's kingdom and the outpouring of the Holy Spirit. The New Testament does not merely affirm a set of ethical standards incumbent on all people by virtue of their common humanity and achievable by the free exercise of the will. It also enjoins standards of conduct and character that go far beyond what is 'naturally' possible and which presuppose participation in the 'new creation' that has broken redemptively into the present in the person of Christ. It teaches the ethics of Christian discipleship, not the ethics of social and political policy.

Many of the so-called hard sayings of Jesus come into this category. Believers are beckoned not simply to respect the rights of their neighbours but actively to love and serve them, including even their enemies. They are not merely to avoid murder and adultery but to eschew lust and anger; not simply to forgive those who hurt them but even to bless their persecutors and pray for those who hate them. The peculiar problem for public theology, then, is to decide how the eschatological values of Christian existence can meaningfully inform the common life of wider, non-Christian society. This is *the* crucial question to which I will return later when discussing the parables.

This brings us, thirdly, to the *problem of determination*. Once all the sources of guidance are consulted and understood, the question remains of what constitutes a truly *Christian* position on the particular issue at hand. Such a position is not simply one that is held by most practising Christians, for sincere believers have done all manner of devilish things in the

---

28. See Christopher D. Marshall, *Beyond Retribution: A New Testament Vision for Justice, Crime, and Punishment* (Grand Rapids: Eerdmans, 2001), pp. 9-16.

name of religious truth. Rather, it is one that is demonstrably consistent with the central norms and values of Christian belief in general and the Gospel narratives of Jesus' life and teaching in particular. Given the diversity and complexity of sources, the irreducible role of human interpretation in appropriating them and the variety of Christian theological frameworks that exist, it is futile to look for *the* Christian view on this or that issue. On any contentious issue there is usually as much disagreement within the Christian community as there is in wider society. It is frequently the case that several different, even opposing, perspectives will claim Christian fidelity for themselves. In this situation, there is no alternative but ongoing dialogue and debate within the Christian family on the matter at hand, in a setting of humility and mutual respect (cf. Acts 15.1-29; Rom. 14.1–15.13).

But even if a Christian consensus on an issue should, perchance, emerge, difficulties remain. There is still the tricky job of determining what pragmatic policy options will produce outcomes that most closely approximate Christian concerns. Christians ought to agree, for example, on care for the weak and indigent as a central obligation for every human society. But determining what social and economic policies will be most effective in protecting and empowering those on the margins is a matter of fallible human judgment. Religious faith guarantees no special expertise for translating moral principle into effective policy.

A fourth problem confronting public theology is the *problem of reception*. All attempts to articulate a theological perspective today must reckon with the long history of Christian political involvement and its frequently baleful legacy. Following the Constantinian settlement, it was expected that Christianity would fulfil the normal task of religion in antiquity of shaping and legitimating political rule. Although there were always features in the Christian narrative that served as an impediment to the total co-optation of Christianity by the state,[29] the church still often prostituted itself to Caesar, advancing its own agenda by what has been called a 'combination of flattery and battery'—flattery towards the emperor and battery against heretics and dissidents.[30]

It is not surprising, then, that with the Enlightenment came the attempt to restrict and moderate the public role of religion in society.[31] It was decided

---

29. These include its central narrative of a saviour crucified by the legitimate authorities, its pervasive fear of idolatry and its eschatological expectations that God's own rule would eventually sweep away all earthly rulers, inaugurating a universal reign of peace and justice.

30. See Alan Kreider, *The Change of Conversion and the Origin of Christendom* (Harrisburg, PA: Trinity Press International, 1999), esp. pp. 91-98, and also 'Beyond Bosch: The Early Church and the Christendom Shift', *International Bulletin* 29.2 (2005), pp. 59-68.

31. William Cavanaugh has argued, however, that the post-Reformation Wars of

that the liberal polity should operate on the basis of reason, positive law and respect for individual rights. Ideas and values deriving from religious belief were to have no normative public role, for religion appeals to revelation rather than to reason, and no one revealed religion can ever command universal assent. Theology was still welcome at the public table but only as long as its voice conformed to the truths of reason and could be validated by social consensus. While that consensus remained nominally Christian, theology continued to play a potent public role in Western societies. But with the steady growth of secularization, the final unravelling of Christendom and the marked increase in pluralism in society, the Christian voice no longer enjoys a positive reception in public debate. Religion and theology are now viewed as a trivial, if not malign, influence in political life and are largely ignored in political deliberations. It is no longer accepted that Christian theology trades in public truth; it simply articulates 'the beliefs of a minority of "cognitive deviants" in the population'.[32] Even if its rights of access to the public forum are protected by democratic principle, the church's voice today is more often tolerated than welcomed, and it is forced to operate under terms dictated by secular rationalism.

These, then, are the daunting methodological problems public theology faces in coming to a credible Christian contribution to public life, even before it confronts the equally challenging task of articulating its views in an intelligible and faithful way. What role, then, do the *parables* have in all of this? In what sense can we look to the parables as paradigms for conceptualizing the task of public theology and the public role of the church?

The Potential of Parables

I began with a broad definition of public theology as the attempt to address matters of common concern in society in light of the special truth-claims, insights and moral convictions of Christian faith, in the pursuit of justice

---

Religion were not engendered by religion at all but 'were fought largely for the aggrandizement of the emerging State over the decaying remnants of the medieval ecclesial order...what was at issue in these wars was the very creation of religion as a set of privately held beliefs without direct political relevance... [which] was necessitated by the new State's need to secure absolute sovereignty over its subjects'. See William T. Cavanaugh, '"A Fire Strong Enough to Consume the House": The Wars of Religion and the Rise of the State', in *Radical Orthodoxy* (ed. Graham Ward, Catherine Pickstock and John Milbank; London: Routledge, 1999), pp. 397-419. This thesis is worked out at length in Cavanaugh's important book, *The Myth of Religious Violence: Secular Ideology and the Roots of Modern Conflict* (Oxford: Oxford University Press, 2009).

32. Duncan B. Forrester, *Christian Justice and Public Policy* (Cambridge: Cambridge University Press, 1997), p. 9.

and peace for all. In this, we have seen, it shares common cause with political theology, though public theology is less preoccupied with the role of government and the political state, and more focused on the diverse organisations, spheres, issues and involvements that comprise civil society. This mandate usually entails, on occasions, articulating its views in the public arena, where it is usually expected to conform to the secular canons of public reason. Even in doing so, public theology may still be considered 'theological', however, *not* because it speaks 'from faith to faith' (as does doctrinal theology), nor because it employs theological language (often it does not), but because it draws on theological resources and authorities when first formulating its views.

The most important of these resources and authorities is canonical Scripture, however diversely it is interpreted and whatever relative weight it may be given vis-à-vis tradition, reason and experience. Now when Scripture is appropriated for the theological task, it is necessarily read through a Christological lens. That is to say, its normative authority resides principally in its witness to the mission, person and work of Jesus Christ. Accordingly, as a theologically grounded endeavour, public theology *must* reckon with, and be finally accountable to, the biblical testimony to the person and work of Jesus Christ. This in turn requires deep engagement with the Gospel traditions, for it is here we find our only reliable record of the life, career and teaching of Jesus.

In turning to the Gospel accounts, we encounter a fascinating fact: at least one third of the recorded teaching of Jesus in the Synoptic tradition comes to us in the form of parabolic discourse of one kind or another. I say 'of one kind or another' because scholars differ in terms of how widely or narrowly they define 'parable'. Some define the category broadly to include all examples of non-literal or figurative speech, including proverbs, metaphors, similes, hyperbole, symbols, analogies, aphorisms, riddles, mysteries and so on. Others limit the category to the short fictional narratives Jesus told, ranging from very brief examples, such as the Parable of the Buried Treasure (31 words) to much longer and more sophisticated examples, such as the Parable of the Prodigal Son (390 words). These story parables are often further subdivided into various categories, either on the basis of their literary type, such as similitudes, example stories and allegories, or on the basis of their content or theme, such as parables of growth, parables of delay, parables of judgment, parables of reversal, parables of refusal, parables of discovery and so on.

Such variety within the parable genre, as well as within the long interpretive tradition that has ensued in their wake, means that it is very difficult to make blanket statements about the parables that apply in every instance. Even if we limit ourselves to the narrative parables, every generalisation will have exceptions or qualifications. But to keep the discussion manageable and pertinent to our subject, I will rely on some broad-brush observations about the character, power and purpose of parabolic discourse in the proclamation of Jesus that have relevance to the task of public theology.

I will not consider the complicated question of how best to adjudicate between diverse readings of particular parables, or how to choose between the various reading strategies that have been brought to bear on them—the allegorical, moralist, historicist, existentialist, literary-critical, socio-political, socio-rhetorical and so on.[33] It will be enough to repeat the broad hermeneutical parameters proposed in *Compassionate Justice*:

> For any particular interpretation of a Gospel parable to be credible, it must be demonstrably faithful to how the story itself is constructed and told, do justice to the historical and cultural points of reference implied in the text, make sense of the narrative and conceptual context in which the parable occurs in the Gospel tradition, and cohere with what we know of the larger message and perspective of its narrator.[34]

There are three observations about Jesus' parabolic communication that invite a comparison with the character and goals of public theology.

A Central Means of Communication

The first observation is that Jesus made such deliberate and frequent use of parables to convey his message that no attempt at public theology can afford to ignore them. In the parables, it is generally agreed, we come closest to the most characteristic and authentic voice of Jesus, so they are by no means of peripheral importance to discerning his standpoint on a wide range of issues. As far as we know, he is the only teacher in Jewish and Christian tradition who employed parables as his central mode of communication. He did not merely use an occasional parable to illustrate or prove some statement; he made parables the very lifeblood of his proclamation. 'With many such parables he spoke the word to them, as they were able to hear it', Mark explains. 'He did not speak to them except in parables, but he explained everything in private to his disciples' (Mk 4.33-34 // Mt. 13.34).

This preference for parable is partly explicable in terms of the distinctive power of storytelling to induce emotional experience and promote self-understanding in an audience. All good stories do this, but Jesus' parables did it to an unrivalled degree. They mediated the very experience of God's presence, and they addressed and evoked in hearers a response that disclosed the state of their hearts, the extent of their spiritual receptivity, their readiness to engage. The parables did not simply convey information about

---

33. The secondary literature on the parables is vast and constantly growing. A particularly useful analysis is Klyne Snodgrass, *Stories with Intent: A Comprehensive Guide to the Parables of Jesus* (Grand Rapids: Eerdmans, 2008).

34. Marshall, *Compassionate Justice*, p. 25; cf. p. 192 n. 39.

the external world; they helped to project an entirely new world of perception and experience, and they invited hearers into that reconfigured world as active participants, both imaginatively and in terms of subsequent social behaviour.

Jesus' heavy reliance on parables is also explicable in terms of the fundamental importance of storytelling to the construction of social solidarity and identity and also to the development of collective morality. Human beings are, by constitution, storytelling creatures, compelled to make sense of experience by recollection and narration. We use narratives to formulate and convey our understanding of ourselves and the world we inhabit. As communities, we use narratives to express our common origins, history, memories and ideals, and we use religious narratives to connect historical experience to matters of ultimate concern. We also use stories to foster moral commitment and to sharpen ethical sensitivities. Stories, it seems, are socially formative and morally effectual in a way that abstract rules and philosophical principles are not.[35] As a master storyteller, Jesus devised a whole repertoire of stories that would convey his own distinctive perspective on the world and would enable listeners to see their present world, and their past history, in a new light (including, sometimes, fresh insight into the oppressive and unjust nature of the prevailing socio-political order).[36] The stories also helped to forge a new sense of identity and solidarity amongst his followers, as collective agents of a new world order intruding on the old.

Not surprisingly, the parables encountered diverse responses from hearers, pictured famously in the Parable of the Sower as seed falling onto different kinds of soil (Mk 4.3-20). Not all who heard the parables were able to discern or accept the deeper insight being disclosed. But some could. Some had 'ears to hear and eyes to see',[37] and for them the parables served to cast further light on the remarkable thing taking place in their midst through the activity of Jesus and their part in it (Mk 4.22-25).

In a sense, public theology encounters a similar situation. Its public nature means its audience is hugely diverse and includes many who are unable to appreciate or accept its undergirding theological convictions. Non-believers may understand what is being said at a pragmatic or policy level, but they will be blind, perhaps even hostile, to its deeper epistemological commitments and implications. On some occasions, even the pragmatic message will be unacceptable to them because it presupposes a completely different way of evaluating reality than is commonly accepted. A case in point, perhaps, is Christian advocacy of nonviolence and love of enemy. Christian

---

35. Cf. Marshall, *Compassionate Justice*, 19.
36. Cf. William R. Herzog II, *Parables as Subversive Speech: Jesus as Pedagogue of the Oppressed* (Louisville, KY: Westminster/John Knox Press, 1994).
37. See Mk 4.3, 9, 13, 23-24; 7.18; 8.17-20; Lk. 14.35.

nonviolence is grounded not simply in obedience to the plain teaching of Jesus (Mt. 5.9, 38-48) but, more fundamentally, in a belief in the objective, disarming impact on the principalities and powers of Christ's life, death and resurrection. Non-believers may (or may not) be sympathetic to utilitarian and moral arguments about the superiority of nonviolence in achieving justice and peace, but they will not grasp the metaphysical dimension of Christian peace advocacy or recognize its deeply subversive consequences. As with Jesus' parables, they will see but not perceive, they will hear but not understand, lest they get more than they bargained for—a demand for radical repentance and faith, towards which public theology must ultimately gesture at some level.[38]

A Real World Focus
A second observation about the parables pertinent to public theology is their markedly this-worldly focus. Though Jesus characteristically used the parables to illuminate the character and activity of God—introducing several with comments like, 'With what can we compare the kingdom of God?' or 'The kingdom of God is like...'—the narratives themselves are extraordinarily secular in character. They deal with the regular routines of everyday life; they include ordinary human actors, involved in normal human relationships and embedded in recognizable social and political settings. Their subject matter reflects the lived experience of the 'little people' of small-scale Palestinian village society to whom Jesus directed his mission.

In one or two stories, religious characters may appear, such as priests, Levites and Pharisees, and at least one of the stories is set in the Jerusalem Temple (Lk. 18.9-14). But even these episodes are not primarily concerned with abstract theological debates or religious rituals. For the most part, the parables deal with the world of fields and fishing, of sowing and harvesting, of feasting and banquets, of household activities and tenancy disputes, of baking bread and looking after sheep, of ruthless landlords and autocratic rulers, of building houses and lighting lamps, of chronic indebtedness and entrenched unemployment, of travel to neighbouring towns and its many perils, of crime, conflict and imprisonment, of losing things and finding them again.

---

38. The so-called 'parable theory' of Mk 4.10-12 (and its variations in Mt. 13.10-16; Lk. 8.9-10; cf. Jn 12.39-40) is notoriously difficult to explain. But the tension it expresses between the parables as a tool concurrently of revelation and concealment is explicable in terms of the wilful resistance on the part of some hearers to the deepest claims of the message—the need for thoroughgoing repentance and forgiveness. See Christopher D. Marshall, *Faith as a Theme in Mark's Gospel* (Cambridge: Cambridge University Press, 1989), pp. 72-74.

There is a notable absence of fantasy elements in the parables.[39] There are no haunted forests or talking animals or wizards casting magical spells or superhuman heroes swooping down in the nick of time to bring miraculous deliverance through preternatural powers. Even God figures as an actor only rarely.[40] The plot may include extravagant details—like ridiculously huge harvests or impossibly massive debts—but even these features are not depicted as the direct outcome of supernatural agency. With the exception of the tale of Lazarus and Dives (Lk. 16.19-31), the parables are more like newspaper stories than fairy stories. Their substance is derived from run-of-the-mill happenings in rural Palestine.

This compelling 'realism' of the parables serves at least two purposes. At a *rhetorical level*, it facilitates the involvement of hearers in the story being told. Listeners recognize the story world as *their* world, the problems portrayed as their problems, the characters depicted as the kind of people they know all too well. Such familiarity draws them imaginatively into the drama and triggers in them the kind of emotional, moral and spiritual responses Jesus wanted to evoke. At a *theological level*, the realism suggests that God's activity—in particular God's action of inaugurating the eschatological kingdom—is located in the midst of everyday affairs.[41] God's reign is not confined to Temple and Torah; it permeates 'secular' life or civil society as well and hence is best understood by means of metaphors and analogies drawn from common life, and tellingly bereft of religious dogma.[42] As Chilton and McDonald explain, 'It does not matter that

---

39. See Gerd Theissen and Annette Merz, *The Historical Jesus: A Comprehensive Guide* (London: SCM Press, 1996), pp. 335-37.

40. God or the Son of Man appears as a character in the parable of the Sheep and Goats (Mt. 25.31-46) and the parable of the Rich Fool (Lk. 12.16-21), while 'Father Abraham' appears in the parable of Lazarus and Dives (Lk. 16.19-31). Even if some critics would want to include the Bible as a whole in the genre of fantasy because that genre alone can accommodate the supernatural events, divine personages and miracles recorded within (cf. Colin Manlove, 'The Bible in Fantasy', *Semeia* 60 [1992], pp. 91-110), the relative absence of such features in the dominical parables is a noteworthy feature of their form.

41. See L. Ryken, *Words of Life: A Literary Introduction to the New Testament* (Grand Rapids: Baker House, 1987), p. 63: 'The realism of the parables is an important part of their religious meaning. There are so few references to religious practices or to the religious professionals of the day that the surface world of the parables is decidedly "secular." On the basis of their literal level, we could not possibly guess that they are designed to teach religious truth. The parables thus assault any "two-world" outlook that divides the spiritual and earthly realms. In the world of the parables, it is in everyday experience that people make their spiritual decisions and that God's grace works.'

42. Theissen and Merz, *The Historical Jesus*, p. 345, observe that the symbolic and metaphorical nature of parables makes them uniquely suited to discourse about God.

some parables are linked explicitly to the Kingdom and others are not. It is evident that all are designed to name, articulate, even to dramatize, some aspects of the reality of life in which everyone is involved, and to discern the activity of God in it.'[43] It is in the rich tapestry of everyday life that the reign of God and its justice are to be found and worked out.

In this feature, the parables constitute a striking anticipation and endorsement of the goal of public theology, which, I suggested, is to show how God's saving intervention in Christ has concrete implications for society as a whole and for how we manage 'the commons'. This civil society focus cautions against a forced over-politicization of the parables, to which some interpreters today are inclined. Even if some parables do allude polemically to contemporary political realities and oppressive practices, others are more irenic reflections on the common stuff of life, rather than coded critiques of systemic injustice and imperial domination.[44]

Perhaps it is this feature that helps account for the phenomenal impact several of Jesus' parables have had in shaping Western culture and society in general, far beyond the realm of power politics. In *Compassionate Justice*, I draw attention to how the parables of the Good Samaritan and the Prodigal Son have furnished the subject matter for numerous works of art, music, choreography, drama, film, literature, philosophy and legal theory, and have also informed research and debate in several academic disciplines, such as social psychology. Indeed, it is difficult to imagine two more influential stories than these two parables in the development of the spiritual, aesthetic, moral, social, political and intellectual traditions of Western civilization. Their generative power, I suggest, stems from the fact that they portray 'universal human fears, faults, and foibles in the face of circumstances that are morally ambiguous and personally demanding',[45] which is what public theology must also seek to do if it is to have any hearing at all in contemporary society.

Ethics and Eschatology
This brings us to a third and most important observation. It is crucial to recognize that, set against the backdrop of his mission and message, Jesus' parables are more than simple moral yarns or dramatizations of popular

---

The parables 'are an undogmatic way of speaking of God. They do not bear witness to the way people have always thought about God. Nor do they prescribe how people should always think of God. They aim to give impulses towards thinking of God in new and different ways'.

43. Bruce Chilton and J.I.H. McDonald, *Jesus and the Ethics of the Kingdom* (London: SPCK, 1987), p. 64.

44. Cf. Mary Ann Beavis, 'The Power of Jesus' Parables: Were They Polemical or Irenic?', *JSNT* 82 (2001), pp. 3-30.

45. Marshall, *Compassionate Justice*, p. 2.

wisdom. Viewed in isolation, some may appear to be straightforward appeals to common sense: 'Which one of you would not go after a sheep lost in the wilderness?' 'Who would ever consider putting new wine into old wineskins?' 'What father would dream of giving his son a stone if he asked for bread?' But viewed in their evangelical context, the parables are typically much more subversive than that, calling into question the reliability of conventional ways of understanding the world and its moral certainties. Even those tales that echo shared values and commonplace experiences still serve a larger transformational agenda.

At one level, the parables are thoroughly realistic reflections of present existence. They usually begin by portraying familiar circumstances, drawing hearers into the story and lulling them into a false sense of security about the way the world operates. But then something baffling occurs, something surprising or shocking, something that reverses expectations or confounds calculations. A rupture rents the realism. Impossibly huge harvests are reaped; debts of astronomical size are forgiven; wedding invitations are declined with unimaginably rude excuses, in breach of every rule of village hospitality; latecomers to the workplace are paid the same wages as early starters; true virtue is exhibited by hated apostates and compromised tax collectors. Things are obviously not as they seem. Something peculiar is happening.

This 'sting in the tail' of many of the parables is intended to stop hearers in their tracks and cause them to question the reliability of their existing frames of reference and dominant narratives. It also serves to tip them off to the fact that the story is about something far more profound than farming or fishing, baking or building, servants and masters, indebtedness and release. It is about *God* and what God is now doing behind the scenes to change the world by bringing his royal justice to earth and what this means practically for those who embrace it. The parabolic shock also underscores the reality that God's impinging kingdom is not a familiar, tame, homely, reassuring spiritual experience. Quite the opposite: it horrifies and appals; it challenges and confounds; it up-ends taken for granted values and overturns established human judgments. It reckons the great to be small and the small to be great, the first to be last and the last first, the least of all to be highest of all and the highest to be of least account. It is, in short, a revolutionary phenomenon that confronts prevailing social, cultural, religious, domestic, economic and political arrangements with the demand for radical change.

It is the interpenetration of eschatology and ethics in the parables that accounts for their characteristic mix of realism and unrealism. (By 'eschatology', I am not referring to parabolic portrayals of end-time events like the resurrection of the dead and Last Judgment but to their underlying presupposition that, with the appearance of Jesus, an eschatological shift in the ages has occurred: God's long awaited kingdom has dawned.) Moreover, it is this combination of reality and unreality, of eschatology and ethics that is critical to appreciating the significance of Jesus' parables for public theology.

The supreme challenge for public theology, I suggest, is to hold in tension the ethically achievable and the eschatologically radical dimensions of the gospel. When speaking into the public square, the temptation is to emphasize what is practically achievable at the social and political level, and to elide the eschatological 'extra mile' dimension that presupposes and necessitates divine empowerment to achieve. When speaking into an ecclesial setting, the temptation is to emphasize the eschatological 'with God all things are possible' dimension and to overlook the question of how such radicalism has practical implications for wider, unbelieving society.

The parables succeed in uniting both elements. By invariably portraying human activity and the normal routines of social life, they show how a fallible human response to the initiative God has taken to establish divine reign in the world is essential to its realization on the ground, so to speak. Human co-operation is implicated in the presence of the kingdom.[46] The parables proclaim what Crossan calls a 'collaborative eschaton', one in which human as well as divine action is required to accomplish God's will on earth.[47] At the same time, the parables beckon an obedience that goes far beyond what is humanly achievable or prudentially justifiable, an obedience that requires hearers to open themselves to the eschatological power of God made available in the person and Spirit of Jesus. This, indeed, is arguably the principal task of the church—to awaken the consciousness of society to the fuller reach of God's restoring justice by striving to embody in its own life and practices the 'higher obedience' to which God's reign calls.

Conclusion

The parables are an important resource for public theology. This is apparent from their prominent and performative function in Jesus' proclamation of the kingdom of God, a proclamation which itself affords public theology its fundamental mandate and normative reference point. The parables have a markedly secular or this-worldly character, though they view this world from a transcendent or divine standpoint. They both reflect everyday reality and refract it through the prism of God's mysterious work behind the scenes to restore the world to wholeness.

---

46. Chilton and McDonald, *Jesus and Ethics*, p. 31.
47. John Dominic Crossan, *God and Empire: Jesus Against Rome, Then and Now* (San Francisco: HarperCollins, 2007), p. 116; cf. p. 235. See also Robert B. Stewart (ed.), *The Resurrection of Jesus: John Dominic Crossan and N.T. Wright in Dialogue* (Minneapolis: Fortress Press, 2006), pp. 31-32, 178-79.

This restorative intervention is an eschatological reality, that is, an act of God proper to the end of the age. But it is also one that elicits, and indeed requires, human collaboration in the present age. This collaboration should be conscious and intentional on the part of the believing community, those who have 'received' the kingdom and have embarked on discipleship. But it will not be so for unbelieving society, which cannot discern the deeper truth at work beneath the surface. The task of public theology, accordingly, is to identify the ways in which God's restoring initiative in Christ impinges on society as a whole, coaxing it to move, albeit unawares, in a direction that is consistent with the redemptive priorities of God's reign and never shrinking, where appropriate, from naming its ultimate hope. Only in this way can public theology satisfy Forrester's proviso that it offers 'something that is *distinctive*, and that is *gospel*, rather than simply adding the voice of theology to what everyone is saying already'.[48]

Drawing from 'its treasury of faith', public theology should strive both to shape a more just and peaceful society for all and to tilt it towards the higher obedience of the kingdom. It will seek to construct a practically viable social ethic for general society, yet without surrendering the 'extra mile' radicalism of Christian discipleship and its meaning. The relevance of the parables to this end lies precisely in their character as *parables*. Parables should not be treated as repositories of normative rules, juridical principles or procedural guidelines that may be translated directly into justice theory or political policy in mainstream society today. Instead, their value lies in the distinctive worldview or hierarchy of values they depict, the universe of meanings they portray. What they afford is not so much a set of conceptual ideas or speculative principles for transposing into public policy but imaginative examples of what is possible in human affairs if we can but grasp— or be grasped by—the restoring and liberating justice of God at work in the teaching and career of Jesus.

Nowhere is this restoring and liberating impulse more powerfully narrated than in the parables of the Good Samaritan and the Prodigal Son, the two stories I examine in *Compassionate Justice* from a restorative justice perspective. In extrapolating from these stories to the task of judicial reflection today, I argue that we need to factor in both sides of the 'striking mix of realism and unrealism' they exhibit. On the one hand, both stories deal with the most *realistic* situations imaginable—an act of criminal violence and a breakdown in family relationships—and both commend practicable ways of resisting the common downward drag of human behaviour toward selfishness and retributive resentment. Both accounts offer realistic moral instruction for everyone. At the same time, the stark *unreality* of the responses of the Samaritan and the forgiving father also needs to be accommodated.

---

48. Forrester, 'Scope of Public Theology', p. 16 (emphasis added).

Both characters display a depth and devotedness of compassion that surpasses anything that is normally seen or naturally attainable. Each exhibits a level of moral excellence that few persons in this life attain to, yet one to which God's reign incessantly summons us.

Put simply, the parables operate on two dimensions, an achievable ethical dimension and what I call an 'eschatological plus' dimension, and it is precisely at the intersection of these two dimensions—the natural and the unnatural, the expected and the unexpected, the possible and the impossible—that the interpretive challenge lies for public theology. The stories simultaneously enjoin a universal moral obligation to pursue restorative or transformative justice in this world ('Go you and do likewise') and underscore the need for divine empowerment to fulfil this obligation to the unlimited extent envisaged. Every individual, and every social institution, is capable of 'going and doing' to a morally significant degree, and is summoned by the parables to move in this direction. But they can only truly do 'likewise' by appropriating the transforming power and restorative priorities of God's eschatological presence manifested uniquely in the person and work of Jesus. Public theology must bear witness to both dimensions, if it is to be truly 'public' and truly 'theology' at the same time.

Luke's Gospel Economics of Restorative Justice

Merrill Kitchen

The Gospel of Luke is a carefully composed counter-narrative written after the destruction of Jerusalem in 70 CE when Jewish faith communities, in both Palestine and the Diaspora, were seeking a new religious identity. As Christopher Marshall's research suggests, this identity search by people of faith involved struggling with received scriptural challenges that could justify both retributive and restorative responses to the social trauma they had experienced.[1] It is in this context that the Lukan author proclaims Jesus as a divinely ordained prophet whose words and actions reminded his followers of their inherited traditions, as well as nurturing in them a hope for the restoration of Israel's longstanding mission to seek justice for all humanity.[2] The Third Gospel is both continuous and discontinuous with the other synoptic Gospels in adopting this distinctive narrative theme. It introduces some political and socio-economic elements that not only challenged the emerging first-century Christian sect[3] to reconsider its goals and values but also continues to confront global Christian communities in the twenty-first century.

The narrative background of the Third Gospel is one of a clash of kingdoms. The kingdom of God is depicted as being obscured constantly by an apparently overwhelming worldly kingdom whose seductively powerful *modus operandi* focuses on economic self-interest rather than an economy

---

1. Christopher D. Marshall, *Beyond Retribution: A New Testament Vision for Justice, Crime, and Punishment* (Grand Rapids: Eerdmans, 2001), pp. 33, 256-59. See also Jeremy Punt, 'Violence in the New Testament and the Roman Empire: Ambivalence, Othering, Agency', in *Coping with Violence in the New Testament* (ed. P.G.R. de Villiers and J.W. van Henten; Leiden: Brill, 2012), pp. 29-41.

2. William R. Herzog II, 'Jesus and the Justice of the Reign of God', in *Prophecy and Passion: Essays in Honour of Athol Gill* (ed. David Neville; Adelaide: Australian Theological Forum, 2002), pp. 31-33.

3. John H. Elliott, 'The Jewish Messianic Movement: From Faction to Sect', in *Modelling Early Christianity: Social-Scientific Studies of the New Testament in its Context* (ed. Philip F. Esler; London: Routledge, 1995), p. 92: '...within a generation of Jesus' death the Jewish messianic faction centred in Jesus of Nazareth eventually began to assume the character of a Jewish sect'.

for the common good.⁴ In response, the Lukan narrative tapestry interweaves prophetic reminders of Israel's socio-economic history as recurring spirals of occupation, repression, separation and dispersion are set alongside memories of rescue, return and new beginnings. In *Compassionate Justice* Christopher Marshall explores two particular Lukan parables, the Parable of the Good Samaritan and the Parable of the Prodigal Son, noting the ways in which both confront economic realities of familial, religious and political allegiances in the context of social dislocation.⁵ Each of these parables offers a challenging narrative framework, allowing readers to reconsider the nature of the Kingdom of God in their midst. This essay explores the wider narrative structure of the Third Gospel in which these parables are embedded, noting that the reader is reminded over and over again of neglected prophetic traditions of Israel that continue to offer holistic economic pathways towards restorative justice for all humanity.

1. *Economics and Covenantal Alignments in Luke's Understanding of Israel's Story*

a. *Power Parameters*

A distinctive theme in Luke's proclamation is the significant relationships that were formed with social, political and religious parameters of power at the time of Jesus, as well as throughout Israel's remembered history. A context of Roman rule is evident at both the beginning and the ending of the Gospel narrative. The story timeline commences in the 'days of King Herod of Judea' (1.5) and refers to a compulsory census ordered by the Emperor Augustus as justification for the temporary relocation of Mary and Joseph from Nazareth to Bethlehem at the time of Jesus' birth (2.1-7). Significant political details are aligned with John the Baptiser's voluntary relocation from Jerusalem to 'the region around the Jordan' (3.1-2), along with Herod's role in his imprisonment and death (3.20; 9.9). At the conclusion of the Gospel, Jesus' death is linked to the 'reign of Emperor Tiberius, when Pontius Pilate was governor of Judea and Herod was ruler of Galilee' (23.1-25).

Woven throughout the Lukan birth and infancy narratives are other significant religious power parameters. Only in Luke's Gospel does the reader

---

4. See Sean Freyne, 'Herodian Economics in Galilee: Searching for a Suitable Model', in *Modelling Early Christianity: Social-Scientific Studies of the New Testament in its Context* (ed. Philip F. Esler; London: Routledge, 1995), pp. 23-46. 'The values of a market economy with all the attendant signs of exploitation of the weak and ostentatious living of the wealthy are easily documented.'

5. Christopher D. Marshall, *Compassionate Justice: An Interdisciplinary Dialogue with Two Gospel Parables on Law, Crime, and Restorative Justice* (Eugene, OR: Cascade Books, 2012).

discover a rich priestly heritage embodied in Jesus' immediate surrogate family. Zechariah, Elizabeth, and presumably her relative (*sungenis*), Mary, are described as being descended from the ancient priestly lines of Abijah and Aaron, while Joseph is depicted as a direct descendent of King David (1.5, 36; 2.4; 3.31). Their traditional religious and royal credentials are clearly impeccable, and this rich priestly and royal heritage is assumed for the two infants, John and Jesus. Interestingly, only in the Third Gospel does the reader discover that Joseph's familial link with Israel's royal line is through David's son Nathan rather than through the more commonly recognized royal heir, King Solomon (2 Sam. 5.14; 1 Chron. 14.4; Lk. 3.31 // Mt. 1.6). Thus the royal lineage of Joseph, emphasized in Matthew's Gospel, is replaced in the Third Gospel by a line of prophetic ancestors[6] and possibly even a Maccabean connection.[7] This is consistent with the ancient prophetic tradition of Israel remembered in the expectant Mary's song to 'the God who has subverted all dominating power and all settled economics'.[8] In addition, the genealogical inclusion of the names of Nathan and Levi reminds the reader of a prophetic promise of restorative justice that had been given to their descendants in Jerusalem after Israel's return from exile in Babylon (Zech. 12.1–13.1).[9] While the annunciation to Mary declares her expected child as a 'son of David' and a promised king (1.32-33), her later canticle sees beyond traditional regal models and embraces a promise of social egalitarianism that is a 'powerful challenge to existing power and oppression' (1.46-55). Consequently, the Lukan narrative gradually discloses a virtual clash of kingdoms, where enemies are seen to emerge from within as much as from outside (1.68-79).

The elimination of Solomon from Joseph's genealogy is also consistent with a Lukan narrative revision of Jerusalem as a place of temporal power. While the temple community in Jerusalem initially offers nurture, hospitality and spiritual formation to Jesus and his family (2.40-47),[10] it later becomes a focus for his prophetic challenges to its understanding of

---

6. Joseph A. Fitzmyer, *The Gospel according to Luke I–IX* (Garden City, NY: Doubleday, 1981), p. 497; Charles H. Talbert, *Reading Luke: A Literary and Theological Commentary on the Third Gospel* (New York: Crossroad, 1987), pp. 46, 488-98.

7. See 1 Macc. 2.1-70.

8. Walter Brueggemann, *Disruptive Grace: Reflections on God, Scripture, and the Church* (Minneapolis: Fortress Press, 2011), p. 300. See also Fitzmyer, *Gospel according to Luke I–IX*, pp. 359-61, who suggests that the origin of the canticle may have been a Maccabean hymnic composition.

9. Noting that only Luke's Gospel includes tribal connections with Nathan and Levi in the assumed genealogy of Jesus (Lk. 3.24, 29, 31).

10. See Bart B. Bruehler, *A Public and Political Christ: The Social-Spatial Characteristics of Luke 18:35–19:43 and the Gospel as a Whole in Its Ancient Context* (Eugene, OR: Pickwick Publications, 2011).

kingship (13.33-34; 20.20-26; 21.20). The religious community in Jerusalem is complicit by co-operating actively in Jesus' betrayal, judgment, death and burial. In an ironic act, they crucify him as 'King of the Jews', confronting the royal expectations held by some of his followers (19.38; 23.2-3, 36-38). But this is not the end of the role of Jerusalem in the larger story. Ultimately, as news of Jesus' resurrection and ascension unfold, Jerusalem is pointed out as a place of renewed hope and the centre from which news of a new kingdom movement will spread throughout the world (22.39–24.49).

It is noteworthy that the Third Gospel was composed at a time when Jerusalem had been destroyed, as Jesus had prophesied (Lk. 21.5-6, 20-24; 23.28). It was no longer the place of economic power and security that had been established by priestly alignments with their Roman occupiers. In spite of that reality, however, the city continues to be depicted in the Third Gospel as a place of hope and promise. Roman military and economic power remained, but the disillusioned followers of Jesus, after his crucifixion, are called to 'turn around' and return to Jerusalem. It is there that they are portrayed as experiencing his resurrection presence, then receiving forgiveness and spiritual empowerment for the future benefit of all humanity (24.33-50; Acts 1.4-26; 2.1-4).[11]

b. *Covenantal Responsibility*

The opening chapters of the Third Gospel offer a dialogical literary framework that recalls a longstanding dynamic covenantal relationship of law and promise between the God of Israel and all humanity. It depicts an ideal community within which resources are shared between 'equals committed to co-operation without authoritarian leadership'.[12] At the same time, this potential community will be confronted constantly by the options of autonomy, privilege and conspicuous consumption—the same temptations that are faced and then resisted by the Lukan Jesus in the wilderness (4.1-13). From that time on, Jesus proclaims an anticipated Kingdom of God that inaugurates a faithful covenantal existence consistent with the received tradition of Israel. Brueggemann describes it as having a vision of 'uncommon generosity and mercy, a community of fidelity and freedom, a community that is not seduced by absolutism and that is not left unrestrained by autonomy'.[13]

The dynamic nature of such a community is imagined throughout Luke–Acts. The followers of Jesus are depicted as being both informed and

---

11. Merrill Kitchen, 'The Good News of Restoration: Reading Luke–Acts Then and Now', *Pacifica* 23.2 (2010), pp. 160-63.

12. Norman T. Gottwald, *The Tribes of Yahweh: A Sociology of the Religion of Liberated Israel, 1250–1050 BCE* (Maryknoll, NY: Orbis Books, rev. edn, 1999), p. 692.

13. See Brueggemann, *Disruptive Grace*, p. 33.

reformed during intense times of active listening and experiential learning. At the same time, it is confronting to those who employ defensive strategies in order to protect their own absolute interpretation of Scripture.[14] It challenges their apparent ownership of a secure communal identity, reminding them that the God of Israel was always present beyond the written possession of any one particular ethnic or cultural group. In a Nazareth synagogue, the Lukan Jesus employs a new and provocative interpretive lens to the Hebrew scripture as he reminds his local Sabbath congregation of God's eternal covenantal interaction with women, Gentiles and the 'unclean' (4.16-30). But this proclamation is not just restricted to the confines of a synagogue. Luke goes on to depict Jesus moving into the more culturally diverse region around Capernaum, where he puts his words into action, physically touching and restoring women, Gentiles and lepers to wholeness, as well as rehabilitating the disabled, the demon possessed, the mortally ill and even the dead.

Jesus' leadership is not concerned primarily with establishing a new local community organisation with a patronising concern for the poor (7.23). Rather, a renewed intimate covenantal alignment between God and all humanity is being announced and realized. As a result, the followers of Jesus see themselves as more than privileged ethnic children of Abraham, Isaac and Jacob. They are reminded that the ancient son of God, Adam, has been realized anew in Jesus, the Son of God (3.22-38), and that the ancient covenantal promises of freedom, justice and salvation will once again empower the entire community to survive and challenge the seemingly unrelenting cycle of oppression, injustice and captivity.[15] Furthermore, their leader, Jesus, does not simply preach an ideology but rather models a response of openness, transparency, nonviolence and passive resistance.

c. *Voluntary Powerlessness and Wealth Distribution*
An hiatus occurs after the Lukan birth and infancy narratives. The voice of Israel's God becomes silent in Jerusalem, but it is heard in other unexpected places. New ideas emerge as expectant crowds, including tax collectors and soldiers, gather around John the Baptist in the 'wilderness around the Jordan' and a renewed hope for restorative justice is proclaimed.

---

14. Anthony J. Saldarini, *Pharisees, Scribes, and Sadducees in Palestinian Society* (Grand Rapids: Eerdmans, 1988), p. 120, explores the writings of Josephus and concludes that in the first century the 'Pharisees functioned as a political interest group which had its own goals for society and constantly engaged in political activity'.

15. Kenneth Duncan Litwak, *Echoes of Scripture in Luke–Acts: Telling the History of God's People Intertextually* (London: T. & T. Clark, 2005), pp. 31-33. 'Scriptures pervade Luke–Acts from its beginning to its end: Scriptures play a hermeneutical role in shaping Luke–Acts.'

Resources are to be shared, appropriate wages are to be distributed and appropriate taxes are to be collected (3.10-14). Jesus is depicted as one of those who responded to the Baptiser's call to submit to a life of 'justice and charity',[16] and his response is affirmed as the voice of God identifies Jesus as his 'beloved Son' (3.21). A new paradigm shift in Israel's story begins as a season of 'the hospitality of God' is inaugurated, offering welcome and acceptance to all.[17]

All of the Synoptic Gospels describe ways in which Jesus' divine commission is tested subsequently in the wilderness, but the Gospel of Luke alone describes Jesus' committed theological response in his manifesto to the Nazareth synagogue community (4.16-19). Isaiah's prophetic challenge for Israel to become 'a light to the nations' (2.30-32; Isa. 49.6-9; 52.10) is remembered and given traction as Jesus proclaims 'the year of the Lord's favour' (4.19; Isa. 61.2). The long-neglected covenantal agreement for a Jubilee redistribution of assets that will benefit all is announced.[18] But while some embrace these expectations of a new community relationship, unsurprisingly, active opposition from others emerges.[19] In addition to his own local religious community, most of the religious hierarchy of Jerusalem as well as a few of Jesus' own disciples become caught in a socio-political web of anxious group survival. For some, the temptation to comply with a powerful few, even at the expense of their own ethical traditions, becomes overwhelming.[20]

The cost of discipleship is addressed in all Synoptic Gospels as one of complete relinquishment. Challenged by Jesus, the fishermen, Simon Peter, James and John, as well as Levi, the tax collector, 'left everything to follow him' (5.11; 27-28). Jesus commissions them, along with eight others, 'to take nothing for your journey, no staff, nor bag, nor bread, nor money', and they continue to follow while becoming dependent on others for the basic necessities of food and shelter (9.3; 10.4 // Mk 6.8-9 // Mt. 10.9).[21] But the ultimate relinquishment demanded by Jesus is their preparedness to give

---

16. Brendan Byrne, *The Hospitality of God: A Reading of Luke's Gospel* (Strathfield, NSW: St Paul's Publications, 2000).

17. Byrne, *Hospitality of God*, p. 50.

18. See Walter Brueggemann, *Theology of the Old Testament: Testimony, Dispute, Advocacy* (Minneapolis: Fortress Press, 1997), p. 190.

19. For a sociological analysis of the human power struggles, see Gerhard Lenski, *Privilege and Power: A Theory of Social Stratification* (Chapel Hill, SC: University of South Carolina Press, 2nd edn, 1984), p. 33: 'Cooperation is certainly a pervasive feature of all human life and so, too, is conflict.'

20. Douglas E. Oakman, *Jesus and the Economic Questions of His Day* (Lewiston: Edwin Mellen Press, 1986). See also Oakman's article, 'The Ancient Economy in the Bible', *BTB* 21 (1991), pp. 34-39.

21. Noting that Mark allows a staff!

their own lives for the greater sake of all (9.23-24; 12.4; 14.27).[22] This all-pervasive countercultural kingdom of God is one in which the poor are blessed (6.20), enemies are treated with respect, loans are made without expectation of any return and a just restoration of over-taxation is expected (6.20, 27-36; 19.1-10). Members of this godly kingdom are encouraged to sell their 'possessions and give alms', a challenge that not all easily accept (12.33; 18.22-25). Even the disciples are unable fully to comprehend the ultimate cost of this style of discipleship articulated and demonstrated by Jesus (18.31-34).

The Gospel of Luke depicts the concerns of Jesus in his final days in Jerusalem as being particularly focused on the misuse of money. As Jesus enters the temple, he drives out 'those who were selling things there' (19.45-46 // Mt. 21.12; Mk 11.15), and reveals the deviousness of the authorities by getting them to reveal the illegal Roman money that is in their possession (20.20-26 // Mt. 22.15-22 // Mk 12.13-17). He accuses the scribes of fraudulently 'devouring widows' houses' (20.45–21.4 // Mk 12.40), but ultimately Jesus is betrayed for a price by one of his own (22.3-6 // Mt. 26.14 // Mk 14.10-11). While these stories are in all three Synoptic Gospels, a final political accusation made against Jesus is found only in the Third Gospel when the 'assembly of the elders of the people' complains that Jesus is 'forbidding us to pay taxes to the emperor' (23.2).

d. *Wealth in the Early Church*
Over five decades ago, the Lukan scholar, Hans Conzelmann, argued for a clearly consistent 'large framework' of narrative theology shared by the Gospel of Luke and the Acts of the Apostles. He proposed that the Lukan 'story of salvation' not only depicts a 'continuity between the period of Jesus on the one hand and the period of the church on the other' but also deliberately connects these eras with the 'period of Israel'.[23] This hypothesis is affirmed when assessing the literary function of wealth in the Acts of the Apostles. The apostle Peter, in the first chapter, recalls ancient prophetic promises of salvation when addressing a gathering of 'believers' in Jerusalem after the ascension of Jesus. He reminds them that the gruesome ending of the life of Judas was a fulfilment of Scripture (Acts 1.16-20). Later, his 'fellow Israelites' repented, sold 'all their possessions and goods' and then shared their common resources with each other (Acts 2.44-45; 4.32-37). Some commentators point out that this practice is in compliance with Platonic ideals,[24] others note a continuity with the inclusive Deutero-

---

22. See parallels also in Mt. 10.26-33, 37-39; 16.24-28; Mk 8.34–9.1.
23. Hans Conzelmann, *The Theology of St. Luke* (trans. G. Buswell; Philadelphia: Fortress Press, 1961), pp. 16-17.
24. Aristotle, *Nicomachean Ethics* IX.8.2 (1168b).

nomic ideals hoped for in Israel (Deut. 15.1-7), while Tannehill asserts that the 'community of goods is not a mere curiosity, interesting in itself but unconnected with the central concerns of Luke–Acts. It relates directly to a major topic of Jesus' teachings in Luke'.[25]

Economic responsibility is emphasized most strongly in the narrative reversal as the faithful generous character, Barnabas, is compared with the devious actions of two fellow travellers, Ananias and Sapphira (Acts 5.1-11). Their calculated deception is attested to twice, and each time the true intentions of these apparently faithful people are disclosed and judged. As Tannehill notes, 'Peter is the prophet who exposes and rebukes the deceptive heart',[26] and in so doing he honours the true tradition of Israel that has been disclosed and demonstrated to him by Jesus. There is clear evidence that the earliest church struggled with issues of money and power. For example, the Pastoral Epistles, probably written about the same time as Luke–Acts, all alert the reader to a number of wealth issues facing the communities to whom they were written. Women are advised not to be ostentatious in the demonstration of their wealth (1 Tim. 2.9-10), and bishops are adjured to resist being a 'lover of money' (1 Tim. 3.3; Tit. 1.7-8). Those who do not share their resources are called 'unbelievers', and the epistles repeatedly emphasize that 'the love of money is a root of all evil' (1 Tim. 5.7-8; 6.10; 2 Tim. 3.2).

2. *Lukan Parables of Recovery and Restoration*

Two decades ago William Herzog asked the question, 'What if the parables of Jesus were neither theological nor moral stories but political and economic ones? What if the concern of the parables was not the reign of God but the reigning systems of oppression that dominated Palestine in the time of Jesus?'[27] Reading the parables again today through this lens can challenge contemporary understandings of social order and the reality of socio-political controls.[28] The Lukan parables invite us not only to reconstruct critically the probable leadership challenges that confronted the emerging Christian movement in the late first century but also to examine

---

25. Robert Tannehill, *The Narrative Unity of Luke–Acts: A Literary Interpretation*, Vol. 2: *The Acts of the Apostles* (Minneapolis: Fortress Press, 1990), pp. 44-46.

26. Tannehill, *Acts of the Apostles*, p. 79.

27. William R. Herzog II, *Parables as Subversive Speech: Jesus as Pedagogue of the Oppressed* (Louisville, KY: Westminster/John Knox Press, 1994), p. 7.

28. David B. Gowler, *What Are They Saying about the Parables?* (New York/ Mahwah, NJ: Paulist Press, 2000), p. 68: 'Parables explore how human beings could respond to break the spiral of violence and the cycle of poverty... Therefore the parables of Jesus were forms of social analysis just as much as they were forms of theological reflection.'

the ethical practices of formal and informal religious organisations today. A major challenge to the reader is the way in which domination and subordination is characterized and perceived. Herzog argues that the focus of the parables 'is not on a vision of the glory of the reign (kingdom) of God, but on the gory details of how oppression serves the interests of a ruling class'.[29] At the same time, using a different interpretive lens, others read the same Lukan parables as justifications for privilege and control.

a. *Remembering, Recovering and Restoring the Bigger Story*
The first parable in Luke's Gospel re-introduces a theme that is woven throughout the narrative. It is told by Jesus to a mixed group of people, including tax collectors, Pharisees and scribes, who have gathered around a meal. The host is Levi, a tax collector with a relevant historic Israelite name, who has just 'left everything' to follow Jesus. In response to some legal concerns expressed by the religious participants about the inclusiveness of the gathering, and the perceived movement away from the ascetic practices of John the Baptist, the Lukan Jesus tells a parable about both the compatibility and incompatibility of things that are old and things that are new (5.33-39). In both continuity and discontinuity with the other Synoptic Gospels, the Lukan parable points out the futility of integrating new and old fabrics, and of using old wineskins to store new wine, with Luke concluding uniquely that 'the old is *good*' (*chrēstos*, 5.39; cf. Mt. 9.17; Mk 2.22). Levi may be seen as a living example of one who appears to have returned to his inherited values, but multiple challenges to Jesus' understanding of Torah law follow from the religious community.

b. *Remembering, Recovering and Restoring Covenantal Relationships*
Christopher Marshall has written extensively on the way in which Lukan parables disclose an ethic of covenantal love.[30] The Parable of the Good Samaritan responds to a question asked by a lawyer about the necessary qualifications for entry into 'eternal life'. He receives a traditional rabbinic response from Jesus, who describes the essence of covenantal relationship between God and others as a distillation and blending of two traditional love commandments from the Hebrew Bible, which some have described as 'the perfect summation of God's will'.[31] It first entails the need to embrace an holistic love of God, but it is also to reflect that love in a generous love of neighbour (10.25-28). The parable follows as Jesus clarifies the meaning of 'neighbour' for the inquiring lawyer, uncovering a way in which restorative covenantal relationships between God and humanity may be embodied

---

29. Herzog, *Parables as Subversive Speech*, p. 3.
30. Marshall, *Compassionate Justice*, pp. 127-33.
31. Marshall, *Compassionate Justice*, pp. 65-76.

more in the actions of perceptive compassionate strangers than the inaction of self-centred religious compatriots who are blind to the needs of others.[32] Importantly, it is the wounded traveller who experiences the actions of restoration. He is helplessly dependent upon the actions of others and, in continuity with covenantal Torah principles, discovers hope and healing in the loving actions of supposed outsiders who embody the unconditional hospitality of God.[33] The victim's personal reactions to the experience of rescue and recovery are not mentioned, and readers are left to decide where they would fit into the story.

The motif of covenantal hospitality continues in the Lukan narrative as diverse characters enact new possibilities. The Parable of the Lost Son (15.11-32), as Marshall points out, 'is unsurpassed in the biblical tradition in its depiction of the love and forgiveness of God'.[34] The reader cannot engage in this story from a distance. It is not about strangers but about family. There are some parallels with the two preceding parables in Luke's Gospel (15.3-10), but it is not about a lost animal or a lost coin but about a lost brother. In the wider story of Israel, it recalls post-exilic separation, the lost tribes of the children of Abraham and perhaps, even further, the lost children of Adam. Issues of honour and shame in dyadic societies emerge, and the apparently absurd celebrations that are described when the lost sheep and the lost coin are found fade into insignificance as a disgraced father forgives, welcomes back and restores his undeserving but seemingly repentant son with a family celebration beyond all expectations. While some readers may identify with the younger son, many more will be taken aback like the older brother. The Lukan challenge to share abundantly one's own rightful possessions with others eternally remains.

c. *Remembering, Recovering and Restoring the Jubilee Ethic*
As mentioned earlier, Israel's Jubilee principle is a recurring narrative theme in the Third Gospel.[35] The primary focus of the Jubilee principle, according to Josephus' interpretation in the first century CE, was to redistribute accumulated wealth so that a new era of equality would restore the injustice prevalent in Israel's community.[36] It was designed to be a

---

32. Anne Elvey, 'Love and Justice in the Gospel of Luke—Ecology, the Neighbour and Hope', *AusBR* 60 (2012), pp. 1-17.

33. Byrne, *Hospitality of God*, p. 101: 'It cuts to the heart of the Law as found in the single commandment binding together love of God and love of neighbour. He has simply shown that to fulfil the Law's true intent the notion of "neighbour" has to be drastically revised.'

34. Marshall, *Compassionate Justice*, p. 187.

35. Hebrew Bible references include Exod. 22.25-27; Leviticus 25; Deuteronomy 15; 23.19-20; Isa. 5.8; Hab. 2.6; 1 Sam. 22.2; 2 Kgs 4.1; Neh. 5.1-5; Prov. 22.7.

36. Josephus, *Ant.* III.12.3 in *The Works of Josephus* (trans. William Whiston;

regular 'turn around' moment, but there is no evidence that it has ever been enacted.

The prevailing injustice at the time of Jesus is illuminated in several Lukan parables. The Story of the Rich Fool (12.13-34) expands on two of Jesus' warnings to his religious and non-religious questioners about the consequences of self-indulgence and greed (11.37-52). The parable discloses that the self-centred accumulation of wealth is ultimately irresponsible and foolish, while the appropriate sharing of resources reflects responsible wisdom with positive eternal outcomes.[37] This is the only parable in which God is depicted as a speaking character, and in so doing its stance influences profoundly the interpretation of the next sequence of parabolic teachings.

The Parable of the Lost Son is followed by the Parable of the Shrewd Manager (15.11-32; 16.1-9). These two parables have been interpreted in many different ways over the years, but in the Lukan context they both address challenging questions that arise from misusing wealth, as well as issues of appropriate wealth redistribution. The shrewd manager is accused of squandering his master's resources in the same way that the younger son squandered the inheritance he received from his father. The question remains also for the older son, who is left to struggle with the reality of the unexpected, generous and unconditional family restoration of his repentant younger brother. The disciples of Jesus, as well as the Pharisees who listen also, are directly challenged by both of these stories.[38] Similar management issues will confront them all as they journey towards Jerusalem. Will they make partial compromises and be 'lovers of money', as Judas chooses ultimately? Or will they dare to make no compromise and serve God's kingdom alone, following Jesus to the cross and faithfully embracing the associated personal risk when aligning with God's restorative justice (16.10-13)?

Peabody, MA: Hendrickson, 1987), pp. 604-608: 'debtors are free from their debts, and slaves are set at liberty'. See also Josephus's comment on the Essenes in *War*, II.8.1-14: 'These men are despisers of riches...it is a law amongst them that those who come to them must let what they have be common to the whole order...they carry nothing with them when they travel...nor do they buy or sell anything to one another.' Cf. Douglas E. Oakman, *Jesus and the Peasants* (Eugene, OR: Cascade Books, 2008), p. 15.

37. Matthew S. Rindge, *Jesus' Parable of the Rich Fool: Luke 12:13-34 among Ancient Conversations on Death and Possession* (Early Christianity and Its Literature 6; Atlanta: SBL, 2011).

38. Joel B. Green, *The Gospel of Luke* (Grand Rapids: Eerdmans, 1997), p. 601: 'As "lovers of money" the Pharisees are implicated in the present world system already characterized as "unjust" or "unrighteous" or "dishonest" in Luke 11:37-44.' See also Byrne, *Hospitality of God*, p. 135.

A third parable about the use of wealth is then presented, and once again there are parallels with that of the Lost Son.[39] Social differences between the wealthy and the poor are accentuated in the Parable of the Rich Man and Lazarus (16.19-31). It depicts the rich man as 'an active agent', who dialogues with Abraham and expects to be obeyed, while the poverty-stricken Lazarus 'is completely passive and is only the object of dialogue'.[40] While the two characters occupy the same household space, they are positioned at extremities over and against one another.[41] In their temporal kingdom, one is wealthy, well fed and privileged (his garments are those of a king),[42] while the other is poor, hungry and sick. One is an insider and the other an outsider.[43] But in God's realm everything is depicted as reversed. Lazarus enjoys a place of privilege while the rich man becomes destitute, with no choices left. He does not even have the capacity to warn significant others of the dangers of conspicuous consumption. It is Lazarus who has identified more closely with the family of Abraham, and the rich man's neglect of the traditions of Israel results in his ultimate absence (Amos 5.12, 15). Once again, an echo of Mary's pre-natal prophecy is given contemporary substance (1.51-53).

Finally, the Parable of the Pounds (19.11-27) is another Lukan parable that addresses issues of wealth and power in the context of the kingdom of God. The character of the Nobleman King bears a close resemblance to the historical Herod Archelaus described by Josephus.[44] Two of his slaves conform to the Nobleman King's ruthless thirst for power, but a third one refuses to exploit others for his master's benefit. This uncooperative slave is almost certainly consigned to death, unlike his other colleagues who are commensurately rewarded. This parable immediately precedes the Lukan passion narrative and there are literary links between the character of the defiant slave and that of the resilient Jesus. They both refuse to submit to the unjust demands of others in order to serve a greater good, and they are both condemned for what they say (19.22; cf. 22.71). Furthermore, the way in which the third slave faithfully preserves the received deposit by wrapping it up in a cloth and then burying it is mirrored in the passion narrative description of Jesus' body being wrapped carefully in cloth and buried

---

39. Note that the Greek *epithumōn chortasthēnai* in Lk. 16.21 echoes the state of the prodigal son in 15.16.

40. Green, *Gospel of Luke*, p. 606.

41. Green, *Gospel of Luke*, p. 605, describes the narrative technique as one of 'extravagant parallelism'.

42. Joseph A. Fitzmyer, *The Gospel according to Luke X–XXIV* (Garden City, NY: Doubleday, 1985), p. 1130.

43. Byrne, *Hospitality of God*, pp. 136-37.

44. Josephus, *Ant.* XVII.8-9.5.

(19.20; cf. 23.53).[45] Once again, the Jubilee ethic is remembered but at considerable personal cost.

3. *The Cost of Punitive and Restorative Justice*

Marshall points out that restorative justice can be a 'predetermined facet of a formalized process' yet also 'paves the way' for real forgiveness to occur.[46] But as we have seen, restorative justice, as portrayed in Luke–Acts, always comes at a price. Two of its main protagonists, John the Baptist and Jesus, are both killed cruelly by the powerful ruling political and religious elite (3.18; 9.7; 23.11, 13-25), as is the apostle Stephen (Acts 7.54-60). On the other hand, this depicted punitive justice does not extinguish the flame of faith and hope. Rather, a new beginning is ignited amongst observant Jews as well as inspired Gentiles. The most significant *metanoia* is recorded in the story of a Shavuot / Pentecost gathering in Jerusalem (Acts 2.1-42) and, subsequently, the martyrdom of Stephen marks a new beginning in the story of the Pharisee, Saul of Tarsus, whose experience of a restorative form of justice empowers him to become the evangelising Apostle Paul (Acts 7.58–9.22).

The cost of following Jesus is made clear in each of the Synoptic Gospels (Mt. 10.38-39 // Mk 8.34–9.1 // Lk. 9.23-27; 14.25-27; 17.33). The rule of the kingdom of God will not occur just through miraculous, instant, painless solutions but as a result of rugged, faithful persistence in the face of seductive challenges. This kingdom is declared as already intimately present in the midst of human reality but at the same time obscured constantly by the dominance of self-centred ambition (10.11; 17.20). God's presence and reign is revealed in a voluntary submission to personal powerlessness for the sake of the greater good. As a religiously observant rich ruler struggles with Jesus' challenge to 'sell all that you own and distribute the money to the poor', so do the disciples who hear the same teaching (18.18-30). At the same time, Zacchaeus, a rich, influential tax collector in Jericho proves himself as a true 'son of Abraham' when he responds to Jesus' invitation of acceptance and spontaneously shares the resources he has accrued at the expense of others (19.1-10).

---

45. Merrill Kitchen, 'Rereading the Parable of the Pounds: A Social and Narrative Analysis of Luke 19:11-28', in *Prophecy and Passion: Essays in Honour of Athol Gill* (ed. David Neville; Adelaide: Australian Theological Forum, 2002), pp. 227-46. See also Elizabeth Dowling, 'Slave Parables in the Gospel of Luke—Gospel "Texts of Terror"?', *AusBR* 56 (2008), pp. 61-68 (67-68).

46. Marshall, *Compassionate Justice*, p. 321.

Conclusion

Like a tapestry, the Gospel of Luke weaves together the multi-coloured strands of Israel's inherited stories of God's restorative justice. Over the past two millennia it has continued to invite readers and hearers to engage in issues of righteousness and truth. Throughout the narrative, the Lukan Jesus confronts the religious and political *status quo*, while at the same time holding faithfully to, and uncovering over and over again, the received traditions of Israel that have always carried good news to all humanity. The reader is encouraged to hold on to the wisdom of 'the old' in order to evaluate the 'new' (5.36-39); to build on strong established foundations rather than short-term pragmatic decisions (6.46-49); and to re-embrace a greater truth that favours indiscriminate compassion over strict religious observation (10.25-37; 15.3-32).

Employing economic terms, the Lukan parables call people to reassess their priorities and to take the risk of being countercultural for greater personal and communal outcomes. Sadly, some interpretations of the New Testament parables changed after the era of the first Christian Emperor of Rome. Powerful characters such as kings, masters and noblemen began to be seen as more positive role models. For some, the accumulation of wealth was, and still is, perceived as a sign of blessing rather than oppression. Similarly, the spirals of violence and cycles of poverty are often seen as divinely ordained retribution in a world that privileges some over others.

Retelling the parables appropriately today can open up possibilities for restorative human action as they invite the reader/hearer to find themselves in the story. They can provide a blank canvas upon which a new picture can be painted and from which a renewed perspective can be gained. In the twenty-first century, we wait to hear and experience contemporary stories of repentant clergy, restored human rights, global hospitality, environmental respect and a fair re-distribution of wealth that will be used for the common good. I will let Walter Brueggeman have the last word: 'Our anticovenantal society wants us to be one-dimensional. But we refuse because covenanting is a different way in the world, always requiring, always waiting, always letting us stand alongside neighbors, full of wonder, love, and praise.'[47]

---

47. Brueggeman, *Disruptive Grace*, p. 37.

Stop, Take, Care:
Reading Luke 10.25-37 with Islanders in Prison

Jione Havea

Many are the joys and challenges in/of reading scriptural texts with people in prison,[1] who are among 'the condemned'[2] and 'the damned'.[3] In prison, people have a lot of spare time to read and reflect, and they are eager to learn. Not all of them have undertaken some structured training in theology or hermeneutics,[4] but most hold biblical and theological opinions. They are respectful of scriptures and of religious traditions, but they are not obsessed with figuring out what the legitimate or credible interpretations are.[5] They are committed, but they are also entertaining (funny, flexible, hospitable). Given their incarcerated settings, reading and holding conversations around scriptural texts are opportunities to be free (at least in their minds): free to read, to think, to talk (through bars) and to scripturalize (authorize). That

---

1. People who have been released from prison are not necessarily free. Their records follow them, with stigma and shame shadowing the rest of their lives. See Sadie Pounder, 'Prison Theology: A Theology of Liberation, Hope and Justice', *Dialog* 47 (2008), pp. 278-91 (282).

2. Michel Foucault, *Discipline and Punish: The Birth of the Prison* (trans. Alan Sheridan; New York: Vintage, 1995), pp. 3-31.

3. See Bob Ekblad, *Reading the Bible with the Damned* (Louisville, KY: Westminster/John Knox Press, 2005), pp. 11-24.

4. The majority of people in prison are 'ordinary readers' (compared to 'trained readers'), on which see Sarojini Nadar, 'Beyond the "Ordinary Reader" and the "Invisible Intellectual": Pushing the Boundaries of Contextual Bible Study Discourses', in *The Future of the Biblical Past: Envisioning Biblical Studies on a Global Key* (ed. Roland Boer and Fernando F. Segovia; Atlanta: SBL, 2013), pp. 13-28.

5. Cf. Christopher D. Marshall, *Compassionate Justice: An Interdisciplinary Dialogue with Two Gospel Parables on Law, Crime, and Restorative Justice* (Eugene, OR: Cascade Books, 2012), p. 25: 'Parables may be polyvalent, in the sense that they are capable of diverse and equally legitimate readings, but they are not infinitely pliable. For any particular interpretation of a Gospel parable to be credible, it must be demonstrably faithful to how the story itself is constructed and told, do justice to the historical and cultural points of reference implied in the text, make sense of the narrative and conceptual context in which the parable occurs in the Gospel tradition, and cohere with what we know of the larger message and perspective of its narrator.'

the prison setting is restrictive does not prevent the mood and the perspectives from being free and freeing (herein is a challenge for contextual thinkers[6]). Reading in prison is freeing for the 'inmated' and for the visitors also.[7]

People in prison are not easily persuaded but they are open to being engaged, and they are eager to tell their stories.[8] Stories of how they were trapped in desperate situations, how they have been robbed of their futures by legal systems that do not respect them, how they betrayed their families and loved ones, how their relatives and friends are ashamed, how they are tossed aside and bypassed by community leaders, and more… They appreciate opportunities to read scriptural texts as windows whereby their stories might be told and engaged. Despite the rigidity of the prison setting, it is an oral world where, to steal the words of Christopher Marshall, 'a story can be told a thousand times, and with a thousand tiny variations, and still be an "authentic" recounting of the same essential, inherited story'.[9] In prison, personal stories are as scriptural (important, authorial) as biblical stories are.

In this essay i present modes of reading learned among islanders in prison.[10] I unravel those through readings of Lk. 10.25-37 (which contains a parable involving a Samaritan and an innkeeper), driven by interests in constructing prison hermeneutics. The ambiguity of how prison is 'public space' motivates this reflection.[11] Who owns prison? This is not a question about sponsorship and management (federal, state, private or church), but about the ideologies and conditions that require prison (institution and system).[12] Behind (the bars of) this essay is a conviction that biblical critics

---

6. I present this view in 'Cons of contextuality…Kontextuality', in *Contextual Theology for the Twenty-First Century* (ed. Stephen Bevans and Katalina Tahaafe-Williams; Eugene, OR: Pickwick Publications, 2011), pp. 38-52.

7. So Pounder, 'Prison Theology', who argues that prison theology should be relevant 'to the oppressed in prison and [to] the entire criminal justice system' (p. 279) and hence should keep in mind the difference between 'freedom from' and 'freedom for' (p. 282).

8. My experience with people in prison is limited to Pacific islanders in the Correctional Facilities at Parklea (New South Wales, Australia). Other prison contexts will foster different perspectives.

9. Marshall, *Compassionate Justice*, p. 30.

10. I use lowercase 'i' because i use the lowercase with 'you', 'she', 'they' and 'others'. I do not see the point in capitalizing the first person when s/he *is* in relation to everyone/everything else.

11. See also the taxonomy of various views on the place of Scripture in Public Theology, with special attention to the pluralistic and post-Christian settings of the current time, and a strong case for inner-biblical critique (which affirms the richness of biblical traditions and views) in David J. Neville, 'Christian Scripture and Public Theology: Ruminations on their Ambiguous Relationship', *IJPT* 7 (2013), pp. 5-23.

12. See Foucault, *Discipline and Punish*, and Ulrich L. Lehner, *Monastic Prisons*

can 'own' (by devotion, by commission) prison through reading and engaging with people in prison. The prison condition invites rethinking five categories that biblical critics often take for granted—space, time, relation, identity, interruption—hence the five sections of this essay.

Space

'Confining' and 'isolating' are the popular adjectives used to explain what it means to be in prison. In fact, people in prison are doubly confined and isolated. They are locked away (inside) from the rest of society (outside); inside prison, they are divided further, into blocks, units and cells. Their access to the outside world depends on what they hear through the closely filtered media and correspondences, the occasional visits by members of family and friends, and their contact with staff who *care for by confining* them in prison. Inside prison, confinement is multi-plied with various shades of removal and separation. Prison is a complex place. Inside the walls of a prison, space is both physical and cerebral.

Confinement and isolation foster awareness of boundaries and surroundings. Prison space is similar to island space. Thrown into the deep blue ocean (*moana*), one is free to swim, dive and surface here and there, at the risk of drowning. In shallow waters, one's movement is limited so one identifies the spots to avoid and learns to maneuver through one's surroundings (course). Constriction of space makes one more aware of the boundaries and the obstructions. Being in prison has the same effect, albeit to the unhealthy extreme. Prisons are so shallow and tight that people's perception of the world fall apart, and spin.

The parable of the Samaritan is set in the open hinterland, between Jerusalem and Jericho, where there would have been a lot of room to move. Jesus gives the impression that there is space by explaining that both the priest and the Levite 'passed by on the other side' of the road (Lk. 10.31, 32). The priest and the Levite saw the victim, but they were not arrested by what they saw. How wide was the road? Was the road wide enough so that they could circle around and not hear or smell the victim, or did they have to step over his half-dead body? The narrower the road, the more crucial the questions are. Whereas robbers (one meets several of them in prison) jump on their victims in narrow paths and dark alleys, victims would crawl into the open so that they could be seen. Reading the parable with people in prison invites these queries, and consideration of other stories as well, two of which are stimulating for this reading.[13]

and Torture Chambers: Crime and Punishment in Central European Monasteries, 1600–1800 (Eugene, OR: Cascade Books, 2013), pp. 1-10.

13. This is *talanoa fakatatau* in practice: One tells a story, and others respond by

A young Tongan man was going to a local shopping centre and was met by other young Tongans running toward him, shouting, *'Lele!'* ('Run!'). Not having enough time to find out what they were running from, he turned and ran along with his friends. The police caught them that evening, refused to believe that he was not involved in the holdup, and to cut a long story short, he ended up in prison. His story raises questions about the parable of the Samaritan: How far behind was the Levite from the priest? Did they travel with their asses? Who else was on the road? What difference would it make if there were other people on the road? These questions are not meant to excuse the priest and the Levite from passing by the victim, but in order to feel for the space that the parable constructs. Jesus' parable focused on people (traveler, robbers, priest, Levite, Samaritan, innkeeper), and the young Tongan man's story invites attention to the difference it makes if other people were on the road also.

The story about the death of Amasa (2 Samuel 20) adds another dimension. Amasa sided with his cousin Absalom when the latter usurped the throne from his father (Amasa's uncle) David (2 Samuel 15).[14] When Absalom died, David appointed Amasa as his commander (2 Sam. 19.3), a move that Joab (who was David's commander) did not approve and he did not hesitate to kill Amasa. Joab was then pursuing Sheba, who led the people of Israel in another rebellion against David (2 Sam. 20.2). Amasa was the 'bonus hit' in the 'Sheba mission'. The description of Amasa's death is deceit-full and gory:

> Joab said to Amasa, 'How are you brother?' and with his right hand Joab took hold of Amasa's beard as if to kiss him. Amasa was not on his guard against the sword in Joab's [left] hand, and [Joab] drove it into his belly so that his entrails poured out on the ground and he died... (2 Sam. 20.9-10a, NJPS)[15]

Joab then continued on the chase, followed by his brother Abishai, but all his men stopped at Amasa's body:

---

telling other stories (which could involve them, or stories that they remember upon hearing the first story). I discuss the *talanoa fakatatau* practice in ' *'Unu'unu ki he loloto*, shuffle over into the deep, into island-spaced reading', in *Still at the Margins: Biblical Scholarship Fifteen Years after Voices from the Margin* (ed. R.S. Sugirtharajah; New York: T. & T. Clark, 2008), pp. 88-97.

14. The web of relations is complex. Amasa was son of Abigail, and Joab was son of Zeruiah; Abigail and Zeruiah were sisters of David. Absalom was son of David and cousin to Amasa and Joab (see 2 Sam. 17.25).

15. Here it helps to hear Neville, 'Christian Scripture and Public Theology', p. 21: 'For those sensitized to the reality that conquest, war, slavery and both racial and gender inequalities have been defended on biblical grounds, the simple fact that something is biblical is insufficient to provide it with theological and moral sanction.'

> *Amasa lay in the middle of the road*, drenched in his blood; and the man [who was hastening the army to follow Joab] saw that *everyone stopped.* And when he saw that *all the people were stopping*, he dragged Amasa from the road into the field and covered him with a garment. Once he was removed from the road, everyone continued to follow Joab in pursuit of Sheba son of Bichri. (2 Sam. 20.12-13, NJPS; my italics)

The differences between Amasa and the robbed and stripped victim in Jesus' parable are telling. Amasa lay in the middle of the road and all of the people stopped. I imagine that they stopped out of respect for one of their leaders, and maybe in astonishment at how easily Joab had discarded a cousin and a commander of David's army. On the other hand, in the parable of the Samaritan it is not clear where the victim was lying half-dead, and at least two travelers passed by. Amasa was named and respected, whereas the robbers' victim was unnamed and avoided, even though he was noticed. Amasa was dragged and discarded on the side of the road because he was an obstruction (2 Sam 20.12), while the robbers' victim was picked up by the Samaritan because 'he was moved with pity' (Lk. 10.33). Was his pity only for the victim, as most readers conclude? Did he have pity also for the other travelers who would come later, so that they wouldn't be troubled by this victim? Did the Samaritan move the victim (as in the case of Amasa) so that other travelers would not have to stop?

Reading these stories of Amasa and the Samaritan with people in prison, where the general drive is to close things down, opens the stories up in part because the interlocutors in prison know what it means to be dragged and discarded, to be seen but not noticed,[16] to be seen but not pitied or to be pitied for unbeknown reasons. Jesus did not identify what the object of the Samaritan's pity was, but the Samaritan did not widen the space between himself and the half-dead victim. Proximity makes people stop and do things out of respect and pity. Separation and isolation, on the other hand, permit people to go on as if nothing is wrong.

Time

It is true that, inside prison, *people do time.* However, 'What does time mean in prison?' is one of the questions for which i have not been able to get a consistent answer.

On some days, for some of the people in prison, time does not exist. They are locked up in cells that give them a taste of what it must be like to live in a grave. Nothing seems to move, there is no evidence of change and there is consequently no sense of time. What does time mean to the dead?

---

16. See Pounder, 'Prison Theology', p. 279, and Alyce M. McKenzie, *The Parables for Today* (Louisville, KY: Westminster/John Knox Press, 2007), p. 56.

On other days, the same people find time to be too slow. They are locked up in cells for, on average, nineteen hours per day, with the other five hours spent s/pacing (walking back and forth within confined space and interacting with others, thereby 'filling' space) common areas in the block or yard. Something in the constricting of space, and filling it with bodies and movement, slows down the ticking of time. Time is even sl-o-wer when the date of release approaches.

On most days, notwithstanding, people in prison experience time not as some rigid temporal calculation but as embodied and loaded 'events' (noticed by means of the bodies, motions and movements). Someone else decides what moves, or does not move, in prison, hence time is controlled and 'spaced out'. Reading with people in prison invites one to pay attention to the rich connotations of time.

The lawyer's question to Jesus, 'What must I do to inherit eternal life?', echoes the kind of challenge that lawyers push upon islanders in prison: what to do to avoid going to court, which usually means accepting a negotiated sentence. Put this way, the lawyer's question is about time (read: what to do to extend life). The same question may be read another way. It also presumes that time does not exist, given the common association of 'eternal life' with 'eternity' and 'otherworldliness'. What does eternal life mean to people doing time in prison? What does the otherworld mean for people serving life sentences? These questions are irritating for islanders who receive the upper range of life sentences.[17]

Attending to time in relation to bodies, movement and space suggests that the victim in Jesus' parable fell on a road that was not deserted. The event is placed in the open hinterland, but barriers and obstacles were nonetheless there—such as hills, boulders, cliffs and valleys—around which one must learn to maneuver. The terrain would be rough and unstable at some places, with a host of creatures hovering and watching the travelers.

The quick succession (over the course of six verses, Lk. 10.30-35) and lively movement in the parable (one after another, there came a traveler, robbers, a priest, a Levite, a Samaritan and then an innkeeper) suggests that the road was well travelled. The stories of the young Tongan man and of Amasa invite us to imagine other people and creatures on the road, that is, to fill the road between Jerusalem and Jericho. Reading with people in prison, it is helpful to s/pace the road because, on the one hand, the lived-prison-world is always crowded and, on the other hand, the more bodies present the more opportunities for movement to be perceived, and for time to be experienced.

---

17. Though convicted for the same crimes as white people, the sentences of islanders tend to be longer (twenty to thirty years for manslaughter, compared to four to six years in the case of white people).

For the victim in Jesus' parable, who i nickname Amasa² in the rest of this reading, time would have stopped.[18] Robbed and bashed, he would drift out and back. Though he was half-dead, the islanders in prison (many of whom know what it's like to be half-dead) suggest that he would have been aware of the noises on the road. With his ears on the ground, he would have heard the movements around him. If the priest and the Levite travelled with their asses, Amasa² would have heard them passing on the other side of the road. The priest and the Levite could tiptoe around, but the asses would not have been able to pass by undetected (no matter how wide the road was). Because time had stopped, Amasa² would have tuned into the ground and to his surroundings; because time is at once embodied and loaded, Amasa² would have known when the asses passed by.

Drifting in and out of consciousness, Amasa² probably ignored the next set of hooves that trod up the road. That set of hooves then stopped! By stopping, the Samaritan made time move again for Amasa². He anointed Amasa² with oil and wine, bandaged his wounds, then checked him into the inn where he paid the innkeeper to give more time for Amasa². In stopping, therefore, the unnamed Samaritan gave Amasa² more time and consequently showed that he too is good.[19]

Despite their distaste for lawyers in general, the islanders in prison noticed that Jesus gave time to the inquiring lawyer. Jesus did not snub him; Jesus entertained his queries. The economy of words and sharpness of Jesus' responses, on the other hand, give the impression that he did not have a lot of time for the lawyer. There is no loitering in the corridors, or beating around the bushes. Hit the target (read: bank) straight on, then move on. This dialectical view about time—time is there and at once not there—is not so strange in prison, where the question about time is: time *for* what and *for* whom? Time is not abstract; time is, when filled.

Relation

One of the popular admissions i hear in prison is that people get into trouble because they were with the wrong people (at the wrong place and at the wrong time). The relations they develop and foster isolate them from healthier relations (e.g., with family, community), and they drift with a crowd that push them toward misbehavior, crime and disorder. They get into trouble because they hang and run with the wrong crowd, and the state admits and holds them in supposed 'correctional facilities'.

18. The nickname Amasa² is inspired by the appropriation of 'double', 'square' and 'cube' in several of the nicknames of islanders that i engage in prison. They find echoes of their stories in the story of Amasa².

19. The ambivalence of this reading is intentional, to allow for both the Samaritan and Amasa² to be good.

I am not convinced that confinement and isolation help people heal and mend broken relations, or substitute healthy for unhealthy ones. It takes two or more for any relation to develop and transform, and i find *talanoa* more effective in influencing people in prison. The word 'talanoa' is used in the islands of Oceania to refer to three things: story, telling (of stories) and conversation.[20] Talanoa is an island-ish trinity: there is no story (talanoa) without telling (talanoa) and conversation (talanoa); no telling without story and conversation; no conversation without story and telling. At the heart of island cultures, talanoa is where story, telling and conversation (read: text, interpretation, and analysis) interflow. In this regard, one needs to account for the (young?) lawyer in order for Lk. 10.25-37 to be talanoa. Without the lawyer, there is no conversation (talanoa) and hence there is no engagement, and no relation. The attention that readers in prison give to the lawyer thus invites us to the drifts of talanoa.

The usual questions that biblical scholars ask are: did the lawyer come in order to learn from, in order to test, and/or in order to trap Jesus?[21] The islanders in prison have different concerns. For instance, they are annoyed with their legal advisors and so the question for them is not, 'Who is my neighbor?', but rather, 'Who will confront my lawyer?' Their lawyers prefer to deal and negotiate for their judgments, rather than to fight their cases in court. Their key question about Lk. 10.25-37 is whether the lawyer came to negotiate with Jesus. If so, then about what and on whose behalf did he come to negotiate? Through talanoa, to borrow island navigation metaphors, these interlocutors set up markers to guide meanings and alternatives to find them (and safely guide unhealthy meanings to depart). My reasons for and thoughts about talanoa engagements with them are conditioned by the fluid context and oral cultures of Oceania, and by the navigation wisdom of my ancestors. So i must divert through some of the markers (or 'interruptions', to anticipate the last section of the essay) that guide my engagement with people in prison, then return to Lk. 10.25-37.

~ ~ ~

Surrounded by water, people on islands are constantly reminded of borders, the things within those borders—especially land, people (past and present), plants, animals, resources—and the need to relate to and co-exist with

---

20. See my 'Welcome to Talanoa', in *Talanoa Ripples: Across Borders, Cultures, Disciplines...* (ed. Jione Havea; Auckland: Masilamea Press and Massey University, 2010), pp. 11-22, and also my 'Diaspora contexted: Talanoa, Reading, and Theologizing, as Migrants', *Black Theology* 11.2 (2013), pp. 185-200.

21. See Klyne Snodgrass, *Stories with Intent: A Comprehensive Guide to the Parables of Jesus* (Grand Rapids: Eerdmans, 2008), p. 339.

those. Surrounded by water from all sides and from below, one tunes in to the borders and takes note of one's surroundings. Fluidity and proximity are therefore active energies in the island world.

Island cultures are said to be oral, but what this means has not been considered deeply. I conceive orality in the realms of fluidity and proximity. One can't be oral if one is rigid; one can't be oral if one keeps distance and does not relate to what surrounds her/him. Orality is a wave that runs alongside another wave, relationality. To be oral is to relate; and to relate requires one to be in proximity.

I draw upon the navigation heritage of my ancestors as well. When they rafted from place to place, whether to another island or to the open sea, they did not see themselves moving toward their destination. Rather, they imagined their destination coming to them.

> Pacific models of ocean navigation differ from western paradigms because they do not flatten and stabilize space through the bird's eye view of nautical charts. Instead, Pacific navigators have developed a complex system of charting a vessel's movement through space where the voyaging canoe is perceived as stable while the islands and cosmos move towards the traveler... Attention to movement offers a paradigm of rooted routes, of a mobile, flexible, and voyaging subject who is not physically or culturally circumscribed by the terrestrial boundaries of island space.[22]

Upon this piece of ancestral wisdom, i argue that we are in relationships not because we find or lose people; rather, people find or leave us. This is a different way of thinking compared to the obsession with 'discovery' that runs deep in the blood of colonialist readers.[23] My task in engaging with people in prison is to help to identify markers whereby meaning and new relations are able to find them. Holding those island-ish tendencies in mind, i return to Lk. 10.25-37.

~ ~ ~

The lawyer provides the oral and relational setting for Jesus' parable, and enables the islanders in prison to be found by new relations. The parable is embedded in negotiation and rebuttal. The critical charge against the priest

---

22. Elizabeth M. DeLoughrey, *Routes and Roots: Navigating Caribbean and Pacific Island Literatures* (Honolulu: University of Hawai'i Press, 2007), p. 3.

23. I argue that 'fixing' and 'discovering' a relation is an illusion. Relation is not like a destination that one finds, but a 'floating scripture' that finds the voyager. Feminists teach us that we re-member things, we put them into form (cf. Gen. 1.1-2), rather than find or discover them. As such, the challenge is to make oneself available to be visited, or to be vacated, by others. No one owns a relation; relation floats, reaching and departing in its time. It helps to set markers that guide others to relate and (using Facebook language) to poke them so that they do not unfriend.

and the Levite is that they did not bless the dying man, Amasa². They need not have touched the half-dead Amasa², and it is not important whether touching him, whether dead or alive, would defile the priest and the Levite or not. Most annoying is the fact that the priest and the Levite walked by *silently*. The priest and the Levite committed two wrongs: they did not do anything, and they did not say anything.

People in prison know what it's like when no one says something to them or on their behalf. This is why the Samaritan was good. Not only did he bind Amasa² but he spoke up on his behalf to the innkeeper: 'Take care of him; and when I come back, I will repay you whatever more you spend' (10.35b, NRSV). In prison, 'take care of him' has two implications. It can be a request for assistance and protection. 'Take care of him' is a request for favor (in a world where favor is the currency), 'Provide for and protect his life'. Second, 'take care of him' can also be an order for payback. Prison is a world in which to take care of someone also means to hurt her/him, and this could be fatal. The Samaritan's words lean toward the first connotation, requesting assistance and protection. In this regard, the words of the Samaritan were both solid and healing, and relation-building.

Islanders doing time at Parklea would appreciate the parable being applied differently. Jesus told the parable in order to teach a certain lawyer something about neighbors: 'Which of these three, do you think, was a neighbor to the man who fell into the hands of the robbers?' (Lk. 10.36). Three people are targeted in Jesus' talanoa: the priest, the Levite and the Samaritan. Reading with islanders in prison draws attention to another character, the innkeeper. Neither named nor placed in an ethnic community, the innkeeper was expected to do more than he was paid (10.35). Two denarii would have covered room and board for up to two weeks,[24] so a lot more was expected of the innkeeper, and neither the Samaritan nor the readers gave him the opportunity to refuse. The innkeeper too is neighborly,[25] and deserves to be an example of characters that readers should 'Go and do likewise' (10.37).[26]

What did Jesus want the lawyer to go and do? The popular reading is that he is to stop and give assistance to the robbed and stripped, but this reading does not serve as a marker for the islanders in prison. What appeals to them is that the Samaritan trusted the innkeeper to care for Amasa². Can't this

24. Snodgrass, *Stories with Intent*, p. 347.
25. Marshall, *Compassionate Justice*, p. 80: 'Neighbors are not chosen or created by law; they are found and cultivated through human encounter.'
26. This openness would be scandalous in contexts where innkeepers are suspect, and for readers who find no significance in, or who would eliminate, the innkeeper in the parable. See Bruce C. Longenecker, 'The Story of the Samaritan and the Innkeeper (Luke 10:30-35): A Study in Character Rehabilitation', *BibInt* 17 (2009), pp. 422-47 (427-34, 443).

also be what Jesus wanted the lawyer to do, to accept that someone else can take better care of his clients and to hand over at the right time?[27] In shifting attention to the innkeeper, the parable balances out: the priest and the Levite walk by, but the Samaritan and the innkeeper relate to Amasa².[28] The parable is not all about the Samaritan. Would he have done the same had he come in the middle of the attack?[29]

Identity

We do not know whether the lawyer went and did whatever Jesus meant for him to do.[30] If he came to negotiate with Jesus, would he have accepted Jesus' direction? What kind of lawyer was he? These questions bring us to the realm of identity.[31] 'The question of identity is never merely a question of what we believe as fact, but what we *are*, particularly what we are in relation to God and what motivates us and controls our being.'[32]

One of the assumptions that annoy islanders in prison is that the robbers in the parable must have been poor bandits who were driven to crime by poverty.[33] The islanders give other reasons. They rob also because of greed (defined as the refusal to be satisfied with what they already have), in order to feed an intoxicating habit or fund a Gangman-style lifestyle, or to experience the addictive thrill of doing something dangerous. Poverty is not the only reason why people rob. The islanders in prison are too proud to admit that they rob in order to escape poverty.[34]

Of all the characters in the parable, the one with which the islanders in prison refuse to identify are the robbers. This is not because they themselves were not robbers, but because (1) Jesus did not explain what kind of robbers they were ('there are robbers, and there are robbers') and (2) readers easily fall into the traps of stereotyping and stigmatizing robbers ('robbers and criminals are bad always').[35] Stigma is one of the shackles that people in prison

---

27. The people behind this reading have families outside, and they learn to trust others to care for them. Also, they are not happy with their lawyers.
28. So Longenecker, 'The Story of the Samaritan and the Innkeeper', pp. 445-56.
29. So Marshall, *Compassionate Justice*, p. 133.
30. McKenzie, *The Parables for Today*, p. 55.
31. In turning to the question of identity, we should not assume that all lawyers were the same (so for Samaritans, innkeepers and people in prison).
32. Snodgrass, *Stories with Intent*, p. 359.
33. See, e.g., Marshall, *Compassionate Justice*, p. 83.
34. Poverty is a common and accepted condition among islanders. There is no shame in admitting that one is poor. Some islanders take pride in announcing that they are poor.
35. See, e.g., Mike Graves, 'Luke 10:25-37: The Moral of the "Good Samaritan" Story?' *RevExp* 94 (1997), pp. 269-75 (270).

find difficult to remove. Upon their release, they remove their prison clothes and walk through the gates, but the stigma of being 'prisoners', 'convicts' or 'inmates' goes with them.[36] The hold of the 'inmatism'[37] stigma is especially strong and damaging in the honor-shame cultures of Pacific islanders. Islanders may be released from prison but they are never free of inmatism.

'Released but not free' is tough on people from minority/minoritized backgrounds, who bear the brunt of the maneuverings of racism in the justice and corrective services. They see racism but they do not always detect the workings of color discrimination. Through talanoa, we help each other to see how racism is one thing and bigotry based on color is another. The features and appearances of Pacific islanders who have a European parent or grandparent are as white as white people's are. Those Pacific islanders (some even have blue eyes and European names) get better treatment. Darker-skin islanders, on the other hand, do not have the respect of the staff or of their legal advisors. They are the ones who are encouraged by Jesus' refutation of the lawyer. 'Jesus responds to the lawyer's request with a counter-question that invites him to *nail his own colors to the mast:* "What is written in the law? What do you read there?"'[38] Jesus was able to do with the lawyer what islanders in prison cannot do with their legal advisors.

Borrowing Marshall's metaphor, what might happen if we nail colors to the parable of the Samaritan? Similar to members of gangs, the priest and Levite would have worn outfits that revealed their religious and cultural colors (status, position). Did the Samaritan wear some cultural outfit or, like Pacific islanders, did his face and features give him away as a Samaritan? What signified him as a Samaritan? The one point of distinction in his characterization is that he had an animal with him (Lk. 10.34). This pricked the attention of the islanders: Was he a farmer? a marketer? a trader? a merchant? a vendor? a pusher? a migrant? In the course of talanoa, it became clear that the islanders in prison did not want to confine the Samaritan into the cells of stigma, but to perceive him in the same range of colors as they also see the robbers and the innkeeper.

The lawyer, on the other hand, did not receive the sympathies of the islanders in prison. Conditioned by their experiences, they imagine the lawyer standing up to convince Jesus to accept responsibility and guilt for something he has done or said. The exchange is quite clever:

- The lawyer pushed Jesus on the question of *eternal life*;
- Jesus responded with the *love commandments*;[39]

---

36. This is why i prefer to refer to 'people in prison' in my writing and talanoa.
37. Pounder, 'Prison Theology', p. 282.
38. Marshall, *Compassionate Justice*, p. 63 (my italics).
39. Cf. Preston M. Sprinkle, 'The Use of Genesis 42:8 (not Leviticus 18:5) in Luke 10:28: Joseph and the Good Samaritan', *BBR* 17.2 (2007), pp. 193-205.

- The lawyer honed in on the *question of neighbor*;
- Jesus responded with the *parable of the Samaritan*.

Jesus dodged the lawyer's highfaluting moves by bringing the conversation (talanoa) to anchor in the familiar world, where some people walk by and a few stop to lend a hand. The shift from the other-worldliness of *eternal life* to the roadside in the *parable of the Samaritan* appeals to the islanders in prison. As talanoa, Lk. 10.25-37 is not about something that is beyond their reach but something reasonable and attainable.

Interruption

Reading with people in prison obliges one to keep her/his ears and eyes to the ground. It helps to set markers, which in prison serve as interruptions, which can direct 'rootedness and belonging' to find the people in prison. Reading with people in prison requires interruptions to occur in space, time, relation and identity, as well as interruptions to break the shackles of imprisoning readings.

Luke 10.25-37 is filled with interruptions: The lawyer interrupts Jesus; Jesus interrupts the lawyer's line of thinking; the robbers interrupt Amasa^2's journey; the fallen body of Amasa^2 interrupts (read: diverts) the Samaritan's journey; and the Samaritan interrupts the innkeeper. Interruptions (diversions) are disruptive and can be hurtful and devastating, but they can also be instructive, transformative and healing.

People wielding power sometimes ignore interruptions, like the two authority figures in Jesus' parable who went around Amasa^2 (an interruption on their path). Stepping back from the parable, i close with an invitation: reading with people in prison obliges readers to interrupt the flight of 'priests and Levites'. Put another way, reading with people in prison requires readers inside and outside of prison to stop, to take, to care and therewith to 'own' prison.

Making Public Theology More Biblical or Biblical Theology More Public? Christopher Marshall's Interpretation of the Parable of the Prodigal Son in Luke 15

Geoff Broughton

The first biblical story outside the garden is the account of two brothers and their father, a story of the father's honour and the brothers' rivalry borne of their different ways of inhabiting the world. The story includes enmity and violence—with the menace of revenge—and concludes in exile (Gen. 4.2-16). Cain's murder of Abel is the 'original crime', and philosophers, anthropologists, theologians and Christian antagonists have found in this story compelling accounts of crime and wrongdoing, victim and wrongdoer, evil and justice.[1] The extant, cross-disciplinary engagement with the Cain and Abel story demonstrates that public theology can be biblical. But are biblical theologians provoked to engage with public issues and policy? The desire to engage public life with the biblical text can be diverted to mere evangelism (serving the pragmatic needs of the church) or mere abstractions (serving the research needs of the academy). A fully public, biblical theology has a deeper and more extensive role to play.

Luke's rendition of the parable of the Prodigal Son (Lk. 15.11-32) is among the most influential and perhaps best loved of all the parables Jesus told. The parable has been painted by a host of artists (most notably Rembrandt), provided the themes for plays (most notably those of Shakespeare), been set to music and most recently served as the subject of motion pictures. The parable's central themes of rebellion and return vividly capture the devastation of becoming lost and the deep longing for home that characterize the human condition. It seems to encapsulate the entire Christian message,

---

1. See Miroslav Volf, 'Original Crime, Primal Care', in *God and the Victim: Theological Reflections on Evil, Victimization, Justice, and Forgiveness* (ed. Lisa Barnes Lampman; Grand Rapids: Eerdmans, 1999), pp. 17-35; Regina M. Schwartz, *The Curse of Cain: The Violent Legacy of Monotheism* (Chicago: University of Chicago Press, 1997); René Girard, *Things Hidden since the Foundation of the World* (trans. S. Bann and M. Metteer; Stanford: Stanford University Press, 1987); Emmanuel Levinas, *Ethics and Infinity: Conversations with Philippe Nemo* (Pittsburgh: Duquesne University Press, 1985).

as illustrated by Tim Keller, a pastor, speaker and author from New York who reaches a global audience. Keller stands in a long and venerable tradition of biblical commentators who interpret Jesus' story as 'the gospel... the heart of the Christian message'.[2] The real challenge in the story, according to Keller's account of the 'Prodigal God', is the reckless generosity of the father-God towards both sons who are lost. Evangelistic preachers and teachers, Keller contends, emphasize the grace and forgiveness bestowed on the younger son who leaves home but pay less attention to the elder son who stays home. Keller locates the true and deeper meaning of the parable in this second 'act' of the story. Lazy preachers, teachers and Bible commentators who interpret the lost son in Lk. 15.11-32 as simply another 'lost and found' story—like that of the lost sheep (Lk. 15.4-6) or the lost coin (15.8-9)—have missed a crucial development in the parable's plot. In narrating the elder son's account of his father's reckless generosity, Keller places the following words of indignation on the dutiful son's lips: 'Where is the justice in that?'[3]

Exactly. *Where is the justice in this much-loved story?* Or more precisely, what kind of justice is shaped by the father-God's 'reckless generosity'? Some commentators suggest that the justice enacted by the father-God's forgiveness precludes traditional notions of atonement.[4] Christopher Marshall is sympathetic to J. Denny Weaver's reading of the parable but does not find it convincing.[5] Keller is more concerned with 'Jesus's radical redefinition of what is wrong with us' so as to explore in a satisfactory way 'why Jesus constructs a story so that one of them is restored to right relationship with the father, and one of them is not'.[6] Preoccupation with the parable's evangelistic message (so, Keller) or its atonement theology (so, Weaver) limits public engagement with Jesus' most famous parable.

More recently, Marshall has constructed a public theology by focusing on Jesus' most *public* parables: the Good Samaritan (Luke 10) and the Prodigal Son (Luke 15). As Keller, Weaver and many others have demonstrated, these are biblical stories that still resonate in the public domain. But can they serve public life?[7] Marshall adopts Stackhouse's three criteria for his

---

2. Timothy Keller, *The Prodigal God: Recovering the Heart of the Christian Faith* (London: Hodder & Stoughton, 2008), pp. xi-xii.

3. Keller, *The Prodigal God*, pp. 26, 107. In his final chapter, Keller notes that 'Christian theologians have spoken about the law-court aspects of Jesus's salvation. Jesus secures the legal verdict "not guilty" for us so we are no longer liable for our wrongdoings'.

4. J. Denny Weaver, *The Nonviolent Atonement* (Grand Rapids: Eerdmans, 2001).

5. Christopher D. Marshall, 'Atonement, Violence and the Will of God: A Sympathetic Response to J. Denny Weaver's *The Nonviolent Atonement*', *MQR* 77.1 (2003), pp. 69-92.

6. Keller, *The Prodigal God*, pp. 43, 46.

7. Chris Marshall, 'What Language Shall I Borrow? The Bilingual Dilemma of

social ethic of compassionate justice: 'theologically sound, publicly accessible, and practically viable'.[8] Marshall believes that 'public theology is necessarily an interdisciplinary exercise'.[9] *Compassionate Justice* is Marshall's most explicit interdisciplinary dialogue between two Lukan parables and 'law, crime, and restorative justice'.[10] A rigorous interdisciplinary approach is the method by which Marshall relates the Bible and justice, but his achievement goes further than a contribution to the academy.

This chapter demonstrates the possibilities of Jesus' parables for public theology because Marshall's biblical theology is *prescient, peaceable and performable*. A prescient reading includes historical interpretations without becoming frozen in another time; a peaceable reading incorporates cultural interpretations without being located in some other place; and a performable reading integrates practical-theological interpretations within concrete, local relationships and community.

Preliminary Reflections on Marshall's Method

The promises and pitfalls of an interdisciplinary approach are beyond the scope of this chapter. An interdisciplinary method is so central to Marshall's *Compassionate Justice*, however, that two preliminary observations are necessary.

First, Marshall's interdisciplinary approach has bona fides in restorative justice and wider law and criminal justice literature. Marshall is neither new to the disciplines of biblical studies, law and justice nor is he only now pioneering an interdisciplinary dialogue between these disciplines. More than a decade ago he established his approach in *Beyond Retribution: A New Testament Vision for Justice, Crime, and Punishment*, in which justice is rehabilitated as one of the Bible's central themes. For Marshall, the promotion of justice is primarily understood as a 'restorative activity'.[11] Marshall's

---

Public Theology', *Stimulus* 13.3 (2005), pp. 11-18 (11) argues that 'the quandary' for public theology is this: 'What language should religious believers use when they engage in public debate? Do they use the language of faith? Or do they adopt the secular language of mainstream political discourse?'

8. Cited in Marshall, 'What Language?', pp. 11, 17. Marshall concludes that 'Christians must be able to speak the language of political discourse effectively, albeit with a foreign accent'.

9. Marshall, 'What Language?', p. 12. See also Christopher D. Marshall, *Beyond Retribution: A New Testament Vision for Justice, Crime, and Punishment* (Grand Rapids: Eerdmans, 2001), pp. 35-47.

10. Christopher D. Marshall, *Compassionate Justice: An Interdisciplinary Dialogue with Two Gospel Parables on Law, Crime, and Restorative Justice* (Eugene, OR: Cascade Books, 2012).

11. Christopher D. Marshall, *The Little Book of Biblical Justice: A Fresh Approach to the Bible's Teaching on Justice* (Intercourse, PA: Good Books, 2005), pp. 35-47.

conclusion to his earlier studies is the perfect segue to his extended engagement with Lk. 15.11-32: 'according to the witness of the New Testament, the basic principle of the moral order is not the perfect balance of deed and desert but redeeming, merciful love'.[12] Significant theorists in both law and restorative justice have recognized and affirmed Marshall's interdisciplinary approach.[13] Furthermore, other New Testament scholars (such as Ched Myers) have followed Marshall in his interdisciplinary endeavour.[14] The happy consequence of Marshall's work is that discourse in the restorative justice movement has not remained superficial (cf. earlier vague notions of its 'spiritual roots') but has become more biblical! As important as this interdisciplinary methodology has been, however, it is my view that Marshall's role as a scholar-practitioner holds even greater significance.

My second preliminary observation, then, is that public theology as a purely academic pursuit is an oxymoron! Miroslav Volf notes trends both within the broader discipline of systematic theology to become more consciously biblical and within biblical studies to be more consciously theological:

> In my judgment, the return of biblical scholars to the theological reading of the Scriptures, and the return of systematic theologians to sustained engagement with the scriptural texts—in a phrase, the return of both to theological readings of the Bible—is *the most significant theological development in the last two decades*.[15]

These converging trends in theological and biblical studies to engage in study of and reflection on the Scriptures has a growing body of literature attached to it—theological interpretation of Scripture![16] The judgment by Volf, a scholar who has reflected deeply on issues of justice and reconciliation, suggests that theological works on justice need to be more thoroughly engaged with Scripture. Marshall answers this challenge with an extended engagement with two Lukan parables for the work of restorative justice.

Despite the positive development of theologians returning to the Scriptures, there remains another issue within biblical studies: mere interdisciplinary research and writing confined within the academy or mere missional

---

12. Marshall, *Beyond Retribution*, p. 259.
13. Exemplified by contributions such as Christopher D. Marshall, 'Terrorism, Religious Violence and Restorative Justice', in *Handbook of Restorative Justice* (ed. Gerry Johnstone and Daniel W. Van Ness; Cullompton, Devon: Willan Publishing, 2007), pp. 372-94.
14. Ched Myers and Elaine Enns, *Ambassadors of Reconciliation*, Vol. I: *New Testament Reflections on Restorative Justice and Peacemaking* (Maryknoll, NY: Orbis Books, 2009).
15. Miroslav Volf, *Captive to the Word of God: Engaging the Scriptures for Contemporary Theological Reflection* (Grand Rapids: Eerdmans, 2010), p. 14.
16. See, e.g., Stephen E. Fowl, *Theological Interpretation of Scripture* (Eugene, OR: Cascade Books, 2009).

goals for the life of the Church. More than a decade ago Saunders and Campbell identified the problem of academic interpretation that resonated with my own reading of the Scriptures alongside homeless people suffering addictions and a range of mental health issues on the streets of inner-city Sydney.[17] In time I would begin to add my own voice to those asking for the liberation of serious study of Scripture from the academy.[18] Most recently friend and mentor Ched Myers has edited a volume demonstrating the need for our contemporary storytellers—from artists to activists—to join in the task of making biblical theology more public.[19] This requires the deliberate straddling of 'the seminary, the sanctuary, and the streets' because such reading 'reshapes...what vantage point, and in whose interests we read and study the Bible'.[20]

I will return to the critical role of scholar-activists at the end of this chapter. Particularly in the Australian context, Marshall's dual roles as biblical scholar and restorative justice practitioner should not be overlooked. Australia boasts some of the world's best restorative justice researchers.[21] Australia has also demonstrated early 'best practice' in restorative justice to the world.[22] Drawing together practice and principles has been a key concern for the restorative justice movement during the last decade.[23] With 'one foot in the academy' and 'one foot in the justice system', Marshall has been attentive to both principle *and* practice,[24] which is demonstrated throughout *Compassionate Justice*. As a scholar-activist, therefore, Marshall demonstrates how biblical studies can serve public life by becoming *prescient*,

---

17. Stanley P. Saunders and Charles L. Campbell, *The Word on the Street: Performing the Scriptures in the Urban Context* (Grand Rapids: Eerdmans, 2000).

18. Geoff Broughton, 'Reading the Bible through the Lens of the Street', in *Reflections on a Remarkable Church* (ed. Katharine Brisbane; Sydney: St John Foundation, 2008), pp. 103-105.

19. Laurel Dykstra and Ched Myers (eds.), *Liberating Biblical Study: Scholarship, Art, and Action in Honor of the Center and Library for the Bible and Social Justice* (Eugene, OR: Cascade Books, 2011).

20. Ched Myers, 'Introduction', in *Liberating Biblical Study* (ed. Laurel Dykstra and Ched Myers; Eugene, OR: Cascade Books, 2011), p. xxiii.

21. See John Braithwaite, *Crime, Shame and Reintegration* (Cambridge: Cambridge University Press, 1989).

22. See Terry O'Connell, Ben Wachtel and Ted Wachtel, *Conferencing Handbook: The New Real Justice Training Manual* (Pipersville: Pipers Press, 1999).

23. Howard Zehr, 'Evaluation and Restorative Justice Principles', in *New Directions in Restorative Justice: Issues, Practice, Evaluation* (ed. Elizabeth Elliott and Robert M. Gordon; Cullompton, Devon: Willan Publishing, 2005), pp. 296-303.

24. Christopher D. Marshall, 'Reflections on the Spirit of Justice', in *Restorative Justice and Practices in New Zealand: Towards a Restorative Society* (ed. Gabrielle Maxwell and James H. Liu; Wellington, NZ: Victoria University Institute of Policy Studies, 2007), pp. 311-19.

peaceable and performable. This may be demonstrated by comparing Marshall's reading of Lk. 15.11-32 with three other representative readings of the parable of the Prodigal Son.

Three Interpretive Approaches to Luke 15.11-32

There are many and varied approaches to interpreting the text of the New Testament. Here I survey three approaches well established within the academy and popular among interdisciplinary theologians and evangelistic preachers. Luke 15.11-32 can be interpreted in historical, cultural and practical-theological contexts.[25] In order to compare the exegetical commentary that is representative of each approach, I have isolated two moments in the drama of the prodigal son's journey to a far country and return home. The first is his request in Lk. 15.12: 'Father, give me the share of property that is coming to me'. The second is the beginning of his return in Lk. 15.17-19:

> But when he came to himself, he said, 'How many of my father's hired servants have more than enough bread, but I perish here with hunger! I will arise and go to my father, and I will say to him, "Father, I have sinned against heaven and before you. I am no longer worthy to be called your son. Treat me as one of your hired servants."'

After surveying representatives of the historical, cultural and practical-theological approaches to the parable of the Prodigal Son, I demonstrate in the following section that Marshall's exegetical commentary in *Compassionate Justice* incorporates all three dimensions but goes further to be more *prescient* than mere historical criticism, more *peaceable* than cultural analysis and more orientated towards *performance* than practical-theological interpretation.

Joachim Jeremias's Historical Approach

In the post-Bultmann age of biblical studies, Joachim Jeremias's *The Parables of Jesus* was a bold investigation into the historical context of not only Jesus' life and teaching but also his parables.[26] Jeremias identified significant details informing his interpretation of the parable. For example, in his commentary on the Prodigal's request, he interprets this as a request to live an independent life:

---

25. Each of these approaches reflects a genuinely dynamic view of the relationship between theology and lived experience (or between theory and practice) which is substantively different from the dialectical approach of earlier generations and goes beyond mere 'praxis'.

26. Joachim Jeremias, *The Parables of Jesus* (trans. S.H. Hooke; London: SCM Press, 3rd rev. edn, 1972).

> The legal position was as follows: there were two ways in which property might pass from father to son, by a will, or by a gift during the life of the father... In v. 12 the younger son demands not only the right of possession, but also the right of disposal; he wants a settlement because he proposes to lead an independent life.[27]

A generation of scholars and preachers followed Jeremias as interpreting the son's request as saying to his father, 'I wish you were dead'.[28] The legal context of inheritance sheds light not only on the son's request but also on the plight he faced in returning home. Jeremias notes that the son has foregone all legal bases for the basic necessities of life (his earlier desire for complete independence was fulfilled!): '"he came back to himself", "he came into himself", is in Hebrew and Aramaic an expression of repentance... [A]fter the legal settlement he has no further claim, not even to food and clothing. He asks to be allowed to earn both.'[29]

Such historical details prepare the hearer to appreciate the utter graciousness of the father in both granting the son's request and welcoming the son's return. These features of Jeremias's analysis represent good exegesis but prepare the ground for public theology. The connection with public and everyday life is made because the historical narrative is a lived experience. The father and son in the parable are not merely spiritual or psychological tropes employed to serve a larger theme of lost and found. They are two people governed by laws of inheritance in a particular time and place. Historical readings of the parable lose their potency for theology to be genuinely public, however, when the story remains frozen in 'some other' time. What twenty-first century father would agree to such a request or refuse to feed or clothe a returning prodigal? Biblical theology must be more *prescient*.

Kenneth Bailey's Cultural Approach

The rhetorical question, 'What twenty-first century father...?', highlights the distance in time and culture between the world behind the text and the world in front of it. Biblical studies have been attentive to the importance of social and cultural readings of Scripture, and Kenneth Bailey's *Poet & Peasant* is a highly regarded and oft-cited interpretation of the parable of the Prodigal.[30] The majority of Western readers of this story are tone-deaf to

---

27. Jeremias, *The Parables of Jesus*, pp. 128-29.
28. See, e.g., Keller, *The Prodigal God*, p. 18.
29. Jeremias, *The Parables of Jesus*, p. 130.
30. Kenneth E. Bailey, *Poet & Peasant and Through Peasant Eyes: A Literary-Cultural Approach to the Parables in Luke* (Grand Rapids: Eerdmans, combined edn, 1983). See also Kenneth E. Bailey, *Finding the Lost: Cultural Keys to Luke 15* (St Louis: Concordia, 1992).

issues of honour and shame. Bailey highlights the extraordinary insult of the son's request, which uncovers a deeper dimension to the son's 'lostness':

> Can it be confirmed from ancient literature that this son's request is an extraordinary insult to the father? [In response to Levison, Bailey aims] to demonstrate that this can be confirmed and that this cultural aspect of the parable sets the stage in a crucial way for all that follows... In the Middle Eastern milieu the father is expected to explode and discipline the boy for the cruel implications of his demand.[31]

Also significant is the role of the wider 'family' on his return: the reception by the elder brother and also by the village. Most Western interpreters concentrate on the father's welcome, but Bailey notes that a bitter price must be paid as the son faces the wider consequences of his action:

> The prodigal's three primary relationships, as he sees them from the far country, can...be summarized [as follows]. He plans to live in the village as a hired servant. With such a position his status will be secure. He can perhaps fulfil his responsibility to his father, and the problem of any relationship to his brother is eliminated. The village with its mockery will have to be faced. He will have to pay this bitter price in order to get home.[32]

The connection with public and everyday life is made because the cultural narrative is a living expression. Unlike inheritance laws of first-century Palestine, cultural readings portray a different way of relating. For the contemporary reader, the immersion in another culture can be a rich and disorientating experience, similar to travelling overseas for the first time. Cultural readings of the parable lose their potency for theology to be genuinely public, however, when the story is set in 'some other' place one does not inhabit but only visits as a tourist. What twenty-first century prodigal has a neighbourhood or village to return to, let alone with which to reconcile? Biblical theology must be more *peaceable*.

Miroslav Volf's Practical-Theological Approach
A practical-theological approach to the parable of the Prodigal Son, with its vision of reconciliation though the image of embrace, is the heart of Miroslav Volf's *Exclusion and Embrace*.[33] Volf's interpretation of the parable as a 'drama of embrace' describes the multiple breaches precipitated by the son's request. The combined effect on father *and* son was that the breach was total:

---

31. Bailey, *Poet & Peasant*, pp. 162 and 165.
32. Bailey, *Poet & Peasant*, pp. 178-79.
33. Miroslav Volf, *Exclusion and Embrace: A Theological Exploration of Identity, Otherness, and Reconciliation* (Nashville: Abingdon Press, 1996).

> the younger son has already done wrong by demanding the parceling out of the inheritance and deciding to depart... [H]e cut himself off from the relations which constituted his very identity... The younger son's breach with the family was total.[34]

For Volf, the process of reconciliation (of being embraced again) begins with the memory of proper relationships. Despite all that he had forfeited and wasted, the son retained the memory of sonship:

> Through departure he wanted to become a 'non-son'; his return begins not with repentance but with something that makes the repentance possible—the memory of sonship. There is no coming to oneself without the memory of belonging... The memory of sonship gives hope, but it also reminds of failure; the bridge that the memory builds is a testimony to the chasm created by departure.[35]

The connection with public and everyday life is made because the practical-theological narrative is a life-giving encounter. The *relational world* evoked by the practical-theological reading has the potential to be deeply transformative. Practical-theological readings of the parable lose their potency for theology to be genuinely public, however, when they suggest 'something other' than faithful discipleship through Christian community. The metaphor of embrace is suggestive of how to restore relationships after wrongdoing, but it does not describe what actions are required. Biblical theology must be *performable*.

Paradigm for Biblical Theology
Each of the three approaches described above fails to render the kind of theological implications for a fully public social ethic. My brief examination of historical, cultural and practical-theological interpretations of the parable of the Prodigal Son suggests that for biblical theology to become fully public, the following paradigm is needed:

- prescient (engaging today's issues)
- peaceable (reconciling enmity and division)
- performable (faithful in word *and* deed)

The prescient, peaceable and performable shape of Marshall's interdisciplinary reading of the parable of the Prodigal Son is achieved by using the lens of restorative justice. Before examining Marshall's commentary on the same verses of request and return in Luke 15, I will briefly describe the importance of the restorative justice lens in Marshall's work.

---

34. Volf, *Exclusion and Embrace*, pp. 157-58.
35. Volf, *Exclusion and Embrace*, pp. 158-59.

The Restorative Justice Lens for Interpreting Scripture

The most common understanding of restorative justice encompasses the theory and practice of justice-making in which relationships are restored. While there is no clear consensus about what this means among leading restorative justice theorists and practitioners, there is some common ground in relation to the following two principles:

> First, justice requires that we work to heal victims, offenders and communities that have been injured by crime. Second, victims, offenders and communities should have the opportunity for active involvement in the justice process as early and as fully as possible.[36]

According to both theorists and practitioners, just outcomes are primarily relational. Biblical justice—interpreted as *shalom*—has consequently been a significant element in much restorative justice literature. Too much of this literature, however, does not adequately account for the great diversity in Scriptural perspectives on justice that are inherent in the crucial distinction between the semantic domains of justice and righteousness. In general terms the restorative justice movement has preferred Scriptures that witness to both *mishpat* and *tsedaqa* as relational and social justice ('delivering, community-restoring justice'), while reinterpreting classic definitions of *dikaiosunē* ('righteousness, forensic justice') along similar lines. The current evaluation of Marshall's *Compassionate Justice* takes place within these broader concerns through an extended investigation of biblical justice in two of Jesus' most loved parables.[37] The reading of Scripture through the lens of restorative justice is *prescient* because it addresses contemporary issues of wrongdoing; it is *peaceable* because it reconciles wrongdoers and victims; and it is *performable* because it transcends the divide between a public debate over 'law and order' (fixing crime as the responsibility of government) or more private, 'therapeutic' resolutions (helping victims as therapeutic intervention). A distinctive feature of Marshall's reading of Luke 15 is his attention to community responsibility in the aftermath of wrongdoing.[38] In the final section I will demonstrate how the relational lens of restorative justice is employed by Marshall to make the parable of the Prodigal prescient, peaceable and

---

36. Daniel W. Van Ness and Karen H. Strong, *Restoring Justice* (Cincinnati: Anderson, 3rd edn, 2006), p. 44, cited in Gerry Johnstone and Daniel W. Van Ness, 'The Meaning of Restorative Justice', in *Handbook of Restorative Justice* (ed. Gerry Johnstone and Daniel W. Van Ness; Cullompton, Devon: Willan Publishing, 2007), pp. 5-23 (14-15).

37. See also Geoff I. Broughton, *Restorative Christ: Jesus, Justice, and Discipleship* (Eugene, OR: Pickwick Publications, 2014).

38. This is explicit in an earlier treatment of Luke 15. See Christopher D. Marshall, 'Offending, Restoration, and the Law-Abiding Community: Restorative Justice in the New Testament and in the New Zealand Experience', *JSCE* 27.2 (2007), pp. 3-30.

performable. The result is that the biblical theology of *Compassionate Justice* is properly public.

Making Biblical Theology More Public

I have argued that the common interpretive approaches to Lk. 15.11-32 are not public enough because they inadvertently focus attention on another time (e.g., Jeremias), another place (e.g., Bailey) or another relational world (e.g., Volf). By contrast, I suggest that Marshall's interdisciplinary dialogue with restorative justice enables his reading of the parable of the Prodigal to maintain a focus that is prescient, peaceable and performable, resulting in a 'better justice'.[39]

Prescient

Marshall's dialogue between Scripture and contemporary principles and practice of restorative justice makes his theology prescient. By engagement with thinkers such as Richard Bell, Marshall connects 'what it means to be a just human being' with 'classical (and biblical) thinkers', which provides the 'capacity to hold justice and mercy together in the domain of corrective or criminal justice'.[40] He shows that the father's response ('a paragon of patient, merciful justice') elucidates the justice-making that eludes contemporary practice: *respect* (for personal agency), *hope, empathy, humility, integrity, honour* and *acknowledgment*.[41] The father's impressive list of virtues extends the meaning of the parable from forgiveness to justice-making but also significantly deepens the implications for enacting justice. Relating the father's actions to contemporary debates on community responses to crime, Marshall asserts:

> There is a legitimate place for external sanctions in the enactment of justice. But if justice relies wholly or predominantly on force, it can never achieve its ultimate goal of promoting human flourishing. It is revealing that what finally moved the prodigal to change his behavior and seek reconciliation was not fear of his father's power to punish him but recollection of his father's generosity of character (v. 17) and the regard he had shown for his moral autonomy, now expressed as a willingness to accept personal responsibility for his wrongful deeds ('Father, I have sinned', vv. 18, 21).[42]

It is not surprising, therefore, that the kind of communities that benefit most from human flourishing—and suffer most from wrongful deeds—are embracing this better justice: schools, workplaces and urban neighbour-

---

39. Marshall, *Compassionate Justice*, pp. 217-45.
40. Marshall, *Compassionate Justice*, p. 218.
41. Marshall, *Compassionate Justice*, pp. 220-33.
42. Marshall, *Compassionate Justice*, p. 221.

hoods.⁴³ By observing the details of Marshall's interpretation of the parable, these deeper concerns of justice-making as *peaceable* are evident.

Peaceable
A central concern of restorative justice is the relational harm caused by wrongdoing. Marshall calls this 'relational rupture'. The description of this familial and communal damage in the story of the Prodigal has been identified as: the quest for an independent life (the historical contribution); an extraordinary insult (the cultural contribution); and the total breach of proper relationships (the practical-theological contribution). Marshall affirms and deepens these descriptions by noticing the 'relational connections and responsibilities': 'His rebellion consisted in a thoroughgoing rejection of his relational connections with, and his responsibilities towards, his father, his brother, and his wider village community.'⁴⁴

With the trained eye of a biblical exegete *and* facilitator of restorative justice conferences, Marshall provides an anatomy of the younger son's offending as primarily 'relational rupture'. The first rupture is the explicit *disrespect* of the request itself. Beyond greed, impatience and the sheer shamelessness of the approach, Marshall describes the 'deeply dishonouring' wounds to the father. While contemporary Western cultures remain somewhat blind to issues of honour and shame, the wounds (or 'harm') that comes from wrongdoing is immediately recognized. Contemporary debates around law and order, crime and punishment have struggled to name either these relational connections or the responsibilities they entail. Peacemaking initiatives begin by exposing a false peace—the illusion that wrongdoing is impersonal or that the impact is limited to the victim. The parable, as interpreted by Marshall, highlights the 'injury of disrespect' caused by the son's wrongdoing: 'The youngest son in the parable had no qualms whatsoever about making his greedy impatience obvious to his father. This would have been as wounding to him as it was deeply dishonouring.'⁴⁵

The second rupture is to the relational order implicit between father and son so distorted by the younger son's request. Parent-child relationships—particularly relationships between parents and their adult children—are often painful, perplexing and result in permanent damage to people on both sides. An entire therapeutic system has developed by analysing the transactions in these parent-adult relationships. Since the 1960s revolution in attitudes to authority, patriarchy and orderly relationships, the mere suggestion

---

43. See Geoff Broughton, 'Restorative Justice and Jesus Christ: Why Restorative Justice Requires a Holistic Christology' (PhD thesis, Charles Sturt University, 2011), p. 35, where I identify each as a 'third place' which have become restorative communities.
44. Marshall, *Compassionate Justice*, p. 196.
45. Marshall, *Compassionate Justice*, p. 199.

that a son might have a 'proper relationship' to his father appears quaint and conservative. Surely his bold approach reflects an old-fashioned, no-nonsense, 'man-to-man' talk? The son's insolence, on the contrary, serves to reveal that he is still only a boy. The father's deep wounds and hurt reveal that he is aging and vulnerable. For this story to enact justice the son cannot remain stuck in his boyish insolence, nor can the father remain an aging victim. Justice-making involves the re-ordering of relationships distorted by wrongdoing: 'He [the younger son] was preparing to deprive [his father] of the ground of his existence and belonging. It was an insolent and emotionally hurtful demand that manifested a profound distortion in a son's proper relationship to his father.'[46]

Wrongdoing is relational rupture because offending wounds people through disrespect and distorts relationships through immaturity and insolence. Wrongdoers persist in their offending because they have become contemptuous of their victims: they do not see or hear the impact of their offending. When offenders are asked in a restorative justice conference, 'What were you thinking about at the time (of committing the offense)?' the answer is never: 'the impact this will have on my victim'. Too many forms of justice-making remain blind to the victim *after* the offense. With little insight into the 'relational rupture' caused by wrongdoing, the victim remains invisible and the wrongdoer unaccountable. At their best, the various *Truth and Reconciliation Commissions* and courts across Africa during the last two decades have demonstrated the possibility that the penetrating vision of the community can engender respect by offering a gift to the victim and wrongdoer, namely, being able to see the other person in a new way. Finally, there is the son's contempt for all his father had ever accomplished: 'for the younger son to sell the family patrimony to an outsider, presumably at a bargain basement price since the deal was struck so quickly, was to express contempt for all that his father had accomplished during his lifetime'.[47]

Performable
What actions are performed by father and son in the parable? What is the relationship between the actions of these two central characters? It is widely understood that the son's *repentance* followed by the father's *forgiveness* are the two critical actions in this story. Marshall suggests it is 'the profoundest insight of restorative justice theory' that recognizes the 'parallel journeys' for victims and offenders.[48] The parallel journeys of father and son are shown to be *mutually honouring* actions. The 'obligation of offenders' is to take responsibility for their wrongdoing. The catalyst for this action in

---

46. Marshall, *Compassionate Justice*, p. 199.
47. Marshall, *Compassionate Justice*, p. 201.
48. Marshall, *Compassionate Justice*, p. 231.

the story of the Prodigal has already been identified as: coming into himself or coming to his senses (the historical contribution); acknowledging the bitter cost of returning home (the cultural contribution); and remembering the proper relationship of father and son (the practical-theological contribution). Marshall narrates the son's return with three actions: contrition, correction and reconciliation.

> *Repentance as confession:*
> Contrition, if it is sincere, will lead to confession and apology... First it requires an acceptance of moral blame... The prodigal also acknowledges, secondly, that his actions have injured others... A third element in the boy's confession is an acknowledgment that his actions have changed the nature of his relationship to his victim.[49]

Contrition without correction of life is little more than 'feeling sorry for yourself'. Without amends, superficial remorse produces forced apologies rehearsed by celebrities, politicians and young children: 'I'm sorry I got caught'. The yearning for renewed relationships is the key to life-changing action.

> *Repentance as correction of life:*
> the prodigal's remorse, his yearning for renewed contact with his father, his journeying home from a great distance, and his verbal confession of sin, all imply a commitment to a corrected lifestyle in the future, no longer marked by the selfishness and rebellion of the past.[50]

A striking feature of the parable is the son's *desire for reconciliation* with his father rather than forgiveness or exoneration that enables his return. Marshall rightly observes the uncertainty of the son's reception by father, brother and village.

> *Repentance as atonement and reconciliation:*
> [The younger son] could be less certain of his father's pardon or his brother's acceptance [than of God's forgiveness]. From the way he treated his hired hands, he knew his father to be a kind and gracious man (v. 17). But his own offending has been unusually grave, and he could not be sure his father's grace would extend that far... What he experiences when he arrives home, however, is a merciful justice that confounds his expectations and restores him completely to the relationships he had so casually renounced.[51]

His journey home honours his father's generosity. The son, in turn, is bestowed great honour in the father's embrace and following actions. To this point, the father's action has remained at the periphery of the parable but now takes centre-stage. Following Volf, Marshall sees the father's

---

49. Marshall, *Compassionate Justice*, pp. 208-211.
50. Marshall, *Compassionate Justice*, p. 211.
51. Marshall, *Compassionate Justice*, pp. 213-14.

'stubborn, passionate yearning' for restoration as stirring the son to action.[52] Following Bailey, Marshall interprets the father's action as compassion for his son.[53] This is no mere sentimentality, however. The father's 'restorative gestures' are central to his compassionate justice: 'It is impossible, then, to miss the message implied by the father's actions. He does not merely supply his son's bare physical necessities; *he makes him an object of honor.*'[54]

For Marshall the story of 'lost and found' in Luke 15 is the lost honour of both sons and the father (which individually and collectively harms relationships). It is the honour of the father and the younger son that is 'found' and their relationship restored, individually and within the wider community of their village. It is the elder brother who stands outside those restored relationships; a place without honour and a stance that pours dishonour on his father. The restoring of honour to victim, wrongdoer and their community is, in my view, prescient, peaceable and performable.

The Christology of Compassionate Justice
The central role of honour in Marshall's interpretation of the parable of the Prodigal Son in Luke 15 invokes the controversial—and widely misappropriated—notion of satisfaction in Anselm's *Cur Deus homo*,[55] so I conclude with a brief appraisal of Marshall's Christological vision in *Compassionate Justice*. New Testament scholar C.F.D. Moule once characterized God's justice as 'restorative justice' and argued that it was 'ultimately the only way to justice—yes, justice!—on the deepest level, and the only ultimately effective reply to wrong'.[56] The restoration of honour—as witnessed in the final scenes of Luke 15—is a gift of grace. This is not because forgiveness and reconciliation cost nothing 'but because the price is willingly…paid by the donor himself'.[57] Moule understood that the parables of Jesus can only be interpreted through the person and work of Jesus Christ. As famously rendered by Eduard Schweizer, Jesus *is* the parable of God.[58] The compassion of Jesus, so wonderfully portrayed in the parables of the Good Samaritan and the Prodigal Son, is even more wonderfully enacted

---

52. Marshall, *Compassionate Justice*, pp. 222-23.
53. Marshall, *Compassionate Justice*, p. 223.
54. Marshall, *Compassionate Justice*, p. 229.
55. Anselm, *Why God Became Man*, in *A Scholastic Miscellany: Anselm to Ockham*, LCC (ed. Eugene R. Fairweather; Philadelphia: Westminster Press, 1956), pp. 100-183.
56. C.F.D. Moule, 'Retribution or Restoration?', in *Forgiveness and Reconciliation and Other New Testament Themes* (London: SPCK, 1998), pp. 41-47 (41).
57. C.F.D. Moule, 'The Theology of Forgiveness', in *Essays in New Testament Interpretation* (Cambridge: Cambridge University Press, 1982), pp. 250-60 (253), where a recurring theme is that 'forgiveness uses you up'.
58. Eduard Schweizer, *Jesus the Parable of God: What Do We Really Know about Jesus?* (Allison Park, PA: Pickwick Publications, 1994).

in his death *for* others—even his enemies. For Marshall, Jesus remains a prophet of compassionate justice, devoting less attention to Christ's death and resurrection.[59] In my view, this distorts the broader New Testament emphasis portraying the Christ event in an entirely integrated way.

Writing a generation after Moule, Marshall recognizes that punishment played a crucial—if limited—role in the enacting of God's justice. Marshall refers to 'restorative punishment' as the 'pain of taking responsibility' where 'judgment works itself out non retributively inasmuch as God "gives people up" to experience the consequences of their own free choices'.[60] This means that 'if God works for restoration up until the very last moment, so too must we'.[61] To what extent does Marshall allow for God's final justice beyond the intrinsic punishment of consequences? The question that remains for Marshall is this: does the 'pain of taking responsibility' fully encapsulate the obligations that result from wrongdoing? A fully biblical account of Jesus' *compassionate* justice must grapple with the demands of God's *eschatological* justice![62]

Conclusion

For biblical theology to be fully public, the social location of scholar-practitioners like Marshall is critical. Happily Marshall occupies two public locations in which theology is under-represented: in the University and also in the delivery of justice as a restorative justice facilitator. I have argued that the strength of his reading of Lk. 15.11-32 is largely due to these roles making the implications of the parable of the Prodigal Son prescient, peaceable and performable. This is an admirable achievement, making biblical theology more public. If the church is the only location for the reading of Jesus' parable, then evangelistic concerns will continue to be the primary focus. The church has another crucial role in making biblical theology more public. The Christian community can and must witness to the kind of mercy, forgiveness, reconciliation and justice narrated in the parable of the Prodigal Son. This demands that public theology be more biblical. Marshall's *Compassionate Justice* is exemplary in proving that public life and contemporary issues are not as remote from the concerns in Scripture as some claim! Ultimately it is the primary task of the church—not scholar-practitioners—to *enact* Jesus' compassionate justice and the daily challenge of Christian discipleship in the footsteps of the compassionate One. We are indebted to Marshall for his challenge to follow faithfully the compassionate Jesus.

---

59. Chris Marshall, 'A Prophet of God's Justice: Reclaiming the Political Jesus', *Stimulus* 14.3 (2006), pp. 28-41.
60. Marshall, *Beyond Retribution*, pp. 145, 195.
61. Marshall, *Beyond Retribution*, p. 195.
62. See further the later chapter in this volume by David Neville.

'BEYOND REASONABLE DOUBT'?[1] AN EXPLORATION OF THE HERMENEUTICS OF ENGAGEMENT FOR JUSTICE

Helen-Ann Hartley

In Christopher Marshall's book *Compassionate Justice*, he examines two Lukan parables that are key to understanding the process of restorative justice in the contemporary world. This essay explores some of the hermeneutical processes at work in the use of biblical texts in the field of (what the book's promotional material describes as) 'the conscientious cultivation of compassion' in the process of the justice system today. These are hermeneutical processes which are also at work in the wider field of biblical debates which affect many decisions made in the relationships between theology and public life. The arguments presented in this essay pay attention to: firstly, that the character of any hermeneutical process is indicative of its interpretative outcome; and secondly, that a more accurate interpretation of a compassionate response favours a *disinterested* understanding of what compassion is. In that sense, many contemporary 'urban myths' of compassion fall wide of the mark. This study explores whether Jewish hermeneutical processes of reading texts as black fire on white tends to favour a more measured, mindful interpretative process in which the individual interpreter has no presenting bias or personal goal invested in the outcome other than the need to adhere to established and accepted rules of debate. The result is a stance that may be located 'beyond reasonable doubt' but which holds not simply to certainty at the exclusion of all other perspectives, but rather is content to sit with a certainty in the fully unknown. While this may seem like an impossible contradiction, it is not, as the doorhandle said to Alice in her adventures in Wonderland, an *impossible* one.

At the outset, viewing biblical texts as a woven tapestry of stories, contexts, encounters and conversations may help us to navigate some of the complexities of using certain texts to judge and condemn but others to forgive and transform. It further frees the Bible itself, as a collection of diverse books of different genres, contexts and theological themes, from becoming

---

1. 'Beyond reasonable doubt' is a legal definition that has been used in the advice given to juries at trials where they are required to reach a verdict that is as certain as can be given the evidence with which they have been presented.

nothing more than a 'court of appeal'. It is all too easy to view the tapestry of texts from the front-side, where the threads are neat and the colours and patterns in order. To view texts from the back of the tapestry however, reveals something more messy and potentially unresolved. Erich Auerbach argues that biblical narratives report actions and words, but in so doing they leave gaps.[2] The work of the interpreter is to explore these gaps and wonder about what may fill them. Interpretation however is not often content to 'sit' with mystery and the unknown. It is often all too easy to take out the proverbial megaphone and engage in an argument that reveals far more about the self-interests of the interpreter than it does about the text under discussion.

Also of particular interest to this essay are the 'conversation(s)' inherent to the parabolic form used by Jesus in the Gospels. Viewed in its Jewish context, the parable itself is an example of the rabbinic motif of 'black fire on white fire' that can offer a transformative challenge to otherwise 'flat' readings of texts, and an illuminating gloss on the processes of justice and restorative justice today. Both the parables of the Good Samaritan and the Prodigal Son are frequently cited for their promotion of a compassionate response. However, that the compassion is rooted in a deep and profound risk on the part of the Samaritan trader in the former and the father in the latter is often overlooked. By recounting these narratives in parabolic form, the hearer is challenged to consider their own reactions and responses afresh. This is important because it suggests that the hermeneutical process is not solely the task of the professional scholar. Philip Esler reflects this in the final chapter of his *New Testament Theology: Communion and Community*: 'For ordinary or everyday religion encompasses the whole range of what it means to be human under God—not just ideas, but also beliefs, values, aspirations, roles and practices, emotions, experience, and identity. Why should the historical analysis of the New Testament not be brought directly into contact with these factors?'[3] To return to the point made above, there is merit in interpretative conversation(s) being held with all manner of interested groups and individuals. The results may create unresolved tensions between those who hold PhDs and those who do not, but those tensions are inherent to the ongoing desire to make sense of biblical texts. This is a point well made in a recent collection of essays edited by Jeff Astley and Leslie Francis, which seeks to explore the whys and wherefores of academic theological discourse.[4]

---

2. Erich Auerbach, *Mimesis: The Representation of Reality in Western Literature* (trans. Willard R. Trask; Princeton, NJ: Princeton University Press, fiftieth anniversary edn, 2003).
3. Philip F. Esler, *New Testament Theology: Communion and Community* (London: SPCK, 2005), p. 274.
4. Jeff Astley and Leslie J. Francis (eds.), *Exploring Ordinary Theology* (Surry: Ashgate, 2013).

How might we describe our terms of reference? English does not distinguish between the two Hebrew words, *mishpat* and *din* (justice and judgment). *Mishpat* has a variety of meanings according to different contexts (justice, judgment, rights, vindication, deliverance, custom, norm). There is strong evidence that *mishpat* in its origins (and drawing from its wider Semitic usage) referred to the restoration of a situation or environment which promoted harmony (*shalom*) in a community. When referring to legal matters, *din* was often used to indicate a decision reached in a legal court. So the former is more about character, and the latter is the practical application of an assessment of the character comprised of a number of factors. The promotion of harmony in any situation is not unique to Semitic contexts, and may indicate something far deeper in human nature. Not all would agree with such a generalist assumption, but Anna Wierzbicka has demonstrated the potential of biblical texts to remain rooted yet *out*cultured in their application and interpretation.[5]

When it comes to the New Testament, English translations often use the word 'righteousness' instead of 'justice'. There is often good reason to substitute 'justice' for 'righteousness' in many instances within the New Testament. Matthew 6.33 provides a good example of this: 'But seek first the kingdom of God and its justice and all these things will be added to you'. In ancient contexts, the final responsibility for doing justice lay with the king whose law promulgated justice within the boundaries of the kingdom. The problem (as presented in Matthew) is that the justice of the kingdom of God does not occur on earth as God in heaven intends. What is apparent across the biblical witness is that the Judaeo-Christian tradition weaves the ideal of justice into the very fabric of creation. Like all ideals however, justice has value only when it is lived out in daily life, and daily life can impact on the processes of justice and judgment in all manner of unforeseen ways.

Regarding themes of justice in the biblical texts, it may be suggested that the following key points emerge. First, the Israelites (like other Semitic people, it may be argued) regarded the deity as the Judge of the whole earth: 'Shall not the Judge of all the earth do right?' (Gen. 18.25). God as Judge of all was rooted in the conviction that it was God who created the world and established justice: 'Mighty king, lover of justice, you have established equity, you have executed justice and righteousness in Jacob' (Ps. 99.4, noting how the terms 'righteousness' and 'justice' are used synonymously). Justice was very important to Israelites because they were concerned with social relationships among themselves as a people covenanted to God and

---

5. Anna Wierzbicka, 'What did Jesus Mean? The Lord's Prayer Translated into Universal Human Concepts', in *Metaphor, Canon and Community: Jewish, Christian and Islamic Approaches* (ed. Ralph Bisschops and James Francis; New York: Peter Lang, 1999), pp. 180-216.

also among the nations surrounding them. It is not piety which God required of humans, but the practising of justice and righteousness: '...let justice roll down like waters, and righteousness like an ever-flowing stream' (Amos 5.24); 'he has showed you, O man, what is good. And what does the LORD require of you? To act justly and to love mercy and to walk humbly with your God' (Mic. 6.8).

Secondly, the Israelites expected God's justice to be fair because it came from God who was a righteous judge: 'God is a righteous judge, and a God who has vindication every day' (Ps. 7.11). In the Hebrew Bible, the so-called judges of the book of Judges were appointed by God to act for him as administrators of justice in military emergencies and in deciding disputes arising among their people. That these judges were just people is implied in the statement that when they died, the children of Israel forgot the way of the LORD (Judg. 2.17-19).

Thirdly, in several biblical passages, particularly in the Psalms and the Prophets, God is portrayed as having a special concern for the poor, particularly the widow, the fatherless, and the oppressed (Pss. 10.17-18; 82.1-8). Justice in these contexts takes on the idea of basic human rights, rather than simply a sense of what the 'moral norm' might be. God judges in order to restore the lost rights of the oppressed: 'when God arose to establish judgment to save all the oppressed of the earth' (Ps. 76.9). God's justice aims at creating an egalitarian community in which all classes of people maintain their basic human rights.

Fourthly, we may note the way Jesus defines his ministry in the Gospel of Luke in terms of justice by the opening statement he makes in the synagogue in Nazareth. There, Jesus tells the crowd that he fulfils the vision in Isaiah of releasing prisoners, giving sight to the blind, and releasing the oppressed (4.18-19). As Luke relates more of Jesus' ministry, we read that he also imagines that as the oppressed find release, the rich will find suffering. This sense of reversal is found throughout Luke's Gospel in particular, in the parables of Jesus and also in Mary's words of the Magnificat. Mary, as one of the poor in Israel, lifts her praise to God for bringing down the proud and lifting up the humble, feeding the hungry and sending the rich away empty (1.52-53). In this view of God's justice, each gets what each deserves. In another of the Gospels (Matthew), visions of the final judgment often have to do with whether a person carried out justice on earth. In the parable of the Sheep and the Goats (25.31-46), Jesus separates those who will enter heaven (sheep) from those who will not (goats) based on whether they cared for the marginal: the hungry, thirsty, naked, sick and imprisoned. The reversal of fortune, then, may not occur in this life but certainly in the next. These stories intend both to offer the oppressed a sense that they will receive their vindication and also to motivate the rich to care for the poor in the present. Character and action are closely related.

It appears that the writers of the New Testament, like the writers of the Hebrew Bible, intend for justice to emerge in their communities, on the earth. The letter of James, for example, deals almost exclusively with developing 'just' communities that contrast with the standards of the surrounding culture. The standards of the Mediterranean world did not allow for much change in social roles. The elite were elite and the poor, poor. Each group served a particular function in society and was obligated to fulfil the duties inherent to their role in society. In James' context, favouring the rich and mistreating the poor was not something James was willing to tolerate because it violated the most basic command from the Hebrew Bible: love your neighbour as yourself. People could not claim to have faith in God through Jesus and then turn around and judge one person better than another (Jas. 2.12-17). It is important, then, to remember that the vision for justice in the early Christian communities emerged from the vision already present in the Hebrew Bible. The New Testament writers drew from a deep well to press their communities to live up to standards they already knew from the God of Israel. This meant that Christian communities were to express justice by showing concern for the oppressed and to expect God to take action against oppressors. Yet, for both God and the Christian communities, just action also meant showing mercy to those in need: to love your neighbour as yourself. To be compassionate involves suffering with the other, not observing need from afar and donating money to a good cause, but getting alongside the one who is in pain. The Greek word *splanchnizomai* implies a deep stirring emotion leading to action.

Although the above overview has painted some very broad brushstrokes over a canvas of varying texture and depth, some deeper rhythms emerge: namely, the importance of relationship, of community, and of the process of justice as somehow 'setting things right' on earth as it is in heaven. Clearly the biblical witness is varied however, and while it may be possible tentatively to suggest some key points and themes, attention does need to be paid to the diverse contexts, genres and images that emerge. It remains problematic that particular verses may be used to argue a point as if indicative of a 'norm'. Furthermore, what should we do about the level of discomfort (for many) suggested by the idea of God (and Christ) as Judge? Berel Dov Lerner suggests that 'a more sophisticated approach to theological language must take into account the traditions in which these metaphors occur'.[6] This

---

6. Berel Dov Lerner, 'Oppressive Metaphor and the Liberating Literal Sense', in *Metaphor, Canon and Community: Jewish, Christian and Islamic Approaches* (ed. Ralph Bisschops and James Francis; New York: Peter Lang, 1999), pp. 233-41 (234). Lerner's argument suggests a close connection between the images of God as King and Master. I add to this the image of God as Judge. Lerner suggests that 'the discomfort of the contemporary faithful with "archaic, false or repugnant" images of God

is where analysis of the character of the hermeneutical process and its conversational tone might begin to shed light on the matter, and suggest a way forward.

A few years ago, I was selected as a jury member for an eight-day crown-court trial in the south of England. Following the jury's deliberations, the defendant was found guilty and sentenced to a significant period of imprisonment. Upon leaving the 'vacuum' of the court ('vacuum' because there are no windows and therefore no natural light), one of the first things I did was to check my e-mails on my mobile phone. The first e-mail I read came from the secretary of a Diocesan Bishop in the Church of England, inviting me to speak to a clergy conference on the theme of 'Judgment'. Worlds collided. I found myself reflecting back on the week's events in court, and thinking forward, imagining a room, full of clergy, with me speaking to them about judgment. I realized that my own experience of the courtroom was now intricately related to both priestly and scholarly aspects of my identity.

The above experience also affirms the varied biblical witness that concepts of justice are rooted in the local and in the particular, and given meaning by contexts and shared understandings that can vary hugely, yet which may tentatively suggest some common import (relationship, the involvement of community and the setting of things 'right' on earth as in heaven). In the example provided above, my own experience of sitting through a trial, listening to the evidence presented, which itself allowed an albeit limited view into the lives of dysfunctional families and communities, gave me a 'local' feel for the processes of justice, juxtaposed with the 'universal' application of that process: there are ways and norms of how crown court trials are conducted, for example. My subsequent speaking engagement to the clergy conference provided another sense of the 'local'. Since then, further 'local' understandings and experiences of justice and judgment have also crossed the paths that I have taken. In so many ways, it may be suggested that God's vision for a just world is rooted where we are, but always in relationship to those around us who search for shared meanings, who strive for *right*-ness and fairness, so often because that is what *justice* is about—it *just is*: it is the right thing to do, or at least by informed intuition seems right and appropriate. That assertion is based in part on an interpretation of an overview of the varied and complex biblical witness to the theme of justice and judgment.[7] Yet that assertion is also rooted much deeper than that.

---

may indicate a deficiency in the cultural grounding of our generation rather than "some inherent deficiency in the symbol itself" (p. 238).

7. To cite a few representative examples: Lev. 19.15; Deut. 16.20; 27.19; Job 37.23; Pss. 33.5; 106.3; Prov. 28.5; Isa. 1.17; 30.18; Ezek. 34.15-16; Amos 5.24; Mic. 6.8; Mt. 12.18; Lk. 11.42; Acts 17.30-32; Jas 1.27.

First, many biblical pericopes tend to create what Christopher Marshall describes as a 'potent cultural legacy'.[8] The narrative arc of the New Testament suggests that God becomes involved in humanity. This makes a difference, a difference which cannot be articulated ultimately beyond that of whoever's 'local' is being used and experienced at any given moment. Secondly, critical biblical scholarship stresses the importance of understanding aspects of the text that explore narrative detail, context and genre, amongst other features. Our present argument however, suggests that critical scholarship alone is not sufficient. Whilst this has the potential to create discomfort at any hint of a 'confessional' belief-oriented approach, as suggested above, the weaving of my scholarly, experiential and priestly selves leaves me with little choice but to discern a way forward with a sense of integrity and transparency. This is precisely the way in which Chris Marshall begins his study of compassionate justice: 'This book evolved from an initial hunch that the Parable of the Prodigal Son, which of course I knew in broad outline but had not given much concentrated time to studying, might have something valuable to say to me as a father of two fine young adult sons.'[9] Both my own admission of perspective and place, and Marshall's presentation of his own wondering are examples of a narrative approach discussed by Alan Jacobs in *Looking Before and After: Testimony and the Christian Life*.[10] Jacobs suggests that what is needed are 'better and more responsible and more coherent personal stories, not the complete subsumption of all personal narratives into group narratives'.[11] Specifically, Jacobs calls for an expansion beyond 'testimonies of conversion' to 'testimonies of imitation and vocation'.[12] Viewed as the basis for any hermeneutical endeavour, surely it might be helpful for any interpreter to begin with a 'testimony of vocation' indicating why the interpretative process has been initiated? Fernando F. Segovia notes: 'it is amazing how resistant, sometimes bordering on the hysterical, male biblical critics from the world of the North Atlantic can be to any admission of contextuality in their own work'.[13] Segovia goes on to 'propose the beginnings of a hermeneutical

---

8. Christopher D. Marshall, *Compassionate Justice: An Interdisciplinary Dialogue with Two Gospel Parables on Law, Crime, and Restorative Justice* (Eugene, OR: Cascade Books, 2012), p. 21.
9. Marshall, *Compassionate Justice*, p. xi.
10. Alan Jacobs, *Looking Before and After: Testimony and the Christian Life* (Grand Rapids: Eerdmans, 2008).
11. Jacobs, *Looking Before and After*, p. 8.
12. Jacobs, *Looking Before and After*, p. 10.
13. Fernando F. Segovia, 'Toward a Hermeneutics of the Diaspora: A Hermeneutics of Otherness and Engagement', in *Reading from this Place: Social Location and Biblical Interpretation in the United States*, Vol. 1 (ed. Fernando F. Segovia and Mary Ann Tolbert; Minneapolis: Augsburg Fortress, 1995), pp. 57-74 (57).

framework for taking the flesh-and-blood reader seriously in biblical criticism, not so much as a unique and independent individual but rather as a member of distinct and identifiable social configurations, as a reader from within a social location'.[14]

You may be forgiven for wondering if this argument is beginning to flow in the wrong direction. Thus far I have focussed almost exclusively, though briefly, on the theme of judgment (and justice) with only a very brief mention of compassion. Marshall's book does not offer fixed definitions of any of these terms at the outset. Reading his book, one gains a clear 'sense' of what he is discussing without having to turn to a dictionary. Marshall's aim, of course, is to explore the relationship between *restorative justice* and *compassionate justice*. The latter may be described as a 'Gospel' manifestation of the latter. Thus, to speak about justice and the role of compassion in its processes, at least from a Christian perspective, may involve a compassionate way of reading texts (as a verb, rather than a noun).[15] Even though not all Christians think the same about justice and how it should be administered, for the most part, if the parables of Jesus are held as in some way indicative of an attitude, then there appears to be a clear message in the Lukan parables of the Good Samaritan and the Prodigal Son as to the place of compassion as a reaction to a situation in which a decision or judgment may be required: to be compassionate *just is* the right mode of response. More than this, as already stated above, both these parables specifically draw attention to the importance of a *disinterested* compassionate response, that is, *compassion that overrides self-interest*. This is seen clearly through the lens of a Mediterranean anthropological perspective. In the parable of the Good Samaritan (Lk. 10.25-37), it is not simply the identification of the individual who helped the injured man as a Samaritan but the underlying assumption that the Samaritan may have been a trader that adds to the twist. Many traders were wealthy, having grown rich at the expense of others, and they were as a result considered to be thieves. Bruce Malina and Richard Rohrbaugh point out that 'both the victim and the Samaritan were thus despised persons, who would not have elicited initial sympathy from Jesus' peasant hearers. That sympathy would have gone to the bandits. They were frequently peasants who had lost their land to the elite lenders whom all peasants feared. The surprising twist in the story is thus the compassionate action of one stereotyped as a scurrilous thief.'[16] In the parable of the Prodigal Son (Lk. 15.11-32), the risk-taking compassion of the father

---

14. Segovia, 'Toward a Hermeneutics', p. 58. One could challenge to what extent all individuals from within a particular social location would speak with a united voice.

15. Marshall, *Compassionate Justice*, p. 252.

16. Bruce J. Malina and Richard L. Rohrbaugh, *Social-Science Commentary on the Synoptic Gospels* (Minneapolis: Fortress Press, 1992), p. 347.

is emphasized in his running to greet his son in verse 20. Again, Malina and Rohrbaugh point out that 'he is not running to welcome his son, as Western readings would have it. By hastening to the edge of the village the father preempts hostile village reaction, signaling by his kiss and embrace that the errant son is under his protection.'[17] Presumably the father exposed himself to both threat and shame in so doing.

Underlying all of the above are some questions regarding the role and place of the biblical texts in our discussions. Of key importance may be interplays between text(s) and culture(s): a sense of rootedness that determines both the perspective and character of the interpreter, and the literal place of the text that is being read and interpreted. Whether we acknowledge it or not, the books of the Bible are never read in isolation. Multiple interpretations may be presented over the translation and meaning of just one word, never mind a selection of verses. Yet it does not follow that one is either right or wrong; it depends on a whole variety of factors. Interpretation of a text can change depending on the physical location of the interpreter. My interpretation of the so-called 'Golden Rule' (Lev. 19.18; Mt. 7.12) may in one week respond to the relatively unimportant domestic situation of tolerating a neighbour who frequently blocks my driveway with their car but in another week may have to address the life and death situation of a large gathering of Zimbabwean Anglican Christians who have been persecuted because of their faith. In each situation, the need to show compassion to the other is vital, yet the challenges and the consequences of so doing are markedly different. Similarly, the particular context in which I worked when writing this study, where daily encounters demanded that I address situations of injustice and inequity, in stark contrast to my previous employment in the comparatively pleasant surround of an Oxford theological college, means that I am continually having to reassess how biblical texts may be used. In order to be effective, a compassionate interpretative stance is required, which is both demanding yet potentially transformative.[18] To engage deeply with 'the other', one so often needs simply to listen, to be attentive and to speak in a calm and respectful tone. If voices

---

17. Malina and Rohrbaugh, *Social-Science Commentary*, p. 372.

18. The Anglican church in Aotearoa New Zealand and Polynesia is constitutionally divided into three 'tikanga' (the Maori word of 'cultural stream'). The arrival of Christian missionaries to New Zealand in the early part of the nineteenth century saw an explosion of colonialism (as well as of the Gospel), which although partially resolved by the resolution of land ownership through the Treaty of Waitangi in 1843, gave rise to years of fighting and land confiscation by the crown, prompting issues that are still being addressed to this day. Tensions of identity, of language and of claims to 'place' in the forms of land and resources are manifested in the life of the Anglican church. The College of St. John the Evangelist is one of the primary places where the 'three tikanga' live and work together.

are raised, there is a process of reconciliation which typically includes the sharing of food. In the breaking of bread, one becomes a 'companion' on the road rather than a combatant.

In the wider scholarly and ecclesiastical world however, the character of biblical interpretation is so often marked by the use of a megaphone rather than a measured word. If my megaphone is not creating a loud enough voice, I will simply obtain a bigger one, and so on. What if hermeneutics itself could be a compassionate endeavour? How would that affect the understandings of biblical texts that may be used to condemn in one context and to bless in another? The furious debates regarding homosexuality throughout the Christian world are a good example of this broad hermeneutical dilemma. Biblical texts are themselves so often used as a court of appeal in these and other debates, and it is impossible to reach a verdict without inflicting some degree of discomfort on the 'opposing' party. This is why A.K.M. Adam's work on 'differential hermeneutics' is so vital in getting beyond an interpretative impasse. Adam suggests that 'differential hermeneutics permits practitioners to see in interpretative variety a sign of the variety in human imagination'.[19] He continues: '[interpretation is] not "who's right and who's wrong" but "what sort of lives and interactions should our hermeneutics engender?"'[20]

Part of the difficulty in making sense of the texts of the Bible is the way in which those texts themselves often present us with one side of a conversation. Sometimes this is quite literally the case, as with the New Testament letters; at other times there is a more general awareness of voices outside the texts or voices within the texts that are silent. This is not an end to meaning; rather it requires awareness and sensitivity to the ways in which the texts are themselves 'unfinished'. At the same time of course, the Bible is full of conversations, and of texts in conversation with each other, often in subtle ways. Alongside all of these conversations are the ways in which we contribute to the ongoing conversation, even in ways that may be inherently risky or perhaps controversial. Yet as Walter Brueggemann observes: 'if we do not keep the conversation going with the script, we shall all be scripted in ways that are neither human nor faithful'.[21]

What does it mean to 'keep the conversation going with the script'? One way of expressing this is to say that our personal stories and interpretations are the 'midrash' to the literal 'plain' text. In Jewish hermeneutics, midrashim are the interpretational conversations that the Rabbis have to

---

19. A.K.M. Adam, *Faithful Interpretation: Reading the Bible in a Postmodern World* (Minneapolis: Fortress Press, 2006), p. 89.

20. Adam, *Faithful Interpretation*, p. 103.

21. Walter Brueggemann, *Interpretation and Obedience: From Faithful Reading to Faithful Living* (Minneapolis: Fortress Press, 1991), p. 113.

make sense of the texts. The word 'midrash' is itself derived from the verb *darash*, meaning 'to seek'. If we take this broad sense of the meaning of the word, then the earliest midrashim can be found in the Hebrew Bible itself. The books of 1 and 2 Chronicles have been considered as midrash on 1 and 2 Kings, 1 and 2 Samuel, and the 'P' (Priestly) document of the Torah (the first five books of the Bible). Midrash is also identified within the New Testament, with the suggestion that the book of Hebrews is midrash on Psalm 110.

Another way of exploring further this insight is with the rabbinical tradition of 'black fire on white fire'. This phrase comes from the Midrash Tanhuma, a collection of texts that were brought together between 400 and 600 CE: the Torah is full of holy fire; it was written with a black fire upon a white fire. The black fire refers to the letters of Torah, the actual words written down. The white refers to the spaces in between the letters. Together, black and white make up the whole of Torah. On another level, the black fire represents the literal meaning of the text, while the white fire represents ideas that we bring to the texts when we read it. The white fire has endless potential for new meaning that can incorporate stories, songs, even silence when meaning cannot be found in its fullness (yet). Betty Rojtman suggests that 'Torah functions as a "deictic text", manifesting its own expectations of an actualisation still to come. Each addressee, "having to reflect that he himself came out of Egypt" authenticates the projection onto the text of his own existential coefficient.'[22] If you look at a rabbinic scroll, the black text is always completely surrounded by white parchment, and in fact this is laid down as an instruction in the Talmud: black fire must always be surrounded by white fire. Given that Hebrew writing is always realized in its vocalisation, more weight is added to the orality of the text: it is written, spoken and interpreted, and there is always potential for ambiguity and indeterminacy in meaning.

The interweaving of stories with interpretation of texts is used by Jesus in the Gospels in the parables. 'Parable' is of course a term loaded with a good deal of theological and scholarly baggage, as David Stern discusses in his study of Midrash and parables. Stern points out that a parable (with its cognate Hebrew form 'mashal') is 'an allusive narrative told for an ulterior purpose'.[23] Daniel Boyarin holds that Midrash (like all interpretation) involves the filling in of gaps in the narrative text. The gap itself is, as Boyarin points out, 'a complex concept, which essentially means any place in the

---

22. Betty Rojtman, *Black Fire on White Fire: An Essay on Jewish Hermeneutics, from Midrash to Kabbalah* (trans. Steven Randall; Berkeley: University of California Press, 1998), p. 2.

23. David Stern, *Parables in Midrash: Narrative and Exegesis in Rabbinic Literature* (Cambridge: Harvard University Press, 1991), p. 6.

text that requires the intervention of the reader to make sense of the story. Gap filling…involves the application of cultural knowledge, i.e., the mobilization of narrative schemata which are in the repertoire or sociolect of the culture in question'.[24]

It is into this 'gap' that the conversation takes place in search of meaning. So when Jesus brings meaning to a situation, he often contributes meaning through the telling of a story (parable), with meaning one assumes would resonate with his audience who might then be expected to contribute their own experiences to the interpretative conversation. Interestingly, it has been suggested that the most famous parables in the Jesus tradition (such as the Prodigal Son in Lk. 15.11-32 and the Good Samaritan in Lk. 10.25-37) may have been stories that took several hours to tell, and that what we have are 'plot summaries'.[25] One suggestion that follows from this recognition of the possibility of there being *more* to the text than first meets the eye is that our own lives in their incompleteness mirror the texts. The idea that Jesus, for want of a better word, 'performed' his teaching (parables and the like) reminds us that as they were first encountered, these were texts that were bound to have produced conversations about their content, aspects of which may have included the use of 'local' understanding, idiom, even dialect.

In the incident of the woman caught in adultery recorded in Jn 8.2-11, Jesus writes on the ground. What was he writing? Much ink has been spilled on this mystery. Perhaps however the answer lies not in *what* he wrote but on the act of writing itself. Archbishop Rowan Williams suggests that Jesus…'hesitates. He does not draw a line, fix an interpretation, tell the woman who she is and what her fate should be. He allows a moment, a longish moment, in which people are given time to see themselves differently precisely because he refuses to make the sense they want'.[26] In a similar vein, the French philosopher Jacques Maritain speaks of how 'things are not only what they are', they 'give more than they have'.[27]

Around about the year 1868, the American poet Emily Dickinson wrote these words: 'Tell all the truth but tell it slant… The truth must dazzle gradually Or every man be blind.' Dickinson's poem reveals her view of the truth as something that must be broken to listeners gently; while the reader is admonished to ultimately reveal everything, the sense is that the

---

24. Daniel Boyarin, in a review essay of Stern's book entitled 'Midrash in Parables', *Association of Jewish Studies Review* 20.1 (1995), pp. 123-38 (130).
25. A point made by J.D. Crossan in his work on the 'historical Jesus' and parables. This rather suggests the type of epic storytelling known to many cultures, and rather less so nowadays in popular Western tradition.
26. Rowan Williams, *Writing in the Dust: After September 11* (Grand Rapids: Eerdmans, 2002), p. 78.
27. Quoted in Rowan Williams, *Grace and Necessity: Reflections on Art and Love* (London: Continuum, 2005), p. 26.

teller should move in circles towards the truth. A colloquial expression for this method might be to 'beat around the bush' before the matter is fully revealed. More than that however, Dickinson's poem shares the reflection that human beings are essentially frail and that truth is too intense for whatever fragile happiness we might now have; truth has an ability to deliver a supreme shock!

If the hermeneutical process is about telling things 'slant', then parables are a good example of this. Often told to illustrate points of Law, Jesus' parables are designed to shock and dazzle. Much of the impact of this is lost on contemporary interpretations that are removed from the original context of the first hearers. In that sense, the slanted meaning comes to us through a more drawn-out process. While this might be frustrating for some, the potential for meaning to unfold over time creates space around the text for deeper understandings to emerge. The process of biblical hermeneutics is not about coming to a fixed conclusion; it is rather more about opening up texts to new possibilities in dialogue with new situations. If the character of interpretation is itself compassionate and, not only that, representative of a risky compassion, a compassion by means of which the individual is willing to un-prioritize their own interests, then conversations may continue, and new and perhaps wiser understandings might appear.

To attend to compassionate justice in this way presents less of a potential challenge to its current processes and more of a recommendation to attend with great care as to the working out of a restorative process. For a compassionate response in the justice system to be truly compassionate, the offending party has to exhibit a complete emptying of self-interest, vulnerability and risk. The vulnerability that results in such circumstances needs to be managed with great care. In the telling of the parables of the Good Samaritan and the Prodigal Son, we might well wonder 'what happened next?', not only with regard to the inner life of the story but most especially in and amongst the crowds of listeners that surrounded Jesus. Of course, this is pure speculation, and biblical interpretation doesn't like to sit with speculation, at least not willingly! Perhaps if we put away our megaphones and attended more to the gaps and the silences, we might be forced to see ourselves in ways that point to the 'beyond-ness' of the working out of justice on earth as it is in heaven? If that is the case, then Christopher Marshall's work surely presents a profound challenge to us all, whatever our viewpoint.

Prophets Performing as Public Theologians

Jeanette Mathews

One of the largely undisputed facts about the historical Jesus is his use of parables in his public ministry. The power of parables lies in their nature as stories, accessible to everyone yet eschatologically pointing beyond themselves to a greater reality. Jesus can be described as both prophet and poet, and his parables often combine those two dimensions. Jesus stood in the tradition of the 'noble fellowship of prophets'.[1] Although we have access to the Old Testament prophets through the prophetic literature preserved in the canon, it is clear that the prophets were more than writers. They embodied their message, sometimes via symbolic acts and sometimes within their own life experiences such as marriage (Hosea), parenthood (Isaiah) and economic transactions (Jeremiah). For the prophets, their lives were parables that communicated their message publicly and eschatologically. This essay explores the risky performances of prophets in the public sphere, argues that these performances enhanced their prophetic message and asks whether such a model of prophetic performance is still appropriate today.

The Turn to Performance

In 2008 Tracy Davis, professor of Performance Studies at Northwestern University, wrote of the 'performative turn' as a movement that has become increasingly influential across a wide range of academic disciplines.[2] While for many the term 'Performance Studies' remains grounded in the aesthetic arts, there is also a broader view of performance as a heuristic device to account for the social and cultural interactions that are being analysed—in linguistics, anthropology and sociology, for example. Theology and Biblical Studies are two academic fields that have recently begun to use performance as a methodological tool in researching the Hebrew Bible and the Christian Scriptures. At times the language of performance is used simply

---

1. A phrase from the *Te Deum laudamus*.
2. T.C. Davis, 'Introduction: The Pirouette, Detour, Revolution, Deflection, Deviation, Tack, and Yaw of the Performative Turn', in *The Cambridge Companion to Performance Studies* (ed. T.C. Davis; Cambridge: Cambridge University Press, 2008), p. 1.

as a metaphor for the message of Scripture or the life of faith, ranging from Hans Urs von Balthasar's five-volume *Theo-drama: Theological Dramatic Theory*[3] to a popular volume by Craig Bartholomew and Michael Goheen entitled *The Drama of Scripture* in which Scripture is divided into six acts, with each Testament comprising three acts divided by an interlude (the Intertestamental period).[4] Other scholars are attempting a deeper engagement with Performance Studies. Some take up terminology and methodology from the broader field of Performance Studies where obvious correlation exists, such as examining rituals or performative speech acts in biblical texts (e.g., 'Let there be light'). Others are seeking to discover intrinsic performative features in the text itself, regardless of whether or not the text was ever a performance piece in its original setting. Such an approach attempts to read a biblical text as a 'script' open to thoughtful and engaged re-enactment through appropriation of its message with small but significant changes brought about by the new setting of contemporary faith communities.[5]

Reading Scripture via Performance Criticism

Performance Criticism is a particularly apt method for reading Scripture. As far back as 1959 Erving Goffman applied the concept of performance to everyday behaviour, claiming that performance happens all the time as a person takes on a role, tells a story, or enacts a set piece of behaviour such as a greeting.[6] Similarly, Ronald Pelias defines all human communication as 'an act of performance' and counters the negative connotations that often arise suggesting performance is fundamentally 'pretence' by arguing that all communication events involve a choice of roles governed by the variety of situations that an individual finds him/herself in each day. 'One's "real self" is a composite of all these roles.'[7] He concludes: '[P]eople fundamentally are performing creatures who engage in an ongoing process of giving speech to their thoughts and feelings. Through the act of performing, people make their lives meaningful and define themselves.'[8] Scripture

---

3. Hans Urs von Balthasar, *Theo-drama: Theological Dramatic Theory*, 5 vols. (trans. G. Harrison; San Francisco: Ignatius Press, 1988–98 [1973–83]).

4. C.G. Bartholomew and M.W. Goheen, *The Drama of Scripture: Finding Our Place in the Biblical Story* (London: SPCK, 2006).

5. See, for example, Jeanette Mathews, *Performing Habakkuk* (Eugene, OR: Pickwick Publications, 2012).

6. E. Goffman, *The Presentation of Self in Everyday Life* (Harmondsworth: Penguin Books, 1959), pp. 15-16.

7. R.J. Pelias, *Performance Studies: The Interpretation of Aesthetic Texts* (Dubuque: Kendall/Hunt Publishing Company, 1992), pp. 5-6.

8. Pelias, *Performance Studies*, p. 6.

is communication: between God and humanity; between faithful scribes and their readers; between communities of faith and subsequent generations for whom and to whom they preserve and pass on their traditions and convictions. In Pelias's terms, those acts of communication may be considered performances.

Audience transformation is a shared goal between those who read Scripture as a performance and those who are engaged in the performing arts. John Glavin claims:

> In this new, modern theatre, not only do the spectators become part of the work of performance but the key goal of that performance becomes the spectators' transformation...self-consciously modern theatre set out to make things not only new but different, to make something happen, in the audience even more than on the stage.[9]

Similarly, William Doan and Terry Giles argue that the performative aspects of embedded songs in a biblical text 'add to the surrounding narrative a powerful element of audience transformation'.[10]

While the presence of an audience is essential to the concept of performance, with its inherent expectation that a public demonstration of skills will be displayed, the above citation from Glavin suggests that the traditional division between actor and audience is breaking down. In Performance Art in particular, the boundaries between artist and spectator have blurred such that the audience often finds itself contributing to the performance. This phenomenon of audience participation is more characteristic of contemporary drama, but Paul Fiddes points out it can be found explicitly in traditional theatre also, such as when Prospero turns to the audience at the end of *The Tempest* and asks for prayer, forgiveness and mercy. Reflecting on this, Fiddes remarks:

> The barriers between art and life are being broken down. We had thought that Prospero was safely locked away on the stage 'in a play', but with a shock we find that he is drawing us into the reality of his own story... The drama has not finished after all, and we feel that it never will be.[11]

When a passage of Scripture is understood as a performance, members of a faithful audience can become actors themselves, embodying the

---

9. J. Glavin, *After Dickens: Reading, Adaptation and Performance* (Cambridge: Cambridge University Press, 2004), p. 32.

10. W. Doan and T. Giles, 'The Song of Asaph: A performance-critical analysis of 1 Chronicles 16.8-36', *CBQ* 70 (2008), pp. 29-43 (29).

11. P.S. Fiddes, 'Story and Possibility: Reflections on the Last Scenes of the Fourth Gospel and Shakespeare's *The Tempest*', in *Revelation and Story: Narrative Theology and the Centrality of Story* (ed. G. Sauter and J. Barton; Aldershot: Ashgate, 2000), pp. 29-51 (30).

script and re-enacting it in their own setting. Despite this reference to a 'faithful' audience, making use of Performance Criticism as a methodological tool reminds us that biblical interpretation should *always* take place in the public arena—the church should not do its theology 'behind closed doors' but instead needs to be engaged with its context: social, political and philosophical.

Prophets as Performers

When turning to biblical texts, the Prophetic Literature is especially open to being read through the lens of Performance Criticism. Whilst the dramatic qualities of narratives have been long recognized,[12] Prophetic Literature contains a great deal from the poetic genre alongside minimal narrative material. Yet the prophets were clearly performers engaged in what might be termed *poetic drama*. Prophets are commonly understood to be mediators between God and the community, including political and religious leaders.[13] Sometimes they addressed their own community (such as Isaiah, Jeremiah and Micah); at other times they came as outsiders and addressed a new community (Amos and Jonah). Whether prophets of doom or of hope they spoke into 'liminal' moments. The term 'liminality', as used in Performance Studies, describes a departure from normal cultural structures and activities, most clearly recognized in initiation rites or in social occasions that depart from the normal structures of life such as carnival.[14] In relation to the prophets, the term 'liminal' can be used to describe times of political and social crisis for the Israelite community. At such times prophets offered a critique or a new vision, requiring a change of behaviour or attitude on the part of their listeners. They used symbolic action and invested meaning in ordinary objects and events. They were not merely channels for mediation but embodied communicators. Their message quite often affected them physically or mentally, and in some cases had life-long implications.

The book of Hosea describes how the prophet married a prostitute to portray the commitment of God to Israel despite the nation's flirtation with foreign gods (Hos. 1, 3). Hosea named his children with symbolic names

---

12. See, for example, S. Levy, *The Bible as Theatre* (Brighton: Sussex Academic Press, 2000).

13. D.L. Petersen, *The Prophetic Literature* (Louisville, KY: Westminster/John Knox Press, 2002), p. 7.

14. V. Turner, 'Are there Universals of Performance in Myth, Ritual and Drama?', in *By Means of Performance* (ed. R. Schechner and W. Appel; Cambridge: Cambridge University Press, 1990), pp. 8-19 (11, 14). See also D. Conquergood who claims 'performance flourishes within a zone of contest and struggle' in 'Of Caravans and Carnivals: Performance Studies in Motion', *The Drama Review* 39.4 (1995), pp. 137-41 (137).

pertaining to his dual message of judgment and restoration. The first child was called *Jezreel* (Hos. 1.4-5), the name of a battleground and the location of judgment on both Ahab's and Jehu's dynasties, thus conjuring up images of bloodshed and death. Later the prophet drew on its literal meaning, 'God sows', with its connotations of fertility to promise restoration to Israel (Hos. 1.11). The name of the second child, *lo-ruhamah*, is often translated 'Not pitied', indicating the withholding of love and protection from the house of Israel (Hos. 1.6), with that of the third, *lo-ammi*, 'Not my people', conveying the negation of the covenant (Hos. 1.9). The message of restoration is communicated via the names again by merely removing the negating prefix *lo*, so that 'Not pitied' *does* receive pity and 'Not my people' is told 'You *are* my people' (Hos. 2.23).

The prophet Jeremiah readily comes to mind when discussing prophetic symbolic action. There is lively scholarly debate over how much of the book of Jeremiah accurately represents a historical figure and how much it reflects Deuteronomistic ideology.[15] It is certainly true to say that the *persona* at the centre of the book uses many symbolic acts, some only brief and some more substantial, and he seems more than many other prophets to embody the message of judgment and hope in his own life. At the time leading up to the Babylonian invasion Jeremiah invited leaders of the Jerusalem community to go to the edge of the city where he took a pot and smashed it to the ground symbolizing the coming destruction of the city (Jer. 19). Taking witnesses fulfilled the need for prophetic action to have an audience and, just as in contemporary Performance Art, the audience was unwittingly drawn into the drama. Their shock at the action of the prophet smashing a newly-bought flask prefigured the shock of those who would see the city fall.

A little later Jeremiah bought a field near Jerusalem at the time when Babylon was besieging the country and when he himself was imprisoned (Jer. 32.1-15). Given that the field was purchased while the land was in the control of the Babylonians, the event actualized the prophet's faith in a future time when Israel would again be living peacefully in her own land.

Ezekiel was instructed on one occasion to boil meat in a rusty pot, remove the meat, then boil the pot dry over a fierce heat to burn away any remaining impurities (Ezek. 24.1-14). The book of Ezekiel is located in Babylon where the prophet is portrayed as a member of the exilic community. In this drama, called in Hebrew a *mashal* (parable or proverb),[16] the pot repre-

---

15. For an argument favouring the first option, see W.L. Holladay, *Jeremiah 1–25* (Philadelphia: Fortress Press, 1986), and as a representative proponent of the second, see R.P. Carroll, *Jeremiah* (London: SCM Press, 1986).

16. In the Masoretic Text the Hebrew word *mashal* is repeated. The NRSV translates 'utter an allegory' but a better translation would be 'allegorize an allegory' or 'say a saying' or 'parabalize a parable'.

sents Jerusalem whose fate was symbolized by the fierce heat, the removal of meat shows how the inhabitants of Jerusalem were carried away to exile and the fiery purification is the judgment on the city. The instructions and prophecy are given in the form of a rhythmic song that might be characterized as a form of protest music. On another occasion Ezekiel was told to bake bread over a fire fuelled by human dung (Ezek. 4.9-15), an instruction to which he as a priest who had never broken purity laws objected. God relented and told him to use cow dung instead. This and several other strange activities by Ezekiel are characterized by Yvonne Sherwood as 'prophetic scatology'.[17]

A final example in this brief survey is found in a narrative recorded in the book of 1 Kgs 11.26-40. The prophet Ahijah sought out Jeroboam, who was at the time in charge of forced labour under King Solomon. Ahijah stripped off a new garment and tore it into twelve pieces representing the twelve tribes of Israel, and gave ten to Jeroboam with the message that he would rule over ten tribes. This was the impetus for the split in the kingdom that occurred in Solomon's reign.

Reading the Prophetic Literature through the lens of Performance Criticism enables us to view the whole communication event, including symbolic actions, family interactions and even economic transactions along with the words of the prophets, as an inclusive performance. When speaking of prophets as performers, however, we might better describe them as Performance Artists than actors in a pre-set drama. Performance Art is often focused on 'developing the expressive qualities of the body'.[18] The message of prophets is frequently portrayed through their own bodies and personalities, and the examples already given show this is often with profound personal effect.

The book of Isaiah offers another prophetic performance that has been described as 'one of the most celebrated prophetic dramas'.[19] When the Assyrian Empire was threatening the Fertile Crescent, the prophet Isaiah was commanded by God to remove his clothes and sandals and to preach naked for three years as a dramatic sign of the conquest of Egypt by Assyria. It was common practice in those days for political prisoners who were being led away captive to be stripped naked as a sign of humiliation. The biblical writer states it explicitly: 'with buttocks exposed' (Isa. 20.4). By prophesying in this condition, Isaiah would be drawing extra attention to his

---

17. Y. Sherwood, 'Prophetic Scatology: Prophecy and the Art of Sensation', *Semeia* 82 (1998), pp. 183-224.

18. M. Carlson, *Performance: A Critical Introduction* (New York: Routledge, 2nd edn, 2004), p. 110.

19. D. Stacey, *Prophetic Drama in the Old Testament* (London: Epworth Press, 1990), p. 122.

prophecies. It is hard not to interpret such symbolic action as provocative, since the prophet would be undergoing the same humiliation and shame experienced by political captives, but doing it of his own free will. Embodiment was taken to such a degree that prophets were prepared to surrender their own pride and dignity for the sake of their message. They seemed to want to shock a complacent audience with a message that was not welcome and would preferably be ignored. But whether such action resulted in conversion or scorn cannot always be determined. It is notable that in the biblical texts so-called 'false prophets' are usually those who were speaking a word that was in favour of the policies or practices of the day.

One of the common Hebrew words for a prophetic oracle, the word *massa'*, can also mean 'burden', giving the impression that the prophet is bearing a physical load when presenting and embodying the word of God. Sherwood points out the contrast between Wisdom and Prophetic genres in the Hebrew Bible. Whereas Wisdom uses phrases such as 'a word fitly spoken is like apples of gold in a setting of silver' (Prov. 25.11), the prophet does not choose which words to use but is governed by the word they are compelled to give.[20] Moreover, they do not just *say* the word, they *do* the word. Like Performance Artists who aim for sensation[21] or the destruction of convention,[22] prophets seem to have an aim of shocking their audience. Frequently their acts are contrary to socially acceptable behaviour, social convention, religious laws and sensibilities. In this regard the prophets allow themselves to become extremely vulnerable: open to ridicule, accusations, rejection and dismissal of their message. Indeed, they were often told to expect such rejection, and at times they were imprisoned or physically punished by the community they were seeking to influence.

The descriptions of the visionary experiences of a number of prophets have led some to suggest that prophets were psychologically disturbed.[23] Strange, often anti-social behaviour, unwelcome and at times shocking speech, physical manifestations such as fit-like symptoms and descriptions of hallucinatory-like visions have given rise to this suggestion. Indeed, passages such as Isaiah 6, Ezek. 3.12-15 and Hab. 3.16 describe prophets who were rendered speechless and paralysed by their encounter with God. But not all prophetic action can be described in such ways, so a better general

---

20. Y. Sherwood, 'Prophetic Performance Art (editorial)', *The Bible and Critical Theory* 2.1 (2006), pp. 1.1-1.4 (1.1).

21. Sherwood, 'Prophetic Performance Art', p. 1.1.

22. B. Giesen, 'Performance art', in *Social Performance: Symbolic Action, Cultural Pragmatics, and Ritual* (ed. J.C. Alexander, B. Giesen and J.L. Mast; Cambridge: Cambridge University Press, 2006), pp. 315-24 (316).

23. M. Daniel Carroll gives a helpful overview of such views of the prophets. See M.D. Carroll, 'A Passion for Justice and the Conflicted Self: Lessons from the Book of Micah', *Journal of Psychology and Christianity* 25.2 (2006), pp. 169-76 (170-71).

description of prophetic performance is found in David Stacey's suggestion that prophets were persons of 'rare mental intensity' so taken up with their message that they manifested it in their own bodies.[24]

Prophecy and Public Theology

Before addressing the question of whether such prophetic action has a place in the public sphere today, it is important to address prior issues of historical context and literary representation. Much debate surrounds the questions of the prophetic characters and their roles in the Hebrew Bible. Were they loners acting as isolated individuals or did they have more widespread community support (bands of disciples and the like)?[25] How closely tied to the cult were they?[26] Does a historical figure underlie prophetic traditions or are they merely *personas* created by scribes of later eras?[27] Is there any historical basis to what is described in the Prophetic Literature? Given the uncertainty on all of these issues, are we justified in using biblical traditions as templates for our own action?

If, on the other hand, we approach the prophetic literature from a literary rather than historical viewpoint, we might ask whether it matters if a historical actuality underlies the prophetic traditions. These are stories that are part of canonical scripture and carry the weight of tradition. Rather than subject them to the scrutiny of the 'quest for the historical prophet', we can let them speak on several levels through the layers of meaning imbued in their canonical preservation and transmission. They are stories that can continue to inspire and motivate our faithful communities, as will be seen in the following contemporary accounts.

Mike Riddell's Story

Mike Riddell, a writer from New Zealand, spent several formative years at the International Baptist Theological Seminary located at the time in Rüschlikon, Switzerland. There the teaching embraced the philosophy that the Bible should be in one hand and the newspaper in the other. During the 1980s and 1990s Mike was in ministry in the Baptist Church in Auckland and was involved in a campaign trying to prevent the city council from selling off inner-city rental stock, occupied by low-income tenants, including

24. Stacey, *Prophetic Drama*, p. 172.
25. Michael Floyd argues that 'the whole notion of prophetic disciples is an entirely speculative one, born of a purely theoretical necessity' in 'Prophecy and Writing in Habakkuk 2,1-5', *ZAW* 105.3 (1993), pp. 462-81 (467).
26. See Paul Redditt's discussion of 'central and peripheral prophets' in his *Introduction to the Prophets* (Grand Rapids: Eerdmans, 2008), pp. 9-11.
27. See W. Doan and T. Giles for a thorough discussion of this question in *Prophets, Performance, and Power* (New York: T. & T. Clark, 2005).

psychiatric patients. The campaign followed all the usual strategies of printing posters, organising petitions, writing letters and submissions, attending council meetings and making representation on behalf of the tenants. At the final meeting where a decision would be made Mike could see that the Councillors had already made up their minds to sell. This is how he describes his reaction:

> In my despair, I was overcome by divine madness. Without forethought, and to the surprise of the gathered dignitaries, I leapt into the centre of the circled benches and began to disrobe. As I removed my clothes, words came to me. I said to the Councillors that this was what they were doing to the poor: removing what little dignity they had left and leaving them naked and vulnerable. You think that nobody is watching, I told them, but God is watching, and you are accountable for your decision.

Standing in his boxers he wasn't sure what to do next, so much to everyone's relief the mayor called a break for a cup of tea. That day the council did make the decision to sell the properties, but due to the publicity that resulted it did not act on the decision for another seven years. In a passage reflecting on the experience, Mike says: 'In some ways, my confrontation of the ruling powers with my own vulnerability was a more effective means of achieving change than all of our more conventional democratic attempts.'[28]

Dave Andrews's Story

Dave Andrews is an Australian Christian community worker, activist and author based in Brisbane. He spent twelve years in India before forming The Waiter's Union in Brisbane's West End that works with the homeless and needy.

Some years ago, Dave was troubled that one of Brisbane's major newspapers carried no stories about major flooding in Bangladesh that had left more than twenty million people homeless—equivalent to the population of Australia. Dave persistently rang the editor, asking that a story be published, and eventually a few lines were allocated on page 10 of the newspaper. Dave thanked the editor but said he felt the response was inadequate, that Brisbane's inhabitants had the right to know about such an event and how they might respond. He said that unless a bigger story was published in the next week, he and some friends would establish a Bengali refugee camp on the steps of the newspaper building. He then contacted other media sources to reiterate this intention. The editor dug in his heels, claiming that the story was of no interest to Australians. So on the allocated day, when nothing more had been published, Dave and his friends established a lively,

---

28. Quotations received in email correspondence with Mike Riddell, but they can be found in his publication, *Sacred Journey: Spiritual Wisdom for Times of Transition* (London: SPCK, 2nd edn, 2010).

colourful camp, including members of the local Bengali population, children and chickens, all the while ensuring that access was not blocked to the building. Although it was Dave and his friends who risked public censure, it was the newspaper editor that was exposed that day as heartless and uninterested in the plight of Australia's suffering neighbours. The next day a much larger article was published on page 3, with contact details for charity organisations involved in flood relief. The editor told Dave that he had received such bad publicity over the event that his paper could not again afford to ignore future catastrophes of that kind.[29] Christian leaders have named Dave Andrews a 'prophetic' figure due to actions such as this that form part of his ministry.

Publicly Performing God's Word

These stories well illustrate the characteristic of the biblical prophets who are conscious of speaking 'God's word' rather than their own word. Sherwood speaks about this in her editorial to a journal focused on prophetic Performance Art:

> Crazy actions and crazy language are prophetic *special effects* designed to create the very *special effect* of the super-natural para-normal, *das Heilige*, which so frequently finds its expression—as Other—through the *un*natural, *ab*normal. Unlike Wisdom, prophecy claims to be the direct word of God, and prophetic language and prophetic bodies reel in the attempt to create a sense of words that, by definition, are not our words, and of actions that, by definition, are not 'our' own.[30]

There are, of course, stories of prophetic figures who claim to speak God's word but are observed with great unease by the majority of the Christian church. One criterion for judging prophets in the contemporary church is to distinguish between those who claim to be fore-tellers in the popular sense of the word 'prophet' (although sometimes, quite conveniently, in retrospect) and those who fit into the more accurate role that emerges from the prophetic literature as that of truth-teller: even, and most especially, when the truth is against the popular action and opinion of the day.

It must be acknowledged that a context of public theology must include a discussion of a Christian's role in the mainstream political processes, including Christian politicians, advisors, bureaucrats and prayer networks. Neither is it uncommon for the Bible to be claimed as an ally of the status quo. For example, in February 2006 in South Africa, the President at that time, Thabo Mbeki, quoted the book of Isaiah in his 'State of the Nation'

---

29. Story conveyed by personal communication with Dave Andrews in Canberra during 2010.
30. Sherwood, 'Prophetic Performance Art', p. 1.2 (author's italics).

speech, and spokespersons from three other political parties also quoted Isaiah or referred to him in their responses.[31] In the Australian Parliament, Senator Vicki Bourne gave a valedictory speech honouring Democratic Senator John Woodley in which she stated: 'John once stated that he would try to get as many quotes from the Bible in *Hansard* as he possibly could.'[32] Undoubtedly, then, many quotations from the Bible are on the public record.

But a discussion of prophetic action inspired by our biblical heritage suggests that there is also a place for prophetic performance in the liminal sphere—on the margins of socially dominant culture. Such performance can be manifest in a range of ways.

Micah Challenge

'Micah Challenge' is a global movement of Christian agencies, churches, groups and individuals that was established in response to the Millennium Development Goals to add a Christian dimension to the aim of reducing poverty by 2015. Micah Challenge holds an annual 'Voices for Justice' campaign in which up to 300 participants meet in Canberra for four days to advocate for the Millennium Development Goals—two days of preparation, prayer and reflection and two days of pre-arranged meetings with Parliamentarians from across the spectrum of political persuasion. Each year public events are held to present the message and advocate on behalf of the poor, events that have included art exhibitions, public rallies, bike rides, a fifth birthday party in Parliament House with balloons and lolly bags to highlight the number of children globally who do not reach their fifth year, and even a giant toilet on the lawns outside Parliament House. There was promotion of a 'Robin Hood tax' in which several Greenwood clad individuals advocated for a tax on financial transactions which then would be redistributed to the poor. Another time a 'Signature Event' was held in which Wilberforce's action against slavery was evoked as a giant scroll was unrolled across the floor of the Great Hall and politicians were invited to add their signatures to those of 112,000 other Australians who had committed themselves to fighting poverty. Such actions taken by Micah Challenge are inspired by the biblical principle of God's preferential option for the poor. One participant, reflecting on the 'Signature event', wrote that 'it was Tony Abbott who made the most profound comment of the morning when he said, somewhat tongue-in-cheek, that we are nags and that people in power need nags like us

---

31. J. Punt, 'Popularising the Prophet Isaiah in Parliament: The Bible in Post-apartheid, South African Public Discourse', *Religion and Theology* 14 (2007), pp. 206-223.

32. Senator Bourne's speech can be found at: http://parlinfo.aph.gov.au/parlInfo/search/display/display.w3p;query=Id%3A%22chamber%2Fhansards%2F2001-08-06%2F0157%22

to keep them accountable. Whether he intended it or not, his words described our prophetic engagement with the powers of the day.'[33]

Illegal Protest Action

Despite their colourful and attention-grabbing nature, the events staged by Micah Challenge at Parliament House have tended to stay within the parameters of legality and decorum, falling short of the shock value that characterizes some of the prophets of the Hebrew Bible. This more provocative type of prophetic performance may be better illustrated by groups such as the Bonhoeffer Four, a group of peacemakers from Victoria who have embodied their convictions by illegally trespassing and disrupting war training exercises at the Swan Island military base, inspired by the text of Isa. 2.4/Mic. 4.3 ('they shall beat their swords into ploughshares and their spears into pruning hooks, nor shall they train for war any more').[34] Similar action was taken by Aotearoa Ploughshare members, who were charged with intentionally damaging government property with criminal intent after destroying a section of a spy-satellite dish in 2008 being used for the US-led wars in Iraq and Afghanistan. The group was acquitted in March 2010, but a likely outcome of the action is that legislation will be tightened to prevent future demonstrations of this nature.[35]

In 1997, at the opening of the Crown Casino in Melbourne, actress Rachel Griffiths stepped out of a limousine, amongst arrivals of other dignitaries, wearing only a bloody 'crown of thorns' and a loin cloth while holding a child who tossed coins on the ground. William Stewart interpreted her protest action as prophetic, as it evoked memories of the temple-clearing incident as well as explicit allusions to a suffering Jesus.[36] When asked to comment on her reasons for protesting in such a way, she claimed that the government of the time had 'succeeded in raping our state of its dignity, compassion and sense of community'.[37]

Conclusion

The contemporary stories related above suggest that it is through such embodied, imaginative and provocative action that the tradition of biblical

33. Blog entry by Nils von Kalm: http://www.micahchallenge.org.au/blog/n/being-a-nag-for-the-poor-100621

34. http://indymedia.org.au/keywords/bonhoeffer-4

35. More details can be found at the Ploughshares website: http://ploughshares.org.nz/.

36. W. Stewart, 'Crown of Thorns: Ancient Prophecy and the (Post)modern Spectacle', *The Bible and Critical Theory*, 2.1 (2006), pp. 4.1-4.24.

37. From the Herald Sun website archives: http://www.heraldsun.com.au/news/victoria/crown-protest-led-to-naked-ambition/story-e6frf7kx-1111113427408.

prophets in public performances compelled by God's word continues. Like Jesus' parables, such prophetic actions can reach beyond themselves, affirming Sherwood's description of them as 'alliances between the Bible and the margins'.[38]

Exposure—whether by disrobing or inviting censure from others—will always attract attention. What would lead us to view such performance as prophetic? One criterion would be the motivation for such action. If it is *only* sensationalism, it remains performance for its own sake. If there is an aim to expose truth and justice, it could be named prophetic. The performances of biblical prophets compelled to risk dignity and social acceptance in their presentation of a message from God can continue to be one of the sources of inspiration for those engaged in public theology today.

---

38. Sherwood, 'Prophetic Performance Art', p. 1.3.

Resurrection and Justice

Thorwald Lorenzen

When children, women and men are brutalized by poverty, torture and enmity, and when the earth is exploited for short-term profit, does the *foundational event* of the Christian faith, the resurrection of Jesus Christ, and the social dimension of the resurrection, the Christian church, have anything to say to these denials of human and ecological justice? There is a wide theological consensus that the resurrection is the foundational event of the Christian movement. Yet when it comes to discussing its nature, meaning and significance, the consensus fades. In recent decades, the resurrection debate has focussed mainly on the following three alternative positions.[1]

For some, the decisive question is whether or not the resurrection of Jesus Christ was a *historical* event, an event in space and time, open to be explored by and confirmed with modern historical methods. Some theologians (for instance, Wolfhart Pannenberg, Carl F.H. Henry, N.T. Wright) and probably the majority of intentional Christians insist that the physical corpse of Jesus was raised from death and transformed into something else, a 'spiritual' body or a body of 'glory' (1 Cor. 15.43-44). The tomb, therefore, into which Jesus' corpse had been placed, would have been empty following Jesus' resurrection. Since the Gospel traditions contain narratives about the empty tomb, it is claimed that these narratives can be investigated with historical-critical scrutiny so as to demonstrate that the tomb was empty. For many Christians, such *historical* enquiry supports, confirms and even grounds their faith in Jesus Christ. The emphasis here is on whether it happened and whether it can be *rationally* affirmed or even proven.

Others (for instance, Rudolf Bultmann, Gerhard Ebeling, Marcus Borg) shift the focus from what may have happened to Jesus' corpse to the disciples' encounter with the risen Christ. For these theologians, the 'empty tomb' is historically unlikely and theologically irrelevant. The important

---

1. I have discussed various theological approaches to the resurrection in Thorwald Lorenzen, *Resurrection and Discipleship: Interpretive Models, Biblical Reflections, Theological Consequences* (Maryknoll, NY: Orbis Books, 1995; Eugene, OR: Wipf & Stock, 2004), pp. 9-111; idem, *Resurrection – Discipleship – Justice: Affirming the Resurrection of Jesus Christ Today* (Macon, GA: Smyth & Helwys, 2003), pp. 11-42.

point is *existential* transformation of the lives of those disciples encountered by the risen Christ. Here the emphasis is on what happened in and to the disciples, inciting and inviting them to a journey of faith.

A third group of theologians (for instance, Karl Barth, Jürgen Moltmann and, more recently, Brian Robinette) insist that the resurrection was *real*, that Jesus was raised 'bodily' and that the tomb was empty. Yet, the reality of the resurrection, being an act of God, cannot be limited to our perception of space and time. It is a *divine event* with historical traces, such as the appearances and the empty tomb. But its reality is much deeper and wider than such traces. The reality of the resurrection of Jesus includes the transformation and healing of God's creation and also the making possible of an appropriate way of tuning into that process.

I want to develop this third approach by arguing that in a world where human beings are brutalized and the earth is exploited, it belongs to the journey of faith in Jesus Christ to liberate the oppressed and to recognize that 'the earth is the Lord's' (Ps. 24.1). With the resurrection of Jesus Christ, God set in motion the renewal of God's creation and with it the implementation of justice. And it belongs to the empowering mystery of faith that those who believe in the God who raised Jesus from the dead are called to be God's 'fellow workers' (1 Cor. 3.9) in the divine work of renewal.

Sui generis

The earliest Christian confessions affirm that the resurrection of Jesus Christ is a special and intentional *act of God* and, as such, must be interpreted *on its own terms*. While Jesus' life and death, despite having divine dimensions, can be portrayed in historical terms, his resurrection can only be understood in a *category of its own*.[2] Jesus was not resuscitated; his resurrection is *qualitatively* different from that of Lazarus (Jn 11.38-44), or of Jairus' daughter (Mk 5.21-24a, 35-43) or of the widow's son at Nain (Lk. 7.11-15). These were understood to be supernatural miracles—uncommon but not unprecedented. It was clearly understood that these persons were raised to an earthly life such that they would eventually die again. Jesus, by contrast, was removed from the realm within which death reigns: 'We know that Christ, being raised from the dead, will never die again; death no longer has dominion over him' (Rom. 6.9).

---

2. See Lorenzen, *Resurrection and Discipleship*, pp. 116-26. Cf. Jürgen Moltmann, *Theology of Hope: On the Ground and the Implications of a Christian Eschatology* (trans. James W. Leitch; London: SCM Press, 1967), pp. 178-80; N.T. Wright, *The Resurrection of the Son of God* (Minneapolis: Fortress Press, 2003), pp. 200-206, and also *Surprised by Hope* (London: SPCK, 2007), pp. 56-57.

Nevertheless, with Barth one can speak of 'a tiny "historical" margin'[3] to the resurrection. I argue that such a historical margin includes not only the appearances of the risen Christ and with these the coming of faith to the earliest Christians, the transformation of Jesus' body and the empty tomb but also the call to mission and the implementation of justice.

The Transformative Power of Resurrection Faith

Understanding the resurrection of the crucified Jesus *on its own terms* includes the recognition that it is portrayed as an event that is open to the future and, as such, shapes and transforms history. Jürgen Moltmann has helpfully retrieved the Hebrew category of 'promise' (rather than historical fact) to understand the resurrection.[4] It includes the promise of God's accompanying and empowering presence and with this the conviction that the struggle for justice is *worthwhile* because *ultimately* justice will triumph.[5] The resurrection of Jesus is not simply 'there' to be rationally affirmed or denied as a historical event. The resurrection of Jesus is a relational and hence 'open' event. It incites participation and as such transforms and shapes history in the direction of justice.

The risen Christ is therefore presented as 'the *firstborn*' and '*first fruits* of those who have fallen asleep' (Rom. 8.29; 1 Cor. 15.20, 23; Col. 1.18; Rev. 1.5). Indeed, there is a saying in the Matthean passion story, originally part of the resurrection tradition, which paints an apocalyptic picture about the consequences of the resurrection of Jesus: 'The tombs also were opened, and many bodies of the saints who had fallen asleep were raised. After his resurrection they came out of the tombs and entered the holy city and appeared to many' (Mt. 27.52-53). We are invited to consider that the power of death has been broken. Reality has been changed, and this change has consequences for the living and the dead.

The well-known resurrection tradition in 1 Corinthians 15.3-5 makes the same point in a more subtle manner. Most of the verbs are in the aorist

---

3. Karl Barth, *Church Dogmatics*. III/2. *The Doctrine of Creation* (trans. G.W. Bromiley *et al.*; Edinburgh: T. & T. Clark, 1960), p. 446.

4. Moltmann, *Theology of Hope*, pp. 95-138. Cf. Lorenzen, *Resurrection and Discipleship*, pp. 198-206.

5. In an insightful analysis of Paul's resurrection treatise in 1 Corinthians 15, Keith Dyer argues convincingly that the apostle wants to proclaim that 'the just righteousness of God embodied in Jesus Christ will ultimately prevail—even beyond death'. This is the hope to which the Christian faith witnesses and which also sustains Christians in their struggle for justice. See Keith D. Dyer, 'Paul and Embodied Resurrection: Rethinking 1 Corinthians 15', in *Resurrection and Responsibility: Essays on Theology, Scripture, and Ethics in Honor of Thorwald Lorenzen* (ed. Keith D. Dyer and David J. Neville; Eugene, OR: Pickwick Publications, 2009), pp. 136-61 (161, also 149).

tense, describing events that have concluded: 'Christ *died* (aorist tense) ... he was *buried* (aorist tense)...he *appeared* (aorist tense)...'. But then, in ostentatious difference from the aorist tense of the surrounding verbs, we find an assertion in the *perfect* tense: 'he has been raised'. This shift from the aorist to the perfect tense is intentionally used to emphasize the 'continuing effect'[6] of the event of resurrection.

It is therefore not surprising that the resurrection narratives in the Gospels and in Acts are interlocked with the call to mission. Participating in God's plan for God's creation is part of the reality of the resurrection. Therefore both Peter's and Paul's respective calls to the apostolic office and indeed the apostolic office as such are interrelated with a call to and participation in the *missio Dei*.

The resurrection, therefore, is an event that effects, transforms and shapes history; it is 'the beginning of the eschatological transformation of the world by its creator'.[7] For Christians, the first and most appropriate response to the event of the resurrection is neither historical reason nor ecclesiastical liturgy but echoing the life of Jesus in justice-oriented discipleship.[8]

The Identity of the Risen Christ

Despite the present popular distinction between the historical, pre-Easter Jesus and the risen Christ of faith, it needs to be insisted that there is only *one* Jesus Christ, who in the power of the Spirit has invited and incited his followers to the journey of faith and whose story is told in the Scriptures of the Christian Church. In that sense, all of the New Testament writings, including the Gospels, are Easter stories.

Nevertheless, it must not be forgotten, overlooked or relativized that it was the crucified *Jesus* who was raised to newness of life. He, Jesus Christ, is the wellspring and content of Christian faith. And on the journey of faith, the *priority* of Jesus Christ needs to be constantly asserted, protected and nourished, lest in the relationship between Christ and the believer the needs and interests of the believer rather than the life-giving power of Christ become determinative. In early Christianity one of the ministries was 'to distinguish the spirits' (1 Cor. 12.10; 1 Jn 4.1), within which the measure was not simply a verbal Christological confession but the concrete, liberating

---

6. F. Blass and A. Debrunner, *A Greek Grammar of the New Testament and Other Early Christian Literature* (trans. and ed. Robert W. Funk; Chicago: University of Chicago Press, 1961), p. 176 (§342).

7. Jürgen Moltmann, *The Crucified God: The Cross of Christ as the Foundation and Criticism of Christian Theology* (trans. R.A. Wilson and John Bowden; London: SCM Press, 1974), p. 162.

8. I have argued this point both in *Resurrection and Discipleship*, pp. 191-235, 240-47, 269-95, and in *Resurrection – Discipleship – Justice*, pp. 65-82, 137-61.

and demanding story of Jesus. The priority of Christ in the encounter of faith is best protected by being constantly reminded of Christ's identity, and since the earliest days of Christianity the *identity* of the risen Christ was asserted by emphasising *continuity* with the story of Jesus of Nazareth.

The earliest testimonies therefore affirm an essential and integral continuity between faith in Christ and the story of Jesus, the man from Galilee who fleshed out God's unconditional love and ended up on a cross that was 'as a rule reserved for hardened criminals, rebellious slaves and rebels against the Roman state'.[9] In the Lukan and Johannine resurrection narratives, the risen Christ identifies himself with the wounds of crucifixion (Lk. 24.40; Jn 20.20). The Apostle Paul interprets his own discipleship in Christological terms as always carrying in his existence (*sōma*) 'the *death of Jesus*, so that the *life of Jesus* may also be made visible in our bodies' (2 Cor. 4.10); he confesses to carrying 'the *marks of Jesus* branded on my body (*sōma*)' (Gal. 6.17). Lest such assertions are individualized and spiritualized, it is worth remembering that Lukan theology is well known for its social and political focus, with a particular interest in Jesus' solidarity with the poor, and the Gospel of John emphasizes that God's light shines in darkness and God's word became flesh (Jn 1.1-18). When the apostle Paul introduced himself to the church in Corinth, he immediately declared his ultimate allegiance to 'Jesus Christ, and him *crucified*' (1 Cor. 2.2); and the social implications of that confession became clear when Paul criticized the Corinthian church leaders for being more interested in self-edification than sharing their lives with slaves, wharfies and nannies. By neglecting 'latecomers', the church failed to recognize that the *crucified* Christ is host at the *Lord's* Supper (1 Cor. 11.23); as such they were emptying the Eucharist of its meaning and therefore in danger of denying their own identity (1 Cor. 11.20).[10]

The earliest testimonies to the resurrection therefore invite us to recognize and to explore *the resurrection in its essential interrelation with the life of Jesus, including his crucifixion*. If that interrelationship is not recognized, the resurrection is easily misunderstood in terms of Jesus being a 'superman' or of God performing a super miracle. The focus then turns to proving Jesus' divinity, with the consequence that the offence his life provoked and his subsequent pathway to Gethsemane and Calvary become

---

9. Martin Hengel, *Crucifixion in the Ancient World and the Folly of the Message of the Cross*, in *The Cross of the Son of God* (trans. John Bowden; London: SCM Press, 1986), pp. 91-185 (175).

10. For further discussion, see Thorwald Lorenzen, 'The Crucified Christ as Lord of the Church: Theological Reflections on 1 Corinthians 11–14', in *Prophecy and Passion: Essays in Honour of Athol Gill* (ed. David Neville; Adelaide: Australian Theological Forum, 2002), pp. 83-125.

theologically irrelevant. The resurrection is not a negation of Jesus' life and passion but rather a confirmation and effective implementation of it.

The Life and Death of the Risen Christ

Since it was the *Crucified One* who was raised from the dead, his resurrection invites us to correlate both cross and resurrection with those aspects of Jesus' life that led to his collision with the religious, political and economic powers of his day—those powers that ultimately brought about his execution. Jesus did not die 'in a good old age...and full of years', as the patriarchs did;[11] nor did he die of a heart attack or even as a result of judicial error. Jesus was opposed, captured, tortured and executed because he was relentless in his struggle for justice. It is noteworthy that Luke intentionally modifies the centurion's confession at the cross, 'Truly this man was the *Son of God*' (Mk 15.39), to 'Certainly this was a *just* (*dikaios*) man' (Lk. 23.47).[12] Interpreting deity ('Son of God') in terms of justice at this crucial point of the narrative grabs our attention. As Willard Swartley comments, 'Thus in Luke's theology, Jesus, like God, emerges as the standard of true justice.'[13]

So, when we speak of the identity of the risen Christ in his essential interlocking with the story of Jesus, we need to recognize that Jesus was criticized, opposed, captured, tortured, sentenced and executed because he intentionally identified with those lying half-dead on the road of life and that in doing so he thereby questioned, criticized and undermined the dominant institutions of his day—the law, the temple, religious authorities and customs—which had placed self-interest before protecting human life and human dignity. Jesus manifested with his life that law and religion are to serve and to implement justice; their essential purpose is to make human life human (Mk 2.27-28).

The religious culture of Jesus' day was *praxis-* rather than theory-oriented. Opposition to Jesus was not provoked because he made a *verbal assertion* about being the Son of God but because his *praxis* privileged human dignity above obedience to law and cult. Our sources may not allow us to write a biography of Jesus, but even a critical reading of the Gospel narratives reveals a causal relation between Jesus' life and his violent death.

---

11. See Gen. 25.8; 35.29; 1 Chron. 29.28; Job 42.17.
12. At this point, English translations are all over the place. KJV: 'this was a *righteous* man'; RSV: 'this man was *innocent*!' (also NRSV, NEB); Phillips: 'this was indeed a *good* man'. A convincing argument that 'just' is the most appropriate translation is provided by Willard M. Swartley, *Covenant of Peace: The Missing Peace in New Testament Theology and Ethics* (Grand Rapids: Eerdmans, 2006), pp. 140-44.
13. Swartley, *Covenant of Peace*, p. 142.

In word and deed, Jesus displayed an authority, authenticity and *parrēsia* (inner freedom, courage) which people rightly interpreted as the arrival of the 'reign of God'. Since for Jesus the 'reign of God' is characterized by passionate and compassionate love, his identification with marginal people, his commitment to restore human life wherever he found it broken, his criticism of the loveless morality of law and cult, and his call to radical discipleship all have their foundation and content in Jesus' understanding of the 'reign of God' as love.

Jesus' passion brought him into conflict with the authorities of his day. The *religious leaders* charged him with being a friend of publicans and sinners. To them it was presumptuous that Jesus (rather than God) granted faith and forgiveness to people; that in the name of God he restored people and conveyed to them hope and dignity; that he claimed those who were socially suspect and religiously unqualified to be the object of God's saving and liberating passion. His opponents rightly understood his lifestyle as questioning and even attacking the final and absolute authority of the foundational pillars of the Jewish religious establishment: Torah, temple and religious customs.

What offended the religious establishment was not so much that Jesus understood and interpreted the regulations of the law and the rules of the cult differently, but rather that he *acted* upon his understanding, that he accepted personal responsibility for his convictions. In the face of human need, he assumed the authority to break Sabbath rules and suspend cultic regulations on ritual purity and fasting. For his religious opponents, Jesus was a blasphemer and seducer of the people (Deut. 13 and 17), and as such he deserved the death penalty (Lev. 24.16).

By blessing the poor and oppressed, by showing solidarity with the wretched of the earth and by proclaiming their liberation, Jesus also challenged the *economic interests* of those in power. Anyone who suggests that the fate of the poor may not be their own fault, or may not be the will of God, but may indeed be the by-product of societal structures that favour the interests of the rich and powerful is perceived as dangerous by the establishment. This also explains why Jesus' activity was brought to the attention of the *political authorities* of his day, whose concern was to maintain social stability and who readily cooperated in removing one person to maintain law and order for the rest of society.

Jesus threatened the religious, political and economic structures of his day by his radical obedience to God and hence his radical commitment to restoring the dignity of human life. This understanding of God and the resultant vision of reality clashed with the views and interests of the religious, economic and political establishments. They could not contain and incorporate the *newness* of Jesus' vision of the 'reign of God'. In their understanding of reality, condemning Jesus to death was not only an act of self-preservation but also a necessary act of obedience to their perception of the will of God.

A New Way of Being

When this particular Jesus, who with his life fleshed out a *specific* understanding of God and of the dignity of human life, was raised from the dead, *this life and the integrally related subsequent death were revealed as having divine and eternal significance.* By raising the crucified Christ from the dead, God revealed that this *particular* person, Jesus of Nazareth and the particular life he lived, must serve to define the *content of divinity* and therewith the *content of resurrection faith.* Concretely, this means that the *deity* of Christ is revealed in his radical openness and obedience to God and also in his radical commitment to the healing and liberating of broken humanity. Deity, therefore, does not withdraw from the world but manifests its healing and reconciling power in the world. The corresponding human response to God's action in raising Jesus from the dead does not, in the first place, mean adherence to religious institutions and observance of religious rules and dogmas, but rather faith in Jesus Christ and, with such faith, holistic worship of God and concrete engagement for the alleviation of human need. For this reason, it is important to insist that the *whole* Jesus—his life, his body, his personality, his inter-activity with the world around him—was raised from the dead.[14] Since with his personhood Jesus was related to God and society and with his body he was woven into the world, into nature, faith in the risen Christ therefore includes the invitation to a new way of being and with it the promise of the transformation of the whole world.

As part of the new way of being, the resurrection of the crucified Jesus calls for a *specific way of knowing.* The apostle Paul interprets his life as analogous to the story of Jesus, 'always carrying in the body the *death* of Jesus so that the *life* of Jesus may also be made visible in our bodies' (2 Cor. 4.10).[15] And when the Gospel writers tell the story of the crucified and risen Jesus, they insist that the appropriate way of knowing him is not merely intellectual assent or liturgical worship but rather following him in *radical life-giving and liberating discipleship.*[16]

Furthermore, by raising the crucified Jesus from the dead, God declared an *end to religious or cultic ways to please or even impress God.* Jesus tuned into

---

14. See Jürgen Moltmann, *The Way of Jesus Christ: Christology in Messianic Dimensions* (trans. Margaret Kohl; London: SCM Press, 1990), pp. 256-57; Brian D. Robinette, *Grammars of Resurrection: A Christian Theology of Presence and Absence* (New York: Crossroad, 2009), pp. 159-78; Wright, *Surprised by Hope*, pp. 64-87.

15. See also Gal. 6.17; 2 Corinthians 10–13.

16. For further details, see Lorenzen, *Resurrection – Discipleship – Justice*, pp. 137-61.

the longstanding tradition that God is a 'God of justice' who 'loves justice' (Isa. 30.18; 61.8) such that the dominance of cult and sacrifice is relativized: 'Obeying the voice of the LORD...is better than sacrifice' (1 Sam. 15.22).[17]

The apostle Paul therefore proclaims Christ as the fulfilment and end of the 'law', while the Epistle to the Hebrews does the same with respect to the religious cult. The apostle transfigures the whole cultic system by insisting that the appropriate response to what God has done in Christ is to present our *'bodies* as a living sacrifice, holy and acceptable to God, which is your spiritual worship' (Rom. 12.1). Jesus was crucified because the religious forces, with their emphasis on Torah, temple and cult, interpreted Jesus' vision of God as blasphemy and also as leading people astray. Jesus therefore 'suffered *outside the gate* in order to sanctify the people through his own blood'. From this arises the imperative: 'Therefore let us go forth to him *outside* the camp and bear the abuse he endured' (Heb. 13.12-13). Neither sacrifice nor ceremony but rather worshipping God in everyday life is the most adequate response to the resurrection of the crucified Christ.

The new way of being is grounded in the life, death and resurrection of Jesus as *eschatological* events. There are *historical* and *eschatological* dimensions to the life, death and resurrection of Jesus. By sharing God's life with the crucified Jesus and thereby raising him from the dead, God made God's very being vulnerable to the forces of death. Since in that encounter with the forces of death, God remained God, *God thereby relativized the powers of death*. On that basis, we believe and proclaim that life is stronger than death, that love outlasts hate and that peace will prove stronger than violence. That *ontological truth* was spoken into the lives of the first Christians through the appearances of the risen Christ. The earliest Christians heard this good news, which transformed their innermost being, and they responded appropriately in word and deed. They told the new and powerful story of Jesus as their ultimate concern and thereby confessed that their God is a God of love, justice, peace and joy. Whatever else the resurrection may be, it is an affirmation of life and the celebration of freedom. The Johannine saying that Jesus 'came that they may have life, and have it abundantly' (Jn 10.10) applies both to the historical Jesus and to the risen Christ.

The 'God of Justice'

The story of Jesus, therefore, is 'good news' (*euangelion*), and when this 'good news' is heard and obeyed, it includes the praxis of discipleship and

---

17. There is a strong theological trajectory in the Hebrew Scriptures emphasizing obedience to God and practising justice rather than observing cultic rules and regulations: Deut. 30.11-20; 1 Sam. 15.22; Isa. 1.11-17; Jer. 7.21-28; Hos. 6.6; 8.13; Amos 5.21-24; Mic. 6.6-8; Ps. 50.7-15.

the implementation of justice. We have seen that the Gospel narratives of the appearances of Christ are all intimately interwoven with the call to manifest the story of Jesus in the public arena. The same Spirit who raised Jesus from the dead elicits faith in followers of Jesus (Rom. 1.4; 8.11) and with it issues the inviting and liberating imperative to become 'fellow workers with God' (*sunergoi theou*, 1 Cor. 3.9), joining God's passion to heal God's creation.

Nicholas Wolterstorff has emphasized that *dikaiosunē theou* in the New Testament—for instance in the beatitudes (Mt. 5.6, 10)—is in most cases not a character reference, as the English words 'righteous' or 'righteousness' suggest, but rather refers to people relating to each other in a certain way and is therefore more appropriately translated as '*justice* of God'.[18]

Given that most Christians and still too many clergy and theologians fail to relate the foundational event of Christian faith to the struggle for justice, we need to recall briefly what difference the resurrection of the crucified Jesus made in early Christianity. The sad facts that it took 1800 years before the Christian church understood that, with the resurrection of Christ, slavery was abolished and that to the present day most churches have not yet affirmed and implemented the equality of women or abrogated war and violence should not blind us to the reality that the seeds for relating faith in Jesus Christ to the struggle for justice were sown by the early Christians as they sought to understand the new reality that God had spoken into their lives. Given that up to the *corpus christianum* in the fourth century the early Christian communities were tiny sprinklings in a massive sea of patriarchy, slavery and violence, it is astounding that the end of patriarchy, slavery, violence, racism and gender privilege was not only proclaimed but also practised, even though hesitatingly and within understandable limits. Although, in hindsight, such words could have been clearer and such practices could have been more courageous, to use this early lack of clarity and hesitancy as an excuse for denying equality to women or for failing to oppose human trafficking, war and violence *today*, when the understanding of human rights is now clear on these points, is one of the tragic failures of the contemporary churches that seriously diminishes their current credibility.

If such credibility is to be restored, Christian churches need to ask themselves whether the theology that shapes and guides them is still in continuity with the wellspring that called them into being. In what follows I survey a few examples of how, in the earliest churches, the transformative power of the resurrection of the Crucified One concretely shaped social behaviour and, as such, witnessed to the liberating justice of God.

---

18. Nicholas Wolterstorff, *Justice: Rights and Wrongs* (Princeton, NJ: Princeton University Press, 2008), pp. 109-131 (110-13).

Victim Focussed

In their recent books on social ethics, Jürgen Moltmann and Nicholas Wolterstorff emphasize yet again that Jesus was *focused* in his activity and that *his focus* was the *victim*. 'The justice...of God manifested in Jesus is *victim-oriented*: God creates justice for those who suffer injustice and violence.'[19] The early theologians portray Jesus as announcing liberation to the oppressed (Lk. 4.18-19), as promising grace to the poor, to the hungry and the sorrowful (Lk. 6.20-21), and as displaying healing and liberating solidarity with the vulnerable and marginalized people of his day. In word and deed he revealed to them the justice and compassion of God. 'Jesus joins the victims; therein, God joins the victims.'[20]

Jesus' praxis of compassion led to his becoming a victim himself. The resurrection proclaims that neither the perpetrators, Caiaphas and Pilate, nor the institutions of state and religion carried the day but rather that God identified with the victim without ceasing to be God. It is consistent with this understanding of reality that the earliest Christian churches located the presence of Christ in the world not only in the preaching of the word and the administration of the sacraments, as the churches generally emphasize, but also in the vulnerable child (Mk 9.36-37) and in the hungry, the stranger and the prisoner (Mt. 25.31-46). Early Christians confessed that their solidarity with and compassion for victims was a reflection of their relation to Christ.

Nevertheless, the claims of justice in Christian perspective are also addressed to the *perpetrator* because the 'oppressed and the oppressor alike are robbed of their humanity'.[21] Mary's *Magnificat* is an eloquent reminder that the 'Mighty One' has not only 'lifted up the lowly' and 'filled the hungry with good things' but has also 'brought down the powerful from their thrones and...sent the rich away empty' (Lk. 1.49-53). While victims need to be invited back to the journey of life by offering them compassion and granting them compensation, perpetrators need to repent of their deeds and grant reparations. In Australia we are confronted with this challenge every day as indigenous people and sexual abuse victims seek justice for the injustice that they have experienced.

And yet the transforming power of the resurrection promises even more.[22] The encounter of the suspiciously rich tax collector Zacchaeus with Jesus and his subsequent transformation (Lk. 19.1-10), as well as the apostle

---

19. Jürgen Moltmann, *Ethics of Hope* (trans. Margaret Kohl; Minneapolis: Fortress Press, 2012), p. 182. The emphasis is in the original German: *Ethik der Hoffnung* (Munich: Gütersloher Verlagshaus, 2010), p. 204. In the English translation, the translator has added 'and righteousness', which is not in the German text.

20. Wolterstorff, *Justice*, p. 110.

21. Nelson Mandela, *Long Walk to Freedom: The Autobiography of Nelson Mandela* (London: Abacus, 1994), p. 751.

22. I am grateful to David Neville for reminding me of this.

Paul's conversion and witness to 'the power of the resurrection' (Phil. 3.4-10), show eloquently how an economic criminal and 'a persecutor of the church' can be *transformed* to a meaningful and flourishing life.

Waging Nonviolence

In the Johannine and possibly the Lukan resurrection narratives, the risen Christ presents himself to the community of believers with the words, '*Peace* be with you'! He identifies himself as the Crucified One (continuity!), empowers his followers with the Holy Spirit and commissions them to a ministry of peace (Jn 20.19-23, 26; Lk. 24.36-53).[23]

There is widespread agreement amongst New Testament scholars that in contrast to the Essenes, Jesus meddled in the affairs of the world, and that in contrast to the Zealots, Jesus opted for the way of nonviolence. When God raised Jesus from the dead, God *validated* Jesus' life-praxis. At the same time, God also *relativized* the powers of violence that led to Jesus' crucifixion.

Responding to the risen Christ, significant theologians in earliest Christianity related the resurrection to nonviolence, naming their God the 'God of peace'[24] and the risen Christ the 'Lord of peace' (2 Thess. 3.16). On the basis of the resurrection of the Crucified One, we may therefore speak of an ontology of nonviolence and peace.[25] On that basis we can affirm, in a world of war and violence, that peacemakers are the children of God. And in a world where political, economic and military expediency seems to rule, we can confess that ultimately the meek will inherit the earth.

Up to the beginning of the fourth century, when Christianity became the official religion of the Roman Empire, Christians largely refused to

---

23. Some ancient manuscripts do not include the peace greeting at Lk. 24.36. It is difficult to understand why it would have been omitted since Luke may be named the 'evangelist of peace'. If it is not original to Luke, it is easy to imagine a scribe familiar with the Johannine narrative inserting the peace motif here because peace is a central theme for Luke. Whatever the case may be, the peace motif is deeply ingrained in Luke's resurrection story. See David J. Neville, *A Peaceable Hope*: *Contesting Violent Eschatology in New Testament Narratives* (Grand Rapids: Baker Academic, 2013), pp. 91, 95, 111, 192-94, 254.

24. See Rom. 15.33; 16.20; 1 Cor. 14.33; 2 Cor. 13.11; Phil. 4.9; 1 Thess. 5.23; Heb. 13.20. Cf. the reference above to the Gospels of John and Luke. For details, see Neville, *A Peaceable Hope*, pp. 50-52, 95-96.

25. See Brian V. Johnstone, CSsR, 'Transformation Ethics: The Moral Implications of the Resurrection', in *The Resurrection: An Interdisciplinary Symposium on the Resurrection of Jesus* (ed. Stephen Davis, Daniel Kendall, SJ, Gerald O'Collins, SJ; Oxford: Oxford University Press, 1997), pp. 339-60 (347-53). Cf. John Macquarrie, *The Concept of Peace* (New York: Harper & Row; London: SCM Press, 1973), chap. V: 'Metaphysics of Peace' (pp. 63-75); John Milbank, *Theology and Social Theory: Beyond Secular Reason* (Oxford: Blackwell, 1990), pp. 380-438; Robinette, *Grammars of Resurrection*, pp. 271-90, 352-64.

participate in war. And even in the *corpus christianum* theologians took over philosophical ideas and developed the so-called 'just war' theory. Ethical guidelines were formulated to implement the Christian vision of life and to avoid war if at all possible. Nevertheless, against its own intention, the 'just war' theory has been used by church and state not to wage peace but rather to justify war. Given modern military technology and the widespread availability of nuclear, biological and chemical weapons, however, there can be no justification for modern warfare. We are waiting for the nations to implement one of the aims of the United Nations, 'to save succeeding generations from the scourge of war'.[26] It is deplorable that Christians fail to understand the reality entailed in the resurrection of Christ that 'the violence of war must be seen as a tragic aberration, contrary to the fundamental nature of reality'.[27] Affirming the resurrection of Christ includes the passion actively to wage nonviolence and peace rather than war.

Race, Slavery and Patriarchy
When the reality of the resurrection of the Crucified Christ becomes manifest in history and its transforming power is lived out in faith, racism, slavery and patriarchy are revealed to be incompatible with God's restoring justice. *Racism* was part of the social reality in antiquity and remains so in the modern world. It was therefore revolutionary when, in early Christianity, it was proclaimed that 'in Christ' there is 'no longer Jew or Greek' (Gal. 3.28). Where Jesus is confessed as risen, privileges based on nationality, culture and race are overcome. Jesus Christ is confessed as *vere homo*, and faith in him entails the commitment to understand oneself as a member of a common humanity. The 'other' becomes interesting for her or his own sake, and 'in Christ' we no longer need to see the other as a threat from which we need to protect ourselves; rather, we need to develop the awareness that we need the other to celebrate life.

When and where the resurrection becomes manifest, *slavery* is abolished.[28] It belongs to the tragedies of the history of Christianity that it took the established churches 1800 years to grasp this implication of the resurrection of the crucified Christ. Affirming the equality of slaves caused major problems in the earliest churches because slavery was an important economic and social pillar of society. Churches wanted to maintain

---

26. Preamble to the *Charter of the United Nations*.
27. Johnstone, 'Transformation Ethics', p. 353.
28. This is explicit in Gal. 3.28, but even in the Hebrew Bible, whenever the issue of slavery is raised, it is always intent on easing the burden of slaves (Lev. 25.39-46; Deut. 15.12-17; 23.15-16). In early Christianity the churches were too few, too small and too vulnerable to abolish the institution of slavery. But their vision of life clearly pointed in that direction.

good relations with society in order both to survive and to communicate the gospel. Moreover, the churches were so small and vulnerable that a social and political revolution was out of the question. Nevertheless, a definite trend can be observed. When, for instance, the slave Onesimus was converted and sought the apostle Paul's advice, theoretically Paul could have counselled him either to assert his newly found freedom 'in Christ' or to understand it as a private, spiritual and individual freedom. Paul does neither. He had no power to suspend the institution of slavery, and faith for him was certainly not merely an internal reality. So although Paul sent Onesimus back to his master, he did so with a letter in which he appealed to his owner, Philemon, to treat his slave as a brother. In Paul's situation, where the church was a vulnerable and fragile minority in an antagonistic world, this was understandable. To use Paul's understandable reluctance as justification for an 1800-year history of slavery is deplorable. Fortunately, both the churches and the human community as a whole now understand and agree that slavery is wrong. The abolition of slavery belongs to the core of human rights that have universal and absolute validity. Even so, reports from Sudan, Saudi Arabia, China and India speak of a lucrative slave trade, and many child labourers are fated to a life of slavery. But there is a worldwide movement with many governmental and non-governmental organizations effectively opposing all forms of slavery.

When the reality of the resurrection becomes manifest in history and its transforming power is acknowledged, the power of *patriarchy* is broken and the equality of men and women is proclaimed and implemented in all areas of life. Justice demands equality. Yet in most contemporary societies, women are still disadvantaged, and in some cultures such disadvantage becomes outright brutality, with violence, rape, genital mutilation and so-called honour killings being the order of the day. It is also deplorable that in many and probably most churches in which Jesus Christ is confessed and proclaimed as *Kurios*, fifty per cent of humanity is excluded from the office of pastor, priest, bishop or pope.

We must therefore never cease to remind ourselves that to affirm the resurrection of Jesus Christ includes the commitment to affirm the equality and dignity of women in all areas of life. It is ironical no less than incongruent that in those circles within which the resurrection is most vehemently defended—among Conservative Evangelicals and in the Roman Catholic Church—the full equality of women is denied.

Among the reasons given for such a denial of equality is that the earliest appearance of the risen Christ occurred to Peter, a male, in Galilee. The earliest formulas (1 Cor. 15.5; Lk. 24.34), the fact that Jesus' male friends fled to Galilee when he was arrested and executed, and the accumulation of Petrine resurrection narratives (Jn 21.1-14 [cf. Lk. 5.1-6, 8], 21.15-17, 18-22 [cf. Lk. 22.31-32; Mt. 16.17-19]) all certainly point in that direction.

Nevertheless, a healthy suspicion also reminds us that living in a patriarchal culture instilled a tendency in the earliest churches to downplay the role of women and to highlight instead the witness of male apostles. We can observe that tendency in the way *male* witnesses began to be associated with major events like the crucifixion (Lk. 23.49, which refers to 'acquaintances' rather than women only, as in Mk 15.40; Jn 19.26-27) and the discovery of the empty tomb (Lk. 24.12; Jn 20.1-10).

It therefore deserves special attention that the resurrection narratives in the Gospels also speak about an appearance of the risen Christ to a woman (Mt. 28.9-10; Jn 20.14-18).[29] Indeed, in a later ending of Mark, this appearance to Mary of Magdala is described or interpreted as being the *first* one, preceding the other appearances (Mk 16.9).[30] Given the cultural suspicion about the credibility of female witnesses, it is unlikely that the early church would have invented a tradition in which the risen Jesus first appeared to Mary. It is more likely that the first appearance of the risen Christ was indeed to a woman—to Mary, in or outside of Jerusalem. Therefore Mark 16.9, although part of a later addition to the earliest Gospel, may in this case contain accurate historical information. The fact that the pre-Pauline tradition in 1 Cor. 15.5-7 does not include this testimony may be due to the juridical situation which discouraged the testimony of women; in a patriarchal culture and a male-dominated church, there was little encouragement to highlight the importance of women. Furthermore, the tradition in 1 Cor. 15.3-7 may reflect or even validate male leadership in the early church (see 1 Cor. 15.5, 7). Yet the transforming power of the resurrection could not be contained altogether. We hear of a female apostle ('Junia' in Rom. 16.7) and a number of (house)churches led by women.[31]

Those who build their theological position regarding women in ministry on texts such as 1 Cor. 14.34-35 and 1 Tim. 2.11-15 have absolutized a situational element of the biblical message and have therefore failed to hear the living and history-changing message of the Word of God. Christians and churches are always in danger of functionalizing texts to serve the *status quo* and to maintain traditional power structures. We need to learn ever again that the authority of biblical texts resides not in themselves but in their witness to the new reality that became manifest in the transforming resurrection of the Crucified One.

---

29. In Matthew there are two Marys, but that is clearly an adaptation to Matthew's version of the 'empty tomb' narrative (28.1-8, esp. 28.1).

30. Luke may have omitted this appearance to Mary because for him the first appearance of the risen Christ occurred to Peter (Lk. 24.34).

31. Specific mention is made of Phoebe (Rom. 16.1), Nympha (Col. 4.15), Lydia (Acts 16.14-15, 40), Mary, the mother of John Mark (Acts 12.12), and Priscilla, who is often named before Aquila (Rom. 16.3, 5a; Acts 18.18, 26; 2 Tim. 4.19).

Poverty

Statistics indicate that between eight and ten million people, mostly children, die every year of poverty-related causes. Statistics are deceiving, however. They keep the cruelty and brutality of poverty at arm's length. They do not directly confront us with the *pain* of watching a mother wanting to nurse her child but having no milk to give and then slowly, relentlessly, seeing her child die. The pain becomes *anger* when we realize that there is enough food, shelter and medical care available to meet the needs of all people. And anger turns to wrenching *frustration* at our inability to develop structures and institutions that ensure that all people have access to the basics for a humane life.

While Christians and Christian churches have all too often supported the *status quo*, protecting their own interests rather than believing in the resurrection of the crucified Jesus, Jesus himself was the *Messiah of the poor*.[32] Jesus tuned into the Jewish understanding that God is on the side of the poor and oppressed, promising them blessing and liberation (Lk. 4.18-19; 6.20-21).[33] Moltmann makes the point that 'the gospel is realistic, not idealistic. It does not bring new teaching; it brings a new reality'.[34] This new reality, grounded in the resurrection of the Crucified One, ordains the poor with a new and indestructible dignity,[35] the awareness of which empowers them to rise up and realize that poverty is not their fate but their misfortune. N.T. Wright relates the *bodily* resurrection of Jesus directly to the *concrete* struggle for justice: 'To hope for a better future in this world—for the poor, the sick, the lonely and depressed, for…the hungry and homeless…the downtrodden and despairing…—is not something *else*, something extra, something tacked on to "the gospel" as an afterthought… It is a central, essential, vital and life-giving part of it.'[36] He illustrates this emphasis with the need for global debt relief: 'Precisely because Jesus Christ rose from the dead, God's new world has already broken in to the present, and Christian work for justice in the present, for instance in the ongoing campaigns for debt remission and ecological responsibility, take the shape they do.'[37] Jesus' 'resurrection, and the promise of God's new world that comes with it, creates a programme for change and offers to empower it. Those who believe the gospel have no choice but to follow'.[38]

---

32. So Moltmann, *The Way of Jesus Christ*, p. 102.
33. For the biblical view on poverty, see Athol Gill, 'Good News to the Poor', in Harold Pidwell, *A Gentle Bunyip: The Athol Gill Story* (Westlake, South Australia: Seaview Press, 2007), pp. 180-275.
34. Moltmann, *The Way of Jesus Christ*, p. 99.
35. Moltmann, *The Way of Jesus Christ*, p. 101.
36. Wright, *Surprised by Hope*, p. 204.
37. Wright, *Surprised by Hope*, pp. 224-33 (p. 224).
38. Wright, *Surprised by Hope*, p. 232.

Ecology

Usually theologians discuss ecological responsibility within the context of the doctrine of creation. Yet our focus on the resurrection suggests a *christological* grounding for ecological responsibility. The urgent need for such responsibility is beyond question. We humans are ontologically interwoven with, and bound into, the natural ecosystem. Nature is not only our environment. We are part of it! The air we breathe, the water we drink, the food we eat, the mountains, the forests and the oceans which stimulate body and soul are necessary for our survival. Recently a group of Nobel Laureates issued 'The St. James Palace Memorandum', in which they speak of the 'fierce urgency of the now', calling all social institutions to cooperate to reduce carbon emissions, lest 'what we value most is lost'.[39]

Two emphases in resurrection theology suggest that people who affirm the resurrection of Christ must be vitally concerned about climate control, biodiversity, protection of species and related matters: the interpretation of the resurrection as '*exaltation*' and '*ascension*'; and the emphasis on the *bodily* resurrection of Jesus.

Early Christians interpreted the resurrection as 'ascension' and as 'exaltation' to the 'right hand of God'.[40] On the basis of Christ's 'ascension' and 'exaltation', they confessed him as *Kurios* of the universe.[41] Such a cosmic understanding of Christ implies that the meaning of the resurrection applies to *all* of reality, not only to humanity but also to nature and the cosmos.[42] The resurrection of the Crucified One must therefore be understood not only in historical and anthropological terms but also in such a way that it includes the promise of healing for all of creation. While in early Christianity anxiety was experienced from 'the elemental spirits of the universe' (Col. 2.8) and healing came from Christ being proclaimed as the *Kurios* over those spirits (Col. 2.10; Eph. 1.20-23; Phil. 2.6-11), today the challenge comes from human greed and the subsequent exploitation of nature for economic profit or personal short-term gain. In the long term, apart from a functioning ecology, human survival is impossible. Faith in Christ, therefore, not only frees

---

39. St. James Palace Nobel Laureate Symposium, London, 26-28 May 2009 (accessed 13 March 2013).

40. Explicit references to the interpretation of the resurrection as exaltation are found in Acts 2.32-35; 5.30-32; Rom. 1.3-4; 8.34; Eph. 1.19-22. Other NT texts reflecting this interpretation are: 1 Thess. 1.10; Rom. 14.9; Col. 3.1; Eph. 2.6; 4.8-10; 1 Pet. 1.20-21; 3.18-22; Heb. 1.3; 4.14; 5.5; 7.26; 8.1; 10.12; 12.2; 1 Tim. 3.16; Mk 16.19; Mt. 28.18b-20; Lk. 9.51-52; 24.26; Acts 1.1-2, 21-22; 3.19-21; 13.32-33; Jn 3.14; 12.32, 34.

41. See, for instance, Phil. 2.6-11; Col. 1.15-20; 1 Tim. 3.16; 1 Pet. 3.22.

42. For more details, see Moltmann, *The Way of Jesus Christ*, Part VI: 'The Cosmic Christ', and also his *Ethics of Hope*, Part III, §3; Lorenzen, *Resurrection and Discipleship*, pp. 284-95.

us from our self-orientation and thus makes a community of human brothers and sisters possible but it also serves as a basis on which a partnership relation with nature can be restored.

While present-day theologians such as Crossan and Borg—despite being passionate about the relation of the resurrection to justice—consider the 'empty tomb' narratives and the implied bodily resurrection of Jesus as irrelevant for a meaningful resurrection faith,[43] Wright and others insist on the necessity of the *bodily* resurrection of Jesus so as to stress that the resurrection of Christ has not only spiritual significance but also entails the promise of 'the redemption of the entire cosmos'.[44]

Today, an active and concrete engagement in the struggle for a sustainable biosphere is imperative for Christians. 'The earth is the Lord's and the fullness thereof, the world and those who dwell therein' (Ps. 24.1). The ecological crisis is the result of human mismanagement, and this mismanagement is the consequence of a deep-seated and misguided self-interest. For that very reason, the healing process must also include a change of human consciousness and with it a modification of human action.

Empowerment

When it comes to justice, a major concern is its *implementation*, the transition from theory to historical and transformative *praxis*. For that we need more than laws and rights. We need not only a grand story that outlines the *imperative* and *content* of justice but also a *spirituality of justice*, a rebellious spirit mitigated with courage and compassion. Simone Weil says it well: 'What we need is for the spirit of justice to dwell within us. The spirit of justice is nothing other than the supreme and perfect flower of the madness of love.'[45]

As Christians we remind ourselves that as the story of Jesus provides the *imperative* for justice and helps to shape the *content* of justice, so the same Spirit of God who raised Jesus from the dead (Rom. 1.3b-4) *empowers* those who seek to implement justice. 'If the Spirit of him who raised

---

43. See, for instance, John Dominic Crossan, 'Historical Jesus as Risen Lord', in John Dominic Crossan, Luke Timothy Johnson and Werner H. Kelber, *The Jesus Controversy: Perspectives in Conflict* (Harrisburg, PA: Trinity Press International, 1999), pp. 1-47 (17-18, 25-26); Marcus Borg, 'The Truth of Easter', in Marcus J. Borg and N.T. Wright, *The Meaning of Jesus: Two Visions* (London: SPCK, 1999), pp. 129-42 (131).

44. Wright, *Surprised by Hope*, p. 83 (also pp. 203-206). Cf. Moltmann, *The Way of Jesus Christ*, pp. 256-57; Robinette, *Grammars of Resurrection*, pp. 367-69.

45. Simone Weil, 'Are We Struggling for Justice?' *Philosophical Investigations* 10.1 (January 1987), cited in Richard H. Bell, *Rethinking Justice: Restoring Our Humanity* (Lanham, MD: Lexington Books, 2007), p. 89. On 'Spirituality and Justice in Simone Weil', see Bell, *Rethinking Justice*, pp. 124-28.

Jesus from the dead dwells in you, he who raised Christ from the dead will give life to your mortal bodies also through his Spirit that dwells in you' (Rom. 8.11).

Conclusion

Will justice prevail—*ultimately*? Is it worthwhile to engage in the struggle for justice, whatever the cost? Looking into the *eye* of a Hazara refugee from Ghazni Province in Afghanistan who risks his life on an Indonesian fishing boat, or engaging with the *face* of a mother who is nursing her dying child makes the latter question superfluous. Nevertheless, aid budgets are cut, military budgets are inflated and refugees are treated like dispensable chattels. Thus the question remains: in the long run, will the passion for justice outlast selfishness, greed, misguided patriotism and disrespect for fellow human beings? I have argued that the foundational event of the Christian faith and the Christian church—the resurrection of the crucified Jesus—contains the promise that justice, both in its content and in its implementation, is related to God and therefore will ultimately prevail.

Jesus' resurrection is related to the struggle for justice on the personal, social and ecological level. The God who raised Jesus from the dead is the 'creator of heaven and earth'. God remains committed to and involved with God's creation and, through the life, death and resurrection of Jesus Christ, has not only manifested God's divine love and faithfulness (Jn 3.16) but was also reconciling the world to Godself (2 Cor. 5.17-21). This reconciliation must not be reduced to personal or spiritual experience. It is the down payment, the pledge, the promise, the 'first fruits' that anticipates the 'new heaven and the new earth'. 'Reconciliation', therefore, can be limited neither to the 'soul' nor to 'heaven'; it includes the whole of God's creation. Affirming the resurrection of Jesus Christ entails a commitment to define, protect and restore human life and dignity in the context of society and nature. By raising from the dead Jesus of Nazareth—the man for God and therefore for victims—God confirms being a 'God of justice', and since it was *Jesus* whom God raised from the dead, such justice can only be compassionate.

JUSTICE AND GENDER:
ON FEMINIST THEOLOGY AND RESTORATIVE JUSTICE

Heather Thomson

Both feminist theology and restorative justice are concerned with compassionate justice and with the restoration or establishment of right relations after wrongdoing has been perpetrated. This wrongdoing includes disrespect, criminal activity, violence and abuse—from the interpersonal to the larger-scale crimes against humanity. The establishment of right relations for both feminist theology and restorative justice includes dealing with the past in such a way that a better future may be made possible and involves not merely the establishment of justice in terms of fairness and reparation but also the healing of the relationships that were hurt or broken by the wrongdoing. Therefore, justice is understood not as an end in itself but as part of a larger framework of reconciliation (in restorative justice terms) or well-being and human flourishing (terms used in feminist theology). The meaning and the practice of justice, in these views, are governed by the desire for healing and wholeness.

Since feminist theology and restorative justice have much in common, it is a surprise to me that there is not much dialogue between the two disciplines. I have been reading in feminist theology for nearly thirty-five years and although justice between genders has been and remains a central theme of feminist theology, justice within the broader horizons of reconciliation and peace is not discussed in the way it is in restorative justice literature (where it is contrasted with punitive or retributive justice and related to reconciliation). In feminist theology, gender justice tends to be set within the broader categories of the 'flourishing' or the 'well-being' of all, or 'mending the world'. 'Reconciliation' is rarely used. Feminist theology is situated against punitive forms of justice, since they are a mark of patriarchy with its interests in maintaining hierarchies between people, the obedience of subordinates, control and violence. Therefore, in feminist theology justice is spoken of as liberation, and along with other liberation theologies, the social and political dimensions of justice-making are prominent themes, with implications for how we view sin (as structural), grace and redemption (as liberation from patriarchy and other forms of distortion and oppression).

What is missing in this view, which is a key feature of restorative justice, is the role of forgiveness in reconciling relationships after wrongdoing. There is virtually no feminist theology that incorporates forgiveness into its justice-making as restorative justice does. When I search in my university library, which has access to thousands of books, ebooks and online articles, for the subjects 'feminist theology' and 'forgiveness', I find there are '0' results. Mary Grey has also noted feminist theology's 'many difficulties around the whole area of forgiveness and reconciliation', and that 'there is still awkwardness and sensitivity around the subject of forgiveness; indeed it is often rejected outright'.[1] Feminist theology could well benefit from the careful biblical and theological work in restorative justice research on the complex, often fraught but at times profoundly constructive role of forgiveness in justice-making and reconciliation, which are all imperatives in the Christian faith and life.

On the other hand, I have been reading restorative justice literature in more recent years and have found that there is not much attention given to gender and the difference that makes when thinking about justice that reconciles and restores after hurt and wrongdoing. The massive wrongdoing against women for most of history, in most parts of the world, in which the Christian tradition is implicated through its support and sanctioning of the subordination of women, is not given the attention it deserves in restorative justice research. Miroslav Volf, influential in the theology of reconciliation, does devote a chapter to 'Gender Identity' in his *Exclusion and Embrace*, drawing on feminist theologians in his 'exploration of identity, otherness and reconciliation'.[2] He offers a trinitarian theology as the grounds for honouring otherness (rather than colonising others for our own interests), while also advocating openness to others for respectful, mutual, fluid gender-identity construction. His contribution is helpful to both feminist theology and restorative justice theology as each seeks ways of reconciling the differences between the genders that cause hurt and harm, and their supporting theological arguments. Generally, though, there is not much I have found in restorative justice theology that overtly deals with the difference gender makes in the work of reconciliation. Restorative justice can well benefit from the feminist theological awareness that we are always already implicated in power relations of exploitation and domination,[3] which need to be taken into account when justice-making in any particular situation.

---

1. Mary Grey, 'To Struggle with a Reconciled Heart: Reconciliation and Justice', *New Blackfriars* 85.995 (2004), pp. 56–73 (58).
2. Miroslav Volf, *Exclusion and Embrace: A Theological Exploration of Identity, Otherness, and Reconciliation* (Nashville: Abingdon Press, 1996), pp. 167-90.
3. Elisabeth Schüssler Fiorenza, *Jesus and the Politics of Interpretation* (New York: Continuum, 2001), p. 4.

I therefore see 'Justice and Gender' as an opportunity to create a mutually challenging and enriching conversation between feminist theology and restorative justice theology. I cannot try to represent 'feminist theology' as one, whole field of research, given its scope and diversity. Here, I will focus on a recent book by Elisabeth Schüssler Fiorenza in which she summarizes feminist theology as 'a theory and practice of justice', in conversation with many others who have contributed to this field.[4] I will add to that some recent work by Mary Grey, one of the few feminist theologians who are thinking through the relation between feminist theology, justice and reconciliation. Nor will I try to take on restorative justice as a whole field. Rather, I will focus on Christopher Marshall's *Compassionate Justice*, and allude also to his earlier work, *Beyond Retribution*,[5] with some reference to other works.

With the Eyes of a Feminist Theologian

In this first part, I consider restorative justice, in particular *Compassionate Justice*, through the eyes of a feminist theologian. Characteristic of feminist theology across its diversity is, first, a critique of androcentricity:

> The 'root experience' of feminism realizes that cultural 'common sense', dominant perspectives, scientific theories and historical knowledge are androcentric—that is, male biased—and therefore not objective accounts of reality but ideological mystification of domination and subordination.[6]

A second characteristic of feminist theology is its critique of patriarchy, 'a social system which maintains "men's social, ideological, sexual, and political dominance" over wo/men'.[7] Internal criticism within feminist theology challenged 'patriarchy' as being too narrow a tool of analysis. Poor white women and women of colour found that class and race were as important as gender in their suffering and desire for liberation.[8] Elisabeth Schüssler Fiorenza thus developed her notion of kyriarchy (the rule of the

---

4. Elisabeth Schüssler Fiorenza, *Transforming Vision: Explorations in Feminist Theology* (Minneapolis: Fortress Press, 2011), pp. 58, 59.

5. Christopher D. Marshall, *Beyond Retribution: A New Testament Vision for Justice, Crime, and Punishment* (Grand Rapids: Eerdmans, 2001); *Compassionate Justice: An Interdisciplinary Dialogue with Two Gospel Parables on Law, Crime, and Restorative Justice* (Eugene, OR: Cascade Books, 2012).

6. Schüssler Fiorenza, *Transforming Vision*, p. 57.

7. Schüssler Fiorenza, *Transforming Vision*, p. 57, citing Caroline Ramazanoglu, *Feminism and the Contradictions of Oppression* (London: Routledge, 1989), p. 33. Schüssler Fiorenza's use of the term 'wo/men' refers to women and men who suffer under patriarchy and other social systems of inequality, yet who struggle for liberation.

8. Mary Grey, 'It all began with Miriam... Feminist Theology's Journey from Liberation to Reconciliation', *FemTh* 20.3 (2012), pp. 222-29 (226-27).

Lords) as a more complex model and tool of analysis than patriarchy. In her words,

> Feminism as I understand it is not concerned only with gender inequities and marginalization. Kyriarchy perpetuates not only dehumanising sexism and gender stereotypes but also other forms of wo/men's oppression, such as racism, poverty, religious exclusion, and colonialism. Feminist studies therefore have the goal to alter fundamentally the nature of our knowledge of the world by exposing its deformations and limitations in and through androcentricism, racism, classism and cultural imperialism as well as by reconstructing more comprehensive and adequate accounts of the world.[9]

Two other characteristics of feminist theology are worth noting here before relating it to restorative justice, and they concern its starting point and end goal. Feminist theology takes as its starting point 'the centuries of wo/men's silencing and exclusion from religious leadership and the*logical studies' and 'the history of wo/men's subordination and exclusion'.[10] It is not abstract and theoretical but embedded in history, social locations and contexts. Women's subordination, silencing and exclusion were and are maintained by theological justifications, which vie continually with alternative theological thinking and practices of liberation and healing. The practices and rhetoric of contemporary theology are already related to the history of subordination and exclusion, whether by reinforcing this history or by transforming it. Feminist theology is committed not only to understanding the world as it is but also to its transformation. Thus feminist theology is concerned with a vision for 'transformative theories and practices of well-being in an unjust and violent world'.[11]

In describing the end goal of feminist theology, Schüssler Fiorenza uses 'a theory and practice of justice' as a key phrase, but she situates this within a broader vision of 'well-being', as seen above. Putting these terms together, she argues that both justice and well-being are political and spiritual matters that include *metanoia*, struggle, vision and world-making.[12] Other key terms for the goal of feminist theology include liberation, emancipation and transformation as well as mending or healing the world, all supported by a 'wisdom spirituality' concerned with wholeness and integrity.[13] Schüssler Fiorenza argues that these goals are genuinely theological (rather than distortions of the gospel message), but, for the power of the

9. Schüssler Fiorenza, *Transforming Vision*, p. 57.
10. Schüssler Fiorenza, *Transforming Vision*, p. 56.
11. Schüssler Fiorenza, *Transforming Vision*, p. 2.
12. Schüssler Fiorenza, *Transforming Vision*, pp. 15-19.
13. Schüssler Fiorenza, *Transforming Vision*, chap. 12: 'Towards a Feminist Wisdom Spirituality of Justice and Well-Being' (pp. 229-42).

gospel to be realized in the world, its 'world of grace', its 'radical democratic, critical-emancipatory vision' needs to be put into practice.[14]

These goals of feminist theology are very close to the goals of restorative justice, to mend or restore relations after wrong-doing and to practise gospel values of justice and grace. Schüssler Fiorenza almost presages the title of Christopher Marshall's *Compassionate Justice* when she argues for a spirituality of the empty tomb as 'a compassionate practice of honoring those who are unjustly killed in body and spirit'. In this she is inspired by the conviction that Jesus' 'struggle and all struggles for justice have not ended in execution and death. The tomb is empty'.[15] In contrast, however, there are no references in this book of Schüssler Fiorenza's, and very little in other feminist theological works, to 'reconciliation' and 'forgiveness' as goals and practices of feminist theology, a point to which I will return.

As I read *Compassionate Justice* with the eyes of a feminist theologian, I am grateful for Marshall's careful scholarship and inspired by his use of the two parables of the Good Samaritan and the Prodigal Son for our understanding of restorative justice through their visions of a graceful, compassionate God. I was also taken on a journey in which I had to wrestle with these parables for their implications in androcentricity and patriarchy. Let me explain.

When the parables of the Good Samaritan and the Prodigal Son are taken out of their context in the Gospel of Luke and put together as paradigmatic texts for restorative justice, what is noticeable is the complete absence of women. The characters in these parables are all male. Now the question is: does that matter? I noted that there were also no Australians in sight, and although I am an Australian, that did not prevent me learning from these parables and being inspired and challenged by them. What is the difference?

For one, 'Australians' as currently constituted did not exist in the first century CE, whereas women most definitely did. What androcentricity does is to write out people who were actually there, thereby making them invisible in story and history. I recognize that in the context within which the parable of the Prodigal Son is told in the Gospel of Luke, there is another parable in which a woman is featured, looking for a lost coin—a symbol of the kingdom of God which seeks out the lost in order to bring them home.[16] Nevertheless, in Luke, and also in *Compassionate Justice*, the overall focus is on male characters as agents of God's revelation, at least inclining one to the view that these parables are implicated in androcentricity.

---

14. Schüssler Fiorenza, *Transforming Vision*, pp. 20, 54.
15. Schüssler Fiorenza, *Transforming Vision*, p. 242 (for both quotations).
16. For the significance of the Lukan parables featuring female characters, see Barbara E. Reid, 'Beyond Petty Pursuits and Wearisome Widows: Three Lukan Parables', *Interpretation* 56.3 (July 2002), pp. 284-94.

What focused my attention in the parable of the Prodigal Son is the absence of the mother of the two sons, whom one presumes is also the wife of the compassionate father. Indeed, biblical scholar Jane Schaberg refers to this text as 'the parable of the missing mother'.[17] We have no idea how the mother feels about her younger son leaving with his inheritance, nor how she reacts when he returns. She is not mentioned when the party is organized to celebrate the return of the son who was lost, who was dead but returned to life. In the focus on the father and his sons, she is obliterated.

If this were not part of a larger—or should I say massive—marginalization and silencing of women in Christian scriptures, history, liturgy, hymnody, church leadership and so on, it might not matter that this parable just happened to focus on a father and his sons. But it is, and it does. And although these matters are being addressed by the contemporary church, we cannot underestimate the effect this history has had on people's identity, both men's and women's. For me to be in the church as a teacher and leader, I have had to live against the grain, wrestling down inner voices that say, 'Who do you think you are, being in leadership, *and* having something to say?' I do not want to visit this upon our daughters.

What makes this situation more difficult is that this is a parable most likely told by Jesus, for who else would tell such an unlikely story of a father's unexpected, abundant and compassionate response? How ironic, then, if this story of restorative justice is implicated in the injustice against women whereby the woman is written out in the interests of the father and the sons.

What are we to make of this? In searching for how to interpret these two parables with the eyes of feminist theology, I was helped by an article Janet Martin Soskice wrote entitled, 'Can a Feminist Call God "Father"?'[18] Soskice details the plight of feminist-minded women and men who find themselves faced with what seems to be, and was named as such by Mary Daly as, an irredeemably patriarchal religion. Soskice points out that although 'God is designated "father" only *11 times* in the entire Old Testament, and is never invoked as such in prayer', God is 'described as "father" over 170 times by Jesus in the New Testament, and is never invoked in prayer by any other title'.[19] Not only is 'father' language dominant in reference to God in the New Testament, but it has the authority of Jesus himself.

---

17. Jane Schaberg, 'Luke', in *Women's Bible Commentary: Expanded edition, with Apocrypha* (ed. Carol A. Newsom and Sharon H. Ringe; Louisville, KY: Westminster/John Knox Press, 1998), pp. 363-80 (370).

18. Janet Martin Soskice, 'Can a Feminist call God "Father"?', in *Speaking the Christian God: The Holy Trinity and the Challenge of Feminism* (ed. A.F. Kimel, Jr; Grand Rapids: Eerdmans, 1992), pp. 81–94.

19. Soskice, 'Can a Feminist call God "Father"?', p. 88.

Some Christian women who have had their consciousness raised find that their only option is to leave the church. For Soskice and other Christian feminists, however, the scriptures are not only, nor are they absolutely, androcentric and patriarchal. They are also the foundational site for justice and liberation. The grounds on which Christian feminists stand to justify the critique of patriarchy and to call for social, political and spiritual transformation are found within the scriptures. What Soskice does is to show how the designation of God as 'father' has undergone a transformation itself, from patriarchal associations, to the yearning of God in hope (see Jer. 3.19: 'I thought you would call me Father'), to Jesus' scandalous address to God as 'abba'. In this 'turning of the symbol' of fatherhood, the patriarchal image of the father is subverted.[20]

What is important, argues Soskice, is not that men or fathers happen to be the characters in biblical parables or stories, or that God is called father and not mother. What is important is whether these depictions and designations contribute to patriarchy or subvert and undermine it. Applying this to the parables in question, especially the Prodigal Son, we can say that it contributes to the subversion of the patriarchal view of fatherhood and hence to the feminist justice agenda of righting the wrongs done to women in the name of patriarchy. The compassionate father in this parable shows no signs of being concerned with his own honour or with the punishment of his prodigal son, putting him in his place and demanding obedience, points drawn out by Marshall in *Compassionate Justice*. Rather, this father risks making a fool of himself as he rushes ignominiously towards his approaching son, driven only by his love for him and his concern that he is alive and has found his way home.

In a feminist reading of the Prodigal Son and its contribution to restorative justice, I remain concerned about the injustice of women's invisibility. Yet this parable also contributes to feminist theology's interest in transforming relationships beyond their construction within patriarchal/kyriarchal systems. When the symbolism of fatherhood is turned into a compassionate one, patriarchal fatherhood can no longer be sanctioned by this parable, either for the father of the prodigal son or, by implication, for the fatherhood of God.

What, then, of the parable of the Good Samaritan in a feminist reading? Again, it involves all male characters, and again, the actions of the Samaritan and the interpretation of him by Jesus undermines and confronts any social relations based on hierarchy, honour and control. It speaks to and inspires the feminist concern for compassion, well-being and human flourishing, beyond the divisions that set us apart and value us differently in relation to each other.

---

20. Soskice, 'Can a Feminist call God "Father"?', p. 90.

It is worth noting, though, that if feminist-minded women want to feel included in this parable, we also have to feel its offence. That is, it is not only a matter of taking our feminist stance and interpreting scripture but also of allowing scripture to interpret us. To get at what that might mean, perhaps this parable could be retold now as a parable inclusive of women. This will be specific to a particular context, but it is also an invitation for others to retell this parable to bring it alive today, including its shock and offence:

> A certain woman was going down to Canberra from Sydney and, stopping for a rest half-way, fell into the hands of some young women who robbed her, stripped her, beat her, and went away, leaving her half dead. Now by chance, a priest was going down that road; and when she saw her, she passed by on the other side. So likewise a theologian, when she came to the place and saw her, passed by on the other side.
>
> But a Muslim, while travelling, came near her; and when she saw her, she was moved with compassion...

The effect on me of hearing the parable told in this way is significant and, indeed, twofold: on the one hand, it is such a refreshing change to have women as the active agents of God's revelation, even if some of them are playing the baddies. On the other hand, it does feel shocking and offensive that a woman priest or theologian would not be moved by compassion, but would rather cross to the other side of the road. *Surely* women priests and theologians would not act like that?

In telling the parable this way I realized that, despite my better self and what I have learned thus far about equality and inclusiveness, it was a challenge to some of my underlying assumptions. I identified with a group whom I believed was just a bit better, more pure and right (that is, feminist-minded women and men), over against others who have not quite got it right, are less pure or are downright wrong (those who are gender-blind or misogynist). But that is precisely what Jesus challenges. We cannot genuinely be engaged in justice and reconciliation until we get over that kind of thinking. We need, in Miroslav Volf's terms, to move from being 'possessors' of the truth to becoming 'seekers' of the truth.[21] And it does help me to realize this when the parable is retold in a way inclusive of women as active agents, including the possibility of me, or my group, being at fault.

I have so far considered these restorative justice texts from feminist perspectives of androcentricity and patriarchy. What might feminist theology learn from restorative justice?

---

21. Miroslav Volf, *The End of Memory: Remembering Rightly in a Violent World* (Grand Rapids: Eerdmans, 2006), p. 57.

Through the Eyes of Restorative Justice

What I have appreciated about restorative justice as a field of biblical and theological work is that it contains the larger vision of reconciliation and peace, while emerging from practice, including from some very difficult situations of wrongdoing: inter-personal disputes, crimes, abuse, long-term enmity and gross violation of human rights. My experience with the work of restorative justice theology and practice are from places like South Africa, Northern Ireland and Israel/Palestine, as well as Volf's work from the former Yugoslavia. When Christian theologians in these contexts see the justice of God as restorative rather than punitive, they are faced with a real struggle, inwardly and in their social and political environments, to put that into practice. They wrestle with how to deal with the past, and with the role of forgiveness, in making reconciliation and peace between former enemies a real possibility. This practical theology has yielded some very wise insights into memory, shame, forgiveness, justice and the cost of reconciliation.

Why, then, does feminist theology not take up these questions in the same terms? It may be that feminist theologians are also involved in restorative justice theology and practice under its own terms, and in pastoral theology which reflects on the role of forgiveness for reconciling human relations after wrongdoing. It may be that the end goal of feminist theology—that is, mending the world, well-being and flourishing—are simply different terms for peace and reconciliation, which are the end goals of restorative justice. My guess is that it is more a matter of feminist theology and restorative justice theology being on different sides of the equation that relates justice to reconciliation. For feminist theology, 'no reconciliation without justice' seems to describe its basic stance, whereas for restorative justice theologians it is more a matter of 'no justice without reconciliation'. For those committed to peace, world-mending and reconciliation, both sides of this equation are of course necessary, and it is important that they be held together. One reason, however, for a lack of attention to reconciliation in feminist theology may well be that justice is yet to be found for many wo/men.

Mary Grey offers some reflections on this question. She notes that feminist theologians have spent 'an immense amount of energy' on what Carter Heyward has called 'a passion for justice-making', relating this also to peace movements in various contexts.[22] Yet there has been a suspicion of the role of forgiveness and reconciliation in this justice-making endeavour. Grey offers three reasons why this may be the case.

First, she draws attention to some of the contexts from which women suffer and which are the focus of feminist theological work: domestic violence, sexual abuse, the trafficking of women and children, and 'the vested

---

22. Grey, 'To Struggle with a Reconciled Heart', p. 58.

interests between government, police, truck-drivers and businessmen that keep it going'.[23] Even the violence against women in the Bible received scant attention until the rise of feminist theology. These were all 'tolerated as part of a deeply patriarchal, or kyriarchal, status quo'.[24]

Second, 'the Church's response, via the confessional or even counselling has been frequently to order the woman to forgive... Such is the emphasis on forgiveness that reconciliation without justice became the norm'.[25] Feminist theology holds the memory of 'reconciliation' and 'forgiveness' as forms of further abuse that lacked justice. This situation was reinforced by gender stereotypes whereby women were expected to be more irenic than men, willing to sacrifice their own needs and desires for the sake of family unity and peace. In a situation of domestic violence, for example, such expectations reinforce and sanction injustice.

The third point Grey makes is that the suffering, endurance and renunciation of happiness of women and other victim groups have been justified by a spirituality of holiness and Christ-likeness. She names this a 'distortion' of the theology of the cross, 'that enduring suffering, never mind its unjust origins, is identifying with Jesus on the Cross, and obtaining a reward in Heaven'.[26] Therefore, feminist Christologies have had to counter such views, including patriarchal views of Jesus' obedience to the authority of the Father, seeing instead Jesus' obedience as relating to the vision of God's restorative justice and the task of healing the world (from the Hebrew phrase, *tikkun olam*).[27]

Given this history of distortion experienced by wo/men whereby forgiveness and reconciliation are often without justice and are theologically justified as such, there is much work to be done if feminist theologians are to embrace forgiveness and reconciliation as genuine expressions of the task of justice-making and mending the world. Restorative justice theory and theology can contribute to this work. It wrestles with the relation between forgiveness and justice such that justice remains a central concern, yet the way justice is *enacted* can itself be part of the healing and mending of relationships that have been distorted by wrong relations and wrongdoing. In a section on forgiveness in *Compassionate Justice*, Marshall reflects that, in the parable of the Prodigal Son, the relationship between the father and the son is restored not because of any punishment that the son had to undertake but because the father, without using any words, showed by his actions that

---

23. Grey, 'To Struggle with a Reconciled Heart', p. 59.
24. Grey, 'To Struggle with a Reconciled Heart', p. 59.
25. Grey, 'To Struggle with a Reconciled Heart', p. 59.
26. Grey, 'To Struggle with a Reconciled Heart', p. 60.
27. Grey, 'To Struggle with a Reconciled Heart', p. 62; see also Grey, 'It all began with Miriam', p. 229.

his son was forgiven. More than that, he threw a feast in his son's honour, the goal of which was 'to lift the cloak of shame from his son's shoulders and underscore his reinstatement as an esteemed member of the family'.[28] On the role of confession, compassion and forgiveness in the work of justice, Marshall has this to say:

> Perhaps the profoundest insight of restorative justice theory, and the secret to the power of its simple mechanism of bringing victims and offenders together to talk about what has happened, is its recognition that offenders and victims are on parallel journeys of dealing with the crushing impact of shame—for one, the shame of *doing* harm, for the other, the shame of *being* harmed—and that each party, paradoxically, holds the key to the other's healing. This key, moreover, is the mutual conferral of honor.[29]

There is a danger in quoting this summary statement out of the context of Marshall's careful qualifications and hard-won wisdom concerning justice and the role of forgiveness, punishment and reconciliation in this work. As he knows, not all victims and offenders find reconciliation in this 'simple mechanism', and in order for it to serve reconciliation as far as possible, well-trained, skilled mediators are required who are sensitive to the particular people and contexts involved. This is not a matter of perpetrators seeking forgiveness or victims being pressured into forgiveness in order to avoid justice, but a mutual, *voluntary* process whereby both the one who has done harm and the one who has been harmed seek the healing of both, which may involve confession, repentance and restitution on behalf of the offender.

While feminist theology holds the memory that 'forgiveness' and 'reconciliation' have been used in the interests of further injustice and abuse, it can perhaps be more open to the healing and positive work contained within restorative justice theology. While the feminist hermeneutics of suspicion can serve restorative justice work by ensuring that justice is not a casualty in the work of reconciliation, and that injustices against wo/men remain central to its work, restorative justice can bring a bit more grace to the feminist passion for justice-making. Miroslav Volf in his *Free of Charge* gives the book the subtitle: *Giving and Forgiving in a Culture Stripped of Grace*. In this book, even the act of forgiveness is set within a larger context of God's grace that precedes it. In the following passage, Volf uses terms reminiscent of the citation from Marshall above, which notes the importance of honour in the healing from wrong-doing:

> But a person with a shattered life…doesn't first need Christ to forgive her or to forgive through her. Before anything else, she needs Christ to cradle her, to nurse her with the milk of divine love, to hold her in his arms like an

---

28. Marshall, *Compassionate Justice*, pp. 231-32.
29. Marshall, *Compassionate Justice*, p. 231.

inestimable gem, to sing her songs of gentle care and firm protection, and to restore her to herself as a beloved and treasured being.[30]

If we live and move and have our being in God's world of grace, then that should govern our practices of forgiveness as well as our justice-making.

I have argued that feminist theology and restorative justice theology would mutually benefit from having closer dialogue about their starting points, end goals, work and practices. They stand to keep each other honest and true to genuinely theological commitments which they hold in common, that is, to the work of justice that will mend the world.

---

30. Miroslav Volf, *Free of Charge: Giving and Forgiving in a Culture Stripped of Grace* (Grand Rapids: Zondervan, 2005), p. 206.

Parable as Paradigm for Public Theology: Relating Theological Vision to Social Life

David J. Neville

The publication of Christopher Marshall's book, *Compassionate Justice*,[1] is important for various reasons. For those interested in the parables of Jesus, Marshall's discussion of two of Jesus' best-known parables is learned, sagacious and compelling, reminiscent of his earlier contributions to biblical scholarship.[2] For those concerned with the theory and practice of restorative justice, this book is a major contribution to the field. And for those in search of resources for articulating a responsible Christian ethic in a pluralist context, *Compassionate Justice* is a landmark work. In short, this is a book characterized by broad vision and deep perceptiveness.

Marshall's book is the fifteenth volume in Wipf & Stock's Theopolitical Visions series, whose stated purpose is to resource the conversation on the role of theology in public life. The opening paragraph of the series preface reads as follows: 'Theopolitical Visions seeks to open up new vistas on public life, hosting fresh conversations between theology and political theory. This series assembles writers who wish to revive theopolitical

---

1. Christopher D. Marshall, *Compassionate Justice: An Interdisciplinary Dialogue with Two Gospel Parables on Law, Crime, and Restorative Justice* (Eugene, OR: Cascade Books, 2012). This essay responds to what this book by Marshall affirms about relating 'parabolic truth' to public issues today. It therefore marks a moment in a continuing conversation that is carried further in Marshall's essay within this volume. Despite Marshall's more explicit and detailed statement regarding parables as paradigmatic for public theology, I consider it worth reiterating that the continuing public pertinence of any one of Jesus' parables depends on discerning how well it expresses the theological cum moral vision of Jesus.

2. See, for example, Christopher D. Marshall, *Faith as a Theme in Mark's Narrative* (Cambridge: Cambridge University Press, 1989); *Kingdom Come: The Kingdom of God in the Teaching of Jesus* (Auckland: Impetus Publications, rev. edn, 1993); *Beyond Retribution: A New Testament Vision for Justice, Crime, and Punishment* (Grand Rapids: Eerdmans, 2001); 'The Moral Vision of the Beatitudes: The Blessings of Revolution', in *Faith and Freedom: Christian Ethics in a Pluralist Culture* (ed. David Neville and Philip Matthews; Adelaide: ATF Press, 2003), pp. 11-33; and *The Little Book of Biblical Justice: A Fresh Approach to the Bible's Teachings on Justice* (Intercourse, PA: Good Books, 2005).

imagination for the sake of our common good.' Whether or not this is precisely how Marshall conceived his contribution to this series, his interdisciplinary dialogue undoubtedly comprises a vital and edifying theopolitical conversation for the common good. This defining dialogical dimension of Marshall's work, which is explicitly referred to in his preface and is characteristic of much of his oeuvre, opens up the question of the role of the biblical witness in what currently goes by the name of public theology.

Relating Parabolic Truth to Public Concerns Today

In view of the church's historic regard for 'Scripture', the relation between the Bible and *public* theology is an important topic because theological discourse in today's predominantly pluralist contexts can no longer presume basic biblical literacy, let alone the traditional privileging of the Bible as a principal source and norm for thought and practice. Although Marshall does not directly address the question of the relation between the Bible and public theology in *Compassionate Justice*,[3] at various points he touches on this issue in helpful ways. For example, in his introduction to *Compassionate Justice*, Marshall begins by noting the influence that the two parables of the Good Samaritan and the Prodigal Son have had on Western thought and culture. He then commends a dialogical process wherein these parables are interpreted in light of insights from present-day developments in such disciplines as social psychology, moral philosophy and legal theory while also continuing to resource contemporary discussion on a range of public concerns, provided biblical parables continue to have 'cultural currency'.[4] Although the cultural legacy of the parables of the Good Samaritan and the Prodigal Son is (historically) significant beyond measure, the future of that legacy in post-Christian Western societies is not assured. Alongside David Bentley Hart's reminder that Western culture continues both to treasure and to trade upon moral values grounded in the Judeo-Christian tradition,[5] Marshall's interdisciplinary dialogue not only honours but also safeguards the cultural legacy of these parables.

In addition, at the beginning of the third and final part of his book, Marshall ruminates on interpretive challenges associated with relating 'parabolic truth' to public issues today. As he observes,

---

3. See, however, his earlier discussions of this topic in *Beyond Retribution*, pp. 17-31, and in 'What Language Shall I Borrow? The Bilingual Dilemma of Public Theology', *Stimulus* 13.3 (August 2005), pp. 11-18, as well as in his feature essay within this volume, 'Parables as Paradigms for Public Theology'.

4. Marshall, *Compassionate Justice*, pp. 1-3.

5. David Bentley Hart, *Atheist Delusions: The Christian Revolution and Its Fashionable Enemies* (New Haven: Yale University Press, 2009).

> There are major complications entailed in moving from the imaginative world of Jesus' parables to the world of normative ethics or the world of institutional practice today, and any attempt to bridge the gap must grapple with the peculiar characteristics and theological intent of Jesus' parabolic discourse. That does not mean that the message of the parables should be restricted to purely private religious or existential concerns alone... The stories themselves mirror the social and political realities of everyday life in first-century Palestine, and their subject matter ought to be allowed to inform reflection on everyday issues of social and political life today as well, including issues of crime and punishment.[6]

Whether the (accurate) observation that the parables of Jesus mirror first-century socio-political realities authorizes the judgment that such parables should inform reflection and debate on present-day socio-political concerns is perhaps open to question or at least qualification. More contentious, however, is what Marshall proceeds to affirm, namely, that 'the relevance of the parables to this end [that is, reflection on everyday issues of social and political life today] lies precisely in their character as *parables*'.[7] Marshall neither imagines nor postulates any direct or straightforward 'translation' of parabolic meaning into social theory or public policy, but he does consider that the parables of the Good Samaritan and the Prodigal Son open up human imagination to what is otherwise inconceivable in social relations made possible by 'the restorative reality of God's justice' displayed in the life-story of Jesus.[8] For that to occur, however, two dimensions of these parables need to be taken into account: their common or realistic ethical dimension and their extraordinary eschatological dimension. At one level, these parables describe commonplace circumstances and realistic, albeit challenging, moral guidance. At another level, however, their moral vision is premised on an understanding of divine character that resources morality analogous to itself. As Marshall puts it, 'In depicting such an extraordinary expression of sacrificial and extensive love [on the part of both the compassionate Samaritan and the compassionate father of his prodigal son], the parables implicitly summon their listeners to open their hearts to the eschatological power of God's kingdom at work in their midst in order to inspire, empower, and sustain a similar, all-surpassing generosity of spirit in their own lives as well.'[9]

Thus, according to Marshall, both the commonplace and extraordinary dimensions of these two parables of Jesus contribute to their continuing relevance to socio-political issues today. Their realistic dimension makes them morally compelling, whereas their 'eschatological' dimension points

---

6. Marshall, *Compassionate Justice*, pp. 249-50.
7. Marshall, *Compassionate Justice*, p. 250.
8. Marshall, *Compassionate Justice*, p. 250.
9. Marshall, *Compassionate Justice*, p. 251.

to the need for divine empowerment both to live up to and to live out their moral challenge. This would seem to imply that the continuing public pertinence of the parables of the Good Samaritan and the Prodigal Son lies less in their character as parables per se than in their character as parabolic expressions of Jesus' theological cum moral vision.[10] In other words, these parables articulate a particular intuition of God's compassionate character that both calls for and calls forth comparable conduct on the part of people. Given this particular theological intuition, however, how do such parables retain their public pertinence within a pluralist context in which many, if not most, people neither share nor honour the theological vision expressed in Jesus' parables?[11] Moreover, is the theological vision expressed in the two Lukan parables explored by Marshall to be found in all of Jesus' parables? Or is it the case that Marshall's focus on the parables of the Good Samaritan and the Prodigal Son is the result not only of their continued familiarity and broad appeal, even in post-Christian times, but also of an apprehension that the theological vision of these particular parables lies at the heart of both Jesus' messianic mission and the Christian gospel?

The question of whether the theological vision of the parables of the Good Samaritan and the Prodigal Son animates all of Jesus' parables might well strike some as strange. Surely the same basic theological vision is represented in all of Jesus' parables. The problem, however, is that the parables attributed to Jesus derive from diverse sources and are transmitted via different traditions, which means that all are filtered through secondary conceptual grids. Although Marshall considers his two selected parables as authentic parables of Jesus, it is necessary for him to acknowledge that they come to us from Luke's special tradition(s), a situation that ordinarily causes consternation in relation to claiming Jesus traditions as authentic.[12]

---

10. In the biblical tradition, theological vision is inseparable from moral responsibility, that is, human response that mirrors divine character and action in social relations. Further references to theological vision within this study presume this theological-moral integrity.

11. Space permitting, I had intended to revisit Karl Barth's appeal to the concept of 'parable' to explore, within a pluralist context, the relation of the Christian community to the broader civil community, an idea I still find potentially fruitful despite the various criticisms levelled against it. And in light of Marshall's Anabaptist convictions, I had also hoped to correlate his perception of the parables of Jesus as paradigmatic for public theology to John Howard Yoder's argument that the church's paradigmatic public role is to bear witness to God's sovereign reign by being its 'first fruits'. A fine starting point for reflecting on such matters is provided by Alain Epp Weaver, 'Parables of the Kingdom and Religious Plurality: With Barth and Yoder toward a Nonresistant Public Theology', *MQR* 72 (1998), pp. 411-40.

12. Multiple attestation is a key criterion in historical Jesus scholarship, although it should not be applied in isolation or inflexibly. For a critique, see Mark Goodacre, 'Criticizing the Criterion of Multiple Attestation: The Historical Jesus and the

Yet something convinces Marshall (and many others) that even though the parables of the Good Samaritan and the Prodigal Son are found only in Luke's Gospel, they are true to Jesus and his understanding of God's ways, especially in relation to people.

With this view I am in basic agreement, but I do not think that all of the parables attributed to Jesus are as transparently true to Jesus and his intuition of divine reign as the parables of the Good Samaritan and the Prodigal Son—at least with respect to justice. Brief consideration of three other parables attributed to Jesus illustrates my reason for making this point. Two of these are contrasting parables found only in Matthew's Gospel, whereas the third is another Lukan parable with a questionable parallel in Matthew. Each of these three parables proffers a perspective on justice, whether divine or human, but only one envisages a conception of justice comparable to the compassionate justice evoked by the parables of the Good Samaritan and the Prodigal Son.

Conceptions of Justice in Three Other Parables of Jesus

The first of these parables is one to which Marshall himself refers because it, like those of the Good Samaritan and the Prodigal Son, features the relatively rare Greek verb for responding to another's plight with pity or compassion, *splanchnizomai*.[13] The parable is the uniquely Matthean parable of the Unforgiving Slave (Mt. 18.23-35), wherein a king initially releases an exorbitantly indebted slave and forgives his unrepayable debt (18.27). Subsequently, after learning that his compassionate mercy was not emulated in relation to another slave's relatively trivial debt, the king asks the morally compelling question: 'Was it not necessary for you also to have shown mercy to your fellow-slave, as I myself showed mercy to you?' (18.33).

In a subsection on 'education for compassion', Marshall comments briefly on the cultural and moral influences of both biblical tradition and classical culture on Western civilization. Within this context, he makes this comparative judgment: 'The stories of Jesus, like the Good Samaritan, the Prodigal Son, and the Unforgiving Servant, have done more historically to inspire and democratize compassion in Western society than was ever

---

Question of Sources', in *Jesus, Criteria, and the Demise of Authenticity* (ed. Chris Keith and Anthony Le Donne; London: T. & T. Clark International, 2012), pp. 152-69.

13. This verb, used symbolically to mean pity, compassion or mercy, occurs twelve times in the Synoptic Gospels but nowhere else in the New Testament. See Mt. 9.36; 14.14; 15.32; 18.27; 20.34; Mk 1.41; 6.34; 8.2; 9.22; Lk. 7.13; 10.33; 15.20. The cognate noun, *splanchnon*, occurs in Lk. 1.78 and ten further times in the New Testament, once in a literal sense in Acts 1.18 and elsewhere symbolically to designate the centre of a person's affective dimension, which in English we refer to as the heart. See Marshall, *Compassionate Justice*, pp. 120-21.

achieved by exposure to classical literature.'[14] Although Marshall's book composes an impressive argument in support of this judgment in relation to the parables of the Good Samaritan and the Prodigal Son, it is debatable, if not doubtful, in relation to the parable of the Unforgiving Slave. This is because neither compassion nor justice—let alone compassionate justice—has the final say in this parable. For at the end of the parable, the slave's lord, angered by the discrepancy between his own magnanimity and his slave's mercilessness, puts him at the 'mercy' of torturers until he repays the entirety of his unrepayable debt. This occurs, moreover, after he has already released the slave and forgiven his debt. Of course, this is a parable, so not every detail should be squeezed for theological or moral meaning. Commenting on this parable in an earlier work, Marshall warns against pressing its logic too far: 'The reaction of the king is intended to underline the eschatological seriousness of the demand placed upon the messianic community to practice forgiveness, as well as to clarify that forgiveness is not a matter of cheap grace or eternal leniency.'[15]

With respect to this parable itself, Marshall's point is fair and well made. Even allowing for the interpretive guideline of end stress,[16] one need not take this parable to mean that forgiveness within God's heavenly reign is enforced by means of torment. Read within its narrative context, however, Marshall's more magnanimous reading of this parable comes aground on Jesus' concluding interpretive application in Mt. 18.35. There, according to Matthew, Jesus affirms that his heavenly father will likewise do to those within the community of faith who do not sincerely forgive others within it. In short, within God's heavenly reign, failure to forgive leads to unremitting torment. One might be inclined to read this concluding application as but another example of Jesus' use of hyperbole to provoke circumspection, except that Matthew's Gospel is peppered with parables that not only end violently but also picture God and God's agents as violent avengers. In other words, both the ending to the parable of the Unforgiving Slave and its application at the culmination of Jesus' fourth discourse in the Gospel are of a piece with a prominent dimension of Matthew's theology—divine judgment as severe and unremitting retribution. So although it is possible to

14. Marshall, *Compassionate Justice*, p. 274.
15. Marshall, *Beyond Retribution*, p. 77.
16. See Klyne R. Snodgrass, *Stories with Intent: A Comprehensive Guide to the Parables of Jesus* (Grand Rapids: Eerdmans, 2008), p. 30: 'For most parables what comes at the end is the clinching indicator of intent.' Snodgrass's interpretation of the parable of the Unforgiving Slave (pp. 61-77) supports Marshall's reading. Cf., by contrast, Warren Carter, *Matthew and the Margins: A Socio-Political and Religious Reading* (Sheffield: Sheffield Academic Press, 2000), pp. 370-75, and 'Resisting and Imitating the Empire: Imperial Paradigms in Two Matthean Parables', *Interpretation* 56.3 (July 2002), pp. 260-72 (262-68).

appeal to the parable of the Unforgiving Slave in support of biblical precedent for compassionate justice, it seems more likely that this parable has played a part in inculcating a retributive conception of justice unmitigated by compassion. With reference to this parable, Dale Allison remarks that 'a king, out of mercy, releases a servant from debt. But when that servant mistreats another, the king intervenes with punishment. In this story the king lets himself suffer wrong; but when it is another who suffers, mercy gives way to justice'.[17] For Allison, this parable features both mercy and justice but not in such a way that justice is qualified by mercy or compassion. Mercy gives way to justice rather than ameliorating justice.

A Matthean parable more in keeping with the Lukan parables of the Good Samaritan and the Prodigal Son is the parable of the Workers in the Vineyard (Mt. 20.1-16). Read by some as depicting the injustices associated with land ownership and tenure in first-century Palestine, such that the figure of the vineyard owner is unlikely to represent God,[18] *Matthew's* perspective, contextually construed, seems to be that this parable displays the counterintuitive justice of God's heavenly reign. Within its narrative context, the parable of the Workers in the Vineyard is framed by mirror-image sayings of reversal (Mt. 19.30; 20.16). This tethers the parable to the preceding passage in which a commandment-keeping person with many possessions asks Jesus what good he must do to possess eternal life (Mt. 19.16-30). Read in relation to Jesus' exchange with the wealthy young man and the subsequent conversation with his disciples about heavenly rewards, the parable emphasizes that the justice of God's heavenly reign surpasses conventional conceptions of justice. As Klyne Snodgrass discerns, 'The parable instructs us that God's treatment of people, his judgment, is not based on human reckoning and human standards of justice.'[19]

Following Marshall's lead, Darrin Snyder Belousek appeals to the two parables of the Prodigal Son and the Workers in the Vineyard as evidence that 'Jesus' parables about God's kingdom...provoke a gestalt shift in our

---

17. Dale C. Allison, Jr, *The Sermon on the Mount: Inspiring the Moral Imagination* (New York: Crossroad, 1999), p. 96.

18. See, e.g., William R. Herzog II, *Parables as Subversive Speech: Jesus as Pedagogue of the Oppressed* (Louisville, KY: Westminster/John Knox Press, 1994), pp. 79-97; Luise Schottroff, *The Parables of Jesus* (trans. Linda M. Maloney; Minneapolis: Fortress Press, 2006), pp. 209-17; and Ada María Isasi-Díaz, 'A *Mujerista* Hermeneutic of Justice and Human Flourishing', in *The Bible and the Hermeneutics of Liberation* (ed. Alejandro F. Botta and Pablo R. Andiñach; Atlanta: SBL, 2009), pp. 181-95. Especially with respect to biblical conceptions of justice and their reception in the history of interpretation, such studies present a necessary challenge to traditional interpretations of the parable of the Workers in the Vineyard.

19. Snodgrass, *Stories with Intent*, p. 376.

seeing and thinking about the aim and substance of justice'.[20] For Snyder Belousek, both of these parables transcend and thereby overturn the paradigm of retribution or proportionate recompense. Regarding the calibre of justice displayed in the parable of the Workers in the Vineyard, he remarks: 'God's justice, the parable reveals, is not rooted in retribution, contrary to human expectation. Justice belongs to God, and God's just will is expressed in generosity.'[21] To interpret the parable of the Workers in the Vineyard as intimating that divine justice transcends the paradigm of retributive justice is alluring. As Nathan Eubank demonstrates, however, divine recompense for human deeds is an integral dimension of Matthew's theological-moral framework.[22] Within its Matthean setting, then, the parable of the Workers in the Vineyard indicates that divine recompense is never less than fair but may also stretch the bounds of what is generally considered just by tempering recompense with mercy. Thus, the justice of the God of Jesus is 'value-enhanced', one might say, such that one must speak of divine justice as merciful or compassionate justice. In the divine economy, as conceptualized by Jesus, strict or bare justice is closer to injustice than to justice tempered or value-enhanced by mercy.[23]

Crucially, however, for such value-enhanced justice to be recognized as justice, the justice of divine reign must also be value-challenging, provoking a change of outlook and shift in moral orientation so as to be able to embrace the counterintuitive calibre of divine justice.[24] After all, for one who operates with a strictly retributive or just-deserts mindset, value-enhanced justice simply seems unfair. (Consider, for example, the reactions of the other son and the workers who did a full day's work in the parables

20. Darrin W. Snyder Belousek, *Atonement, Justice, and Peace: The Message of the Cross and the Mission of the Church* (Grand Rapids: Eerdmans, 2012), pp. 381-88 (382). For Snyder Belousek, the parable of the Prodigal Son addresses commutative justice, the parable of the Workers in the Vineyard distributive justice.

21. Snyder Belousek, *Atonement, Justice, and Peace*, p. 388.

22. Nathan Eubank, 'What does Matthew Say about Divine Recompense? On the Misuse of the Parable of the Workers in the Vineyard (20.1-16)', *JSNT* 35.3 (2013), pp. 242-62. Eubank demonstrates that the logic of the parable of the Workers in the Vineyard, which points to the generosity of positive divine recompense, is shared by the parable of the Unforgiving Slave, which warns of the severity of negative divine recompense.

23. Cf. Willard M. Swartley, 'The Relation of Justice/Righteousness to *Shalom/ Eirēnē*', *Ex auditu* 22 (2006), pp. 29-53 (30): 'Compassion and mercy are inherent to justice in the biblical understanding.' Although I find it difficult to speak of *the* biblical understanding of justice, I nevertheless agree that compassion and mercy inhere in biblical conceptions of justice that are theologically and morally compelling.

24. For a study that explores this dynamic in terms of grace and commitment within Luke's Gospel, see John T. Carroll, 'Welcoming Grace, Costly Commitment: An Approach to the Gospel of Luke', *Interpretation* 57.1 (January 2003), pp. 16-23.

of the Prodigal Son and the Workers in the Vineyard, respectively.) In any case, with respect to the theme of justice, theologically construed by Jesus, a Matthean parable from which the vocabulary of compassion is absent is more in keeping with the parables of the Good Samaritan and the Prodigal Son than the one that explicitly features compassion.

Returning to Luke's Gospel, there is another parable of Jesus that bears on the theme of justice, albeit rather differently from the parables of the Good Samaritan and the Prodigal Son. The parable appears to amalgamate two storylines, although this might be because its alleged Matthean parallel, the parable of the Talents (Mt. 25.14-30), features only one clearly parallel plotline. The parable appears in Lk. 19.11-28 and is known by various names, among them the parable of the (Ten) Minas or Pounds, the parable of the Nobleman-King or King-Judge, the parable of the Throne Claimant or, more simply, Luke's kingship parable. To my mind, the most apposite of these is the parable of the Throne Claimant because this descriptor captures the concept that the man of means by birth craves yet more power and recompenses those who oppose his self-aggrandizing aspirations with royal ruthlessness.[25]

Within Luke's narrative, this parable occurs in a crucial context, that is, toward the culmination of Jesus' journey to Jerusalem (9.51–19.46). As is well known, Luke's central section comprising Jesus' journey to Jerusalem is both distinctive and critical to his shaping of the Jesus story. In Lk. 9.51 Jesus fixes his face for Jerusalem, and in 19.45 he enters the temple precincts within Jerusalem. The close proximity of Jesus to Jerusalem is apparently decisive for the Lukan perspective on the parable of the Throne Claimant. In Lk. 19.11 the rationale provided for this parable is that Jesus was near Jerusalem and it seemed to his audience that the reign of God was about to appear forthwith (*parachrēma*). Immediately following the parable, moreover, Luke recounts that on saying these things Jesus journeyed ahead, going up to Jerusalem (19.28). Then follows Jesus' non-triumphal approach to Jerusalem (19.29-40),[26] his lament over Jerusalem (19.41-44) and his 'occupation' of the temple to teach people in Jerusalem (19.45-48). The parable of the Throne Claimant thereby concludes Jesus' instruction within the section of Luke's Gospel most evidently devoted to the teaching of Jesus on various themes. As such, it is something of a capstone to

---

25. Cf. Darrell L. Bock, *Luke 9:51–24:53* (Grand Rapids: Baker Books, 1996), p. 1525: 'Often called the "Parable of the Pounds", a more precise title might be the "Parable of Stewardship and Judgment upon the Return".'

26. See Brent Kinman, 'Parousia, Jesus' "A-Triumphal" Entry, and the Fate of Jerusalem (Luke 19:28-44)', *JBL* 118 (1999), pp. 279-94. Kinman argues that in Lukan perspective Jesus does not enter Jerusalem in triumph, but his interpretive inference that Jesus' prophecy of Jerusalem's destruction was provoked by his failure to receive a celebratory welcome to the city is unconvincing.

the teaching of Jesus en route to Jerusalem. Yet its content perplexes and perturbs.[27]

Numerous features of this parable invite comment, including the parable's relation to its alleged Matthean parallel, its apparent allusion to the attempt by Archelaus to secure for himself his father Herod's title as king,[28] its redaction to serve Luke's purposes and its significance for Luke's (and perhaps even Jesus' own) eschatology. Only what serves to probe what this parable intimates about justice can be addressed here, however.

The parable of the Throne Claimant is commonly understood as an eschatological parable, cautioning against imminent eschatological expectation (at least at the time of Luke's composition) while also warning of eschatological judgment for inaction during the time granted by the apparent delay of the *parousia*.[29] Such an interpretation is perhaps inevitable if this parable is read as but a variation on Matthew's parable of the Talents.[30] Taken alone and read in its narrative context, however, various features of this parable resist not only the standard eschatological interpretation but also the alternative eschatological interpretations of Luke Timothy Johnson and N.T. Wright, in which this parable is understood to signal imminent eschatological resolution, whether when Jesus enters Jerusalem as king (Johnson) or when divine reign in Jesus is shown to have been established by the destruction of Jerusalem (Wright).[31]

Two fundamental features of the parable of the Throne Claimant prove problematic for any eschatological interpretation. The first of these is that the explicit rationale for the parable in Lk. 19.11 apparently militates against

---

27. See Merrill Kitchen, 'Rereading the Parable of the Pounds: A Social and Narrative Analysis of Luke 19:11-28', in *Prophecy and Passion: Essays in Honour of Athol Gill* (ed. David Neville; Adelaide: ATF Press, 2002), pp. 227-46. Cf. Elizabeth V. Dowling, *Taking Away the Pound: Women, Theology and the Parable of the Pounds in the Gospel of Luke* (London: T. & T. Clark, 2007).

28. See Josephus, *War* 2.1-38, 80-111, and also *Ant.* 17.208-249, 299-323.

29. In defence of this traditional interpretation, see John T. Carroll, *Response to the End of History: Eschatology and Situation in Luke–Acts* (Atlanta: Scholars Press, 1988), pp. 97-103. Cf. John T. Carroll, *Luke: A Commentary* (Louisville, KY: Westminster/John Knox Press, 2012), pp. 377-82, in which his earlier interpretation is further nuanced by suggesting that the throne claimant's conduct is not congruent with the operation of God's reign but rather intimates what lies ahead for Jesus in Jerusalem and, a generation later, for Jerusalem itself.

30. Cf. Snodgrass, *Stories with Intent*, pp. 519-43. On balance, Snodgrass considers these two parables to be unrelated, but he discusses them together among a group of parables concerned with 'future eschatology'.

31. See Luke Timothy Johnson, 'The Lukan Kingship Parable (Lk. 19:11-27)', *NovT* 24 (1982), pp. 139-59, and also *The Gospel of Luke* (Collegeville: Liturgical Press, 1991), pp. 288-95; N.T. Wright, *Jesus and the Victory of God* (Minneapolis: Fortress Press, 1996), pp. 631-39.

any interpretation along the lines of imminent resolution. Jesus presents this parable to counter his audience's supposition that, since he was nearing Jerusalem, the reign of God must be near and about to appear. As for the view that this parable expresses Luke's revised eschatological schema that the return of Jesus is purposefully delayed and was not envisaged by Jesus as occurring hard on the heels of his departure, the parable is unconcerned with the duration of the throne claimant's time away. Indeed, in terms of the parable's storyline, the throne claimant returns as king in no time.

Since the parable focuses on the industriousness of slaves during their master's absence, it is possible to argue that this emphasis supports the traditional eschatological reading. The (extended) time between ascension and return makes provision for ever-expanding witness to Jesus. A second fundamental feature of the parable also grates against this reading, however. Any eschatological interpretation of the parable of the Throne Claimant must envisage the royal aspirant who secures his kingship as analogous to Jesus as (returning) Lord or, less commonly, God as judge. Yet everything we learn about the throne claimant and his actions contravene Jesus' instructions for living in accordance with divine reign.[32]

In the first instance, the throne claimant pursues power and position, in stark contrast to Jesus' teaching on what constitutes genuine greatness (see Lk. 9.46-48; 22.24-26). If the parable has an eschatological dimension, therefore, perhaps it comprises Jesus' warning against eschatological expectations associated with conventional royal rule, that is, expectations equating divine reign with imperial or at least 'lording over' modes of ruling. It can hardly be gainsaid that this parable mirrors what is constitutive of conventional kingdoms and fiefdoms, which might well have been what Jesus' audience had in mind if, as Luke intimates, nearness to Jerusalem prompted its supposition that the arrival of God's kingdom was near.

Moreover, the parable makes it abundantly clear that the throne claimant is preoccupied with wealth. Immediately upon his return from securing his regal title, he assembles slaves to whom he has entrusted money to ascertain how much has been made by trade. This is in stark contrast to Jesus' instruction on the dangers of wealth, a prominent theme in Luke's central section. Further to this, the throne claimant instils fear by reinforcing his reputation for unjust gain. He is known as one who takes out what he does not put in

---

32. See Kitchen, 'Rereading the Parable of the Pounds', p. 232: 'The character of Jesus Christ is portrayed consistently in Luke's Gospel as "the centre of the story of salvation" and is therefore the hermeneutical key for interpreting all symbolic or metaphorical literary material within the Gospel of Luke… If he is a consistent character, his speech will affirm his imputed ethics. It is Jesus who tells the parable of the pounds, so the reader must assume that the ethic depicted in the parable is intentional and careful, directly reflecting the ethical intention of the Lukan Jesus.'

and reaps what he does not sow. Indeed, Luke ensures that this detail is first uttered by the fearful slave and subsequently reiterated by his master without disagreement or qualification. In the manner of one accustomed to lord it over others, he revels in his capacity to get what he wants. And finally, the manner in which the throne claimant deals with those who opposed his rule—by ordering their execution in his presence—is at complete odds with Jesus' instruction on loving enemies (Lk. 6.27-36; 10.25-37).[33]

As with other parables, particular details within Jesus' parable of the Throne Claimant are not to be understood literally or allegorically but rather analogically.[34] Even so, it is worth reflecting on whether Luke could have conceived of Jesus returning in the manner of the triumphant throne claimant and thereby subverting central dimensions of his own moral instruction: the dangers of amassing both power and wealth, concern for underprivileged people (justice) and peaceable love of enemies. Certain eschatological texts might be forwarded as comparable in their content to the parable of the Throne Claimant, most notably the comparisons between the future day or days of the Son of humanity and the past days of Noah and Lot (Lk. 17.22-37), but most Lukan eschatological texts bespeak a peaceable hope.[35] As a result, there is reason to dispute the traditional interpretation in which the returning throne claimant is aligned with the returning Jesus.

Put differently, various levels of incongruity between Jesus' teaching, as recorded by Luke, and the characterization of the throne claimant lead me to question interpretations of this parable in which the figure of the throne claimant reflects analogically on Jesus. Yet, as David Seccombe reminds us, incongruity, hyperbole and the bizarre are characteristic of Jesus' teaching.[36] Commenting on the parable of the Throne Claimant, Seccombe finds a comparison between Archelaus and the reign of God consistent with the rest of the Jesus tradition. And within this overarching shock-inducing comparison, he considers the note of slaughter on which the parable ends to be apposite to Jesus' first-century context, both to spice up the story and to provoke the question: 'What might the King Messiah do to those who oppose his kingdom?'[37]

---

33. Jeremias could not countenance Jesus comparing himself with such a 'rapacious', 'brutal oriental despot' and therefore placed responsibility for this comparison with Luke. See Joachim Jeremias, *The Parables of Jesus* (trans. S.H. Hooke; London: SCM Press, 3rd edn, 1972), pp. 58-60.

34. See Snodgrass, *Stories with Intent*, pp. 1-31, 540-41.

35. See David J. Neville, *A Peaceable Hope: Contesting Violent Eschatology in New Testament Narratives* (Grand Rapids: Baker Academic, 2013), pp. 89-173.

36. David Seccombe, 'Incongruity in the Gospel Parables', *TynBul* 62.2 (2011), pp. 161-72.

37. Seccombe, 'Incongruity in the Gospel Parables', p. 171.

What, indeed?! Perhaps twenty-first-century squeamishness over brutal violence needs to be set aside in favour of hearing this parable with first-century ears. Perhaps in the absence of the various social, democratic and legal institutions we now take for granted, we must simply accept that divine justice is sometimes synonymous with arbitrary retribution that is beyond moral appraisal. This seems to be the end effect of accepting an analogical association between the actions of the throne claimant and Jesus' understanding of divine reign. As a result, even if it could be demonstrated that Jesus intended such an analogical association, the influence of such an association places interpreters today in the uneasy position of having to assess the theological and moral value of this legacy, features of which include: arbitrary power as characteristic of divine reign; justice as retributive judgment; and the moral validity of violent retaliation. Insofar as the parable of the Throne Claimant inculcates or reinforces such theological and moral 'values', the interpretive imperative might well be to read against the parable in the service of a more edifying theological vision.

Although the parable of the Throne Claimant reflects an understanding of justice, such an understanding is not the vision of justice one finds in the parables of the Good Samaritan, the Prodigal Son or even the Workers in the Vineyard. For this reason, I read the parable of the Throne Claimant in light of the value-enhanced conception of justice in other parables, that is, in view of a theological vision found in some of Jesus' parables but not necessarily—or at least not so brightly—in all. As a result, my reading of the parable of the Throne Claimant comprises an 'against the grain' reading or, perhaps better, a reading conditioned by a theological perspective derived from elsewhere in the gospel traditions.

Reflection on the parables of the Unforgiving Slave, the Workers in the Vineyard and the Throne Claimant leads (me) to the conclusion that one must critically evaluate any particular parable of Jesus in light of a coherent theological vision before parading its pith in public.[38] In other words, what makes a parable of Jesus pertinent to public theology is not simply that it is a parable attributed to Jesus but rather the extent to which it conveys or reflects a vision of God and God's way in the world consistent with the theological-moral vision of Jesus, critically appraised. This is not because such vision is comforting to contemporary ears but because the theological vision of Jesus is discernibly a vision of life with the potential to serve the common good.

---

38. Although I find it problematic to appeal to the parables of the Unforgiving Slave and the Throne Claimant as paradigmatic for public discourse on justice, except perhaps as negative illustrations, that is not to preclude their potential paradigmatic pertinence for theological reflection in relation to other public concerns.

Theological Vision in Luke's Gospel

Does Marshall ever appeal to something like a normative theological vision that might serve as an evaluative criterion for appealing to parables of Jesus as paradigmatic for public theology? In my view, he does, even if subtly. For example, early on he remarks:

> Significantly, 'compassion' in Luke's Gospel is used only of God (1.78; cf. 1.50, 54) and of Jesus (7:13), and of the two most extraordinary parabolic characters of all: the father of the Prodigal Son (15.20) and the Good Samaritan (10.33). Both these parables are used to dramatize a divine reality invading the conventional world of first-century society, a reality activated by and embodied most fully in the larger gospel story by the person of Jesus himself.[39]

Subsequently, in a section entitled 'The Gospel within a Gospel', Marshall comments on the theological value of the parable of the Prodigal Son.[40] This parable is so memorable and so cherished because it pictures 'the costly love and restoring justice of the reign of God', because it offers a glimpse of 'the radical generosity and implicit justice of God's forgiving mercy'. Its vision of God's compassion for wayward people is what sets it apart.

Beyond these explicit statements regarding the dynamic theological vision that animates the parables of the Good Samaritan and the Prodigal Son, Marshall points in the direction of a decisive thematic association within Luke's Gospel that lends theological no less than moral weight to the motif of compassion. 'In Luke's Gospel', he writes fairly early on, 'compassion is supremely a divine attribute.'[41] Later, building on a study by M.J.J. Menken, Marshall points out that the relatively rare references to compassion in Luke's Gospel are positioned with compositional care, thereby signalling its thematic significance.[42] Prior to the two references to compassion in Lk. 10.33 and 15.20, however, compassion is inextricably linked to the distinctively Lukan motif of (divine) 'visitation'.[43]

---

39. Marshall, *Compassionate Justice*, p. 27. Following on from this affirmation of both parables, Marshall says of the parable of the Good Samaritan: 'Certainly it is primarily a didactic tale about moral responsibility towards outsiders. But there is a theological weight or christological texture to the account that should not be missed, even if it is not the governing concern.' Indeed!

40. Marshall, *Compassionate Justice*, pp. 187-91.

41. Marshall, *Compassionate Justice*, p. 121.

42. Marshall, *Compassionate Justice*, p. 222-23, esp. n. 10.

43. This connection is also noticed by Anne Elvey, 'Legacies of Violence toward the Other: Toward a Consideration of the Outsider within the Lukan Narrative', *Colloquium* 34.1 (2002), pp. 21-34 (33). See also Anne Elvey, 'Love and Justice in the Gospel of Luke—Ecology, the Neighbour and Hope', *AusBR* 60 (2012), pp. 1-17, in which she draws attention to 'the quality of excess characteristic of the Lukan divine visitation' expressed in forgiveness, compassion, mercy and love.

Out of eleven occurrences of the verb *episkeptomai* in the New Testament, seven are to be found in Luke–Acts. Of Luke's seven usages of this verb, however, only four convey the sense of *divine* visitation (Lk. 1.68, 78; 7.16; Acts 15.14). To these four theologically significant occurrences of this verb, one should also add Luke's use of the cognate noun, *episkopē*, in Lk. 19.44. Within the New Testament, the only other comparable occurrence of this word family to signify divine visitation is in 1 Pet. 2.12, which refers to the eschatological 'Day of Visitation'. Precedents for Luke's usage of this word family appear in the Septuagint and also in other Jewish literature roughly contemporaneous with Luke–Acts, including Wis. 3.7; *Pss. Sol.* 3.11; 10.4; 11.6; 15.12; *T. Levi* 4.4; *T. Ash.* 7.3; *T. Jud.* 23.5; and the Qumran text known as the *Damascus Document* (CD 1.7-11). In such texts, the vocabulary of 'visitation' conveys the sense of divine approach for the purpose of deliverance or, at times, judgment.

In Lukan perspective, the motif of 'visitation' has rich theological associations. Early in the narrative, Zechariah's Spirit-inspired prophecy (Lk. 1.67-79) begins and ends with the theme of divine visitation for human salvation. 'Blessed be the Lord God of Israel, because he has *visited* and thereby effected redemption for his people', is how Zechariah's prophecy begins (1.68). It ends poetically, affirming that through the compassionate mercies of God, the dawn from on high will *visit* or break in to give light to those in darkness and to guide people's feet into the way of peace (1.78-79). Here *visitation* is not only for human liberation, salvation and peace but is also the inevitable concomitant of divine mercy and compassion. In short, divine mercy and compassion comprise the rationale for life-saving visitation.

In Lk. 7.16 those who witness the raising of the young man at Nain praise God by exclaiming, 'A great prophet has been raised up among us.' And from this they infer that 'God has visited his people'. The presence in their midst of a great prophet signals divine visitation. Furthermore, what elicits this exclamation of praise and recognition is the restoration of a young man to life, prompted by Jesus' compassion for the dead man's mother (7.13). In Zechariah's prophecy of praise, visitation is associated with life-saving liberation; here visitation is associated with restoration to life. And in both instances, discernment of visitation for human benefit is perceived as the outworking of divine compassion. Little wonder, then, that at the culmination of Jesus' journey to Jerusalem, Jesus laments Jerusalem's inevitable demise because of the failure of its inhabitants to recognize in his mercy-motivated mission the appointed time of 'visitation' (19.41-44).

Acts 15.14 makes clear that Luke did not regard divine visitation as restricted to Jesus' mission and message. There James sums up Peter's appeal before the Jerusalem assembly by characterizing the conversion of Cornelius as visitation for the purpose of drawing from the nations a people to represent the divine name. In Lukan perspective, the visitation of Acts 15.14 is clearly associated with the work of the Spirit (Acts 10.44-48; 15.8). So even though divine visitation is not restricted to Jesus' own mission, it is integrally related to it, since in Acts the Spirit is dispensed by the ascended Jesus (2.32-33) to empower apostolic witness to the risen Jesus and hence the continuation of all that Jesus began to do and to teach (1.1-8).

The motif of divine visitation in the prophetic-messianic mission of Jesus is central to Luke's theological vision. Located at the heart of that theological vision, moreover, is compassion as both the rationale for God's initiative and the appropriate—because analogous—human response to that initiative in the sphere of social relations. The close association between visitation and compassion in Lk. 1.78 and 7.13 carries over into the later references to compassion in 10.33 and 15.20. By responding with compassion to one left for dead, the Samaritan of Jesus' parable reflects Luke's understanding of God, and by responding with compassion to a son who was metaphorically dead, the father of two sons likewise mirrors divinity in Lukan perspective. Perhaps Marshall concentrates on the parables of the Good Samaritan and the Prodigal Son not simply because they are parables attributed to Jesus but because they capture something quintessential to Luke's theological vision that Marshall considers to be faithful to Jesus' own theological vision. Although not provable, the intuition that compassion is integral to Jesus' understanding of God is historically, theologically and morally compelling. And insofar as such a theological vision resources moral commitment to work for a more compassionately just social order, any parable of Jesus that taps into such a vision of God's way in the world is paradigmatic for public theology.

JUSTICE: THIN PRAGMATISM BETWEEN THICK PRACTICES

Philip J. Matthews

The theme of the seminar from which this collection of essays derives, *The Bible, Justice and Public Theology*, evokes a different emphasis for philosophers than it does for theologians or biblical scholars, primarily because philosophers use a different toolkit for articulating a concept like justice. Moral philosophers are primarily concerned with distributive justice, and all major theories of ethics posit the meta-ethical principle of universalisation as a preliminary test of justice or fairness. Some types of moral universals are absolutist and some are not. Universalisation is a process that expands the weight of moral claims to all other like cases, regardless of culture, religion, gender, etc. This essay defends moral pluralism because a *thin* level of agreement exists over universals even when people are in sharp disagreement over the *thick* application of those universals.

In a secular liberal democracy, religious pluralism is taken for granted but few people appreciate the level of philosophical pluralism that exists. Stephen Toulmin illustrates the need for philosophical pluralism when he compares natural scientists, who share in agreed-upon tasks, with the agenda of philosophy, which does not, even among its classic authors.[1] The Modern project, according to Toulmin, did not provide certainty for 'intellectual problems—let alone, practical ones', and the claim that philosophical or scientific problems could be de-contextualized was itself based on a historical motivation. He contends that the criticism of leading philosophers 'undermines the whole "foundationalist" program', and thus a new *Cosmopolis* is now required that favours a research program 'concentrated on *narrative* and *practice*'.[2] Toulmin argues that the search for 'common grounding', based either on Cartesian rationalism (clear and distinct ideas) or on Lockean empiricism, has not produced common results and hence a new 'grounding' is required that focuses on the 'overall narrative of conceptual history'.[3]

---

1. Stephen Toulmin, *Cosmopolis: The Hidden Agenda of Modernity* (Chicago: University of Chicago Press, 1990), p. 10.
2. Stephen Toulmin, 'Theology in the Context of the University', *Theological Education* 26.2 (Spring, 1990), pp. 51-65.
3. Toulmin, 'Theology in the Context of the University', pp. 51-65.

After looking back on what he calls the 'received view' of Modernity Toulmin says he is inclined to say, 'Don't believe a word of it!' because 'that whole story was one-sided and over-optimistic'.[4] Following successes in the natural sciences Modern philosophers were confident that disengaged rationality would eventually transcend traditional religious or cultural moral claims as well.[5] Toulmin rejects the Modern assumption that rationality was commonly available to anyone 'who sets superstition and mythology aside' in ways 'free of local prejudice and transient fashion'.[6] He also rejects three other historical assumptions of seventeenth-century rationalism: the myth of social progress; freedom from ecclesiastical tyranny; and the intellectual break with the Middle Ages.[7]

Toulmin says the self-doubt of philosophy, and thus his own, necessitated a fresh start because the 'burden of proof' shifted once agreement over theory-centred moral philosophy failed to materialize.[8] Taking his cue from Wittgenstein, Toulmin suggests that the theory-centred focus of Modernity is over and done with because the 'destructive work of Dewey, Heidegger, Wittgenstein, and Rorty' has left philosophy with limited options. It can cling to a discredited research program that will eventually drive it out of business, it can look for new post-modern practical methods of decision making, or it can return to pre-modern traditions 'that were sidetracked by Descartes, but can be usefully taken up for the future'.[9] Toulmin has in mind here a way of doing philosophy that re-contextualizes the moral claims that Modern philosophers took pride in de-contextualising.[10] He claims that throughout the Middle Ages and the Renaissance, clerics and educated laypeople understood that problems in social ethics were not resolved by appeal to any single universal tradition so they appealed to multiple considerations and coexisting traditions that were weighed against one another.[11] His suggestion is that philosophy ought to 'reappropriate the reasonable and tolerant' legacy of humanism because humanity 'needs people with a sense of how theory touches practice at points, and in ways, that we feel on our pulses'.[12]

Toulmin, with Albert Jonsen, advocates a return to casuistry as a means to sidestep the incommensurability problems of philosophy. Toulmin and Jonsen contend that the benefit of casuistry is that it allows a moral agent

---

4. Toulmin, *Cosmopolis*, p. 16.
5. Toulmin, *Cosmopolis*, p. 9.
6. Toulmin, *Cosmopolis*, p. 11.
7. Toulmin, *Cosmopolis*, pp. 18-20.
8. Toulmin, *Cosmopolis*, p. 178.
9. Toulmin, *Cosmopolis*, p. 11.
10. Toulmin, *Cosmopolis*, p. 21.
11. Toulmin, *Cosmopolis*, p. 135.
12. Toulmin, *Cosmopolis*, p. 180.

to appeal to type-cases or paradigm cases without becoming absolutist.[13] A type-case uses standard cases as referential markers so that an individual case can be compared and contrasted with the typical. Maxims such as 'don't use violence against innocent human beings', 'don't lie' and 'don't take unfair advantage of other people's misfortune' can, according to Toulmin and Jonsen, serve as 'markers or boundary stones that delimit the territory of "moral" considerations in practice'.[14]

Another philosopher to highlight the extent of philosophical pluralism is Alasdair MacIntyre. He contends that because moral theories appeal to different premises—that are themselves incommensurable from each other—moral debates are 'unsettlable' and 'interminable' and therefore debates degenerate into what he refers to as 'the mere and increasingly shrill battle of assertion with counter assertion'.[15] In *After Virtue* (1981), the first of a trilogy of books on moral incommensurability, MacIntyre states that moral philosophy is in crisis because arguments properly constructed are all logically valid, 'conclusions do indeed follow from the premises' but we possess no rational way of 'weighing the claims of one as against another'.[16] In the second book, *Whose Justice? Which Rationality?* (1988), MacIntyre extends this critique and argues that the incommensurability problem is internal to philosophy itself and not simply a problem between rival moral traditions. He claims that although contemporary academic philosophy provides a more accurate and informed explanation of moral disagreement, it does not provide a means for its resolution because philosophers, when applying themselves to questions of justice and practical rationality, 'disagree with each other as sharply, as variously, and so it seems, as irremediably upon how such questions are to be answered as anyone else'.[17] In the third book, *Three Rival Versions of Moral Enquiry* (1990), MacIntyre restates the problem in even starker terms when he posits that moral debates will remain inconclusive because advocates of one moral theory think that advocates of another have not sufficiently appreciated the role that reason plays in resolving moral disputes.[18] Australian preference utilitarian philosopher, Peter Singer, illustrates MacIntyre's point when he claims that

---

13. Albert R. Jonsen and Stephen Toulmin, *The Abuse of Casuistry: A History of Moral Reasoning* (Berkeley: University of California Press, 1988), p. 307.

14. Jonsen and Toulmin, *The Abuse of Casuistry*, p. 307.

15. Alasdair MacIntyre, 'Why is the search for the foundations of Ethics so Frustrating?', *Hastings Center Report* 9.4 (1979), pp. 16-21.

16. Alasdair MacIntyre, *After Virtue: A Study in Moral Theory* (Notre Dame: University of Notre Dame Press, 3rd edn, 2007; 1st edn, 1981), p. 8.

17. Alasdair MacIntyre, *Whose Justice? Which Rationality?* (Notre Dame: University of Notre Dame Press, 1988), p. 3.

18. Alasdair MacIntyre, *Three Rival Versions of Moral Enquiry: Encyclopaedia, Genealogy, and Tradition* (Notre Dame: University of Notre Dame Press, 1990), p. 7.

impartial consideration is a uniquely rational basis for ethical decision making.[19] If this bold claim was as self-evident as Singer seems to think then moral philosophers, who are in the business of rational deliberation, would have taken on board his 'new understanding of ethics'[20] in much the same way as physicists took on board Einstein's theory of general relativity. This has not happened because Singer's 'new understanding' of ethics is neither unique nor definitive.

MacIntyre's pessimism over the present state of moral enquiry is significant because it highlights a key epistemic problem associated with applied ethics. Philosophers do not hold in common a method for evaluating the rightness or wrongness of a moral proposition and therefore philosophy cannot be used to solve particular cases. However, Macintyre's pessimism is focused too finely on incommensurability and difference between rival moral traditions. When MacIntyre states that professors of philosophy disagree with each other just as much as other people do, he overstates the problems associated with this level of disagreement. While it is clear that professors of philosophy exhibit a diversity of conclusions about moral claims, this is exactly what one should expect in a complex discipline like moral philosophy. When MacIntyre portrays practical ethics as a shrill battle of 'assertion with counter-assertion' and states that agreement is both 'rare' and 'accidental', he misrepresents what happens when moral debate is conducted among serious thinkers, even when they do come from diverse philosophical traditions.[21] Certainly disputes in applied ethics exhibit the shrillness that MacIntyre refers to but it is also common for thinkers from diverse moral traditions to agree on many things. Perhaps the reason this often goes unacknowledged is that when people have a common view on moral issues, they do not spend time debating why they agree, whereas when people disagree the debate can be interminable.

The third philosopher in this short review, Bernard Williams, defends pluralism when he rightly argues that any attempt to simplify moral enquiry is mistaken because complexity and conflict is a basic fact of moral deliberation. He describes moral deliberation as a complex mix of local and universal concerns that includes the psychological and emotional concerns of the moral agent.[22] Williams further argues that the desire for a discrete moral theory, and an accompanying decision making protocol, is misguided.[23] He

---

19. Peter Singer, *The Expanding Circle* (New York: Farrar, Straus & Giroux, 1981), p. 111.

20. Singer, *The Expanding Circle*, pp. 148-73.

21. MacIntyre, 'Why is the search for the foundations of ethics so frustrating?', p. 17.

22. Bernard Williams, *Morality: An Introduction to Ethics* (Cambridge: Cambridge University Press, 1972), pp. 23-24.

23. Bernard Williams, *Moral Luck* (Cambridge: Cambridge University Press, 1981), pp. ix-x.

asks, 'If there is such a thing as the truth about the subject matter of ethics—the truth, we might say, about the ethical—why is there any expectation that it should be simple?' Furthermore, 'Perhaps we need as many concepts to describe it as we find we need, and no fewer.'[24] Williams says that the fact that we appeal to a variety of ethical considerations is precisely what one would expect to find in the complex world we inhabit. Ethical considerations, according to Williams, are 'genuinely different from one another', and this is precisely what moral agents should expect because all of us are 'heirs to different long and complex ethical traditions, with many different religious and other social strands'.[25]

Moral pluralism is often aligned with moral relativism but this is a mistake. A moral relativist argues that there are no morally significant universals (other than the one just made). A moral pluralist, on the other hand, argues that moral universals do exist but that they are derived from a diverse range of philosophical and theological traditions. A universal such as 'don't be unnecessarily cruel' is *thinly* shared between philosophers and theologians, regardless of the philosophical or theological tradition to which they belong. This *thin* maxim has vast explanatory power because it covers unnecessary cruelty wherever and whenever it is found. This minimalist universalism cannot be used to resolve all cases, however, because unnecessary cruelty to one person might be necessary cruelty to another. The utilisation of animals for medical experimentation, for instance, is necessary cruelty for some and unnecessary for others. Whatever stance a philosopher takes on this issue, the epistemic weight of the argument will be insufficient to convince those with an opposing view to concede ground because the tools that moral philosophy has at its disposal do not allow for this level of precision.

The desire for precision was itself as aspect of the flawed agenda of Enlightenment philosophers and their various attempts to simplify moral agency. Immanuel Kant, for instance, arguably the finest philosopher since Aristotle, exaggerates the efficacy of the categorical imperative as a means to establishing rules of conduct. The various forms of the categorical imperative that Kant provides are not equivalent but the most common form, 'Act only on that maxim through which you can at the same time will that it should become a universal law', has absurd implications. In his essay, *On a Supposed Right to Tell Lies from Benevolent Motives*, Kant defends the moral duty to be truthful to a murderer, even when lying could prevent harm. He states that honesty and truthfulness are a 'sacred and unconditional

---

24. Bernard Williams, *Ethics and the Limits of Philosophy* (London: Fontana Press, 1985), p. 17.
25. Williams, *Ethics and the Limits of Philosophy*, p. 16.

command of reason, and not to be limited by any expediency'.[26] Kant's overstatement here is well accepted because in certain circumstances it is relatively easy to justify lying in order to satisfy a higher moral imperative.

Similarly, the best of the consequentialist philosophers, Jeremy Bentham, exaggerated the efficacy of quantitative calculus for resolving particular cases. His most famous disciple, John Stuart Mill, had to modify the narrow interpretation of quantitative calculus because he thought that a moral agent should give some pleasures a higher moral consideration than others. The oft-quoted argument against quantitative utilitarianism, that it is 'pig's philosophy', rings true if we stick to the idea that pleasure is the only intrinsic good. The epistemic shifts in utilitarian calculus—quantitative (Bentham), qualitative (Mill) and preferences (Singer)—are significant because moral conclusions drawn in particular cases can differ depending on what type of calculus one employs. However, the epistemic problem of particular cases does not nullify the efficacy of quantitative utilitarianism for social policy, particularly if pleasure is thought of more broadly than crude hedonism.

Both the categorical imperative and the hedonic calculus are useful but neither is definitive. Given this lack of agreement there are limitations on what philosophy can achieve and thus the term 'moral expert' ought only to be used in a highly qualified sense.[27] Clearly moral philosophers can and do contribute to complex moral debates but philosophy as a discipline does not have the tools for resolving such debates.

The *thin* consensus over universals, referred to above, is best articulated by Michael Walzer's 1994 publication, *Thick and Thin: Moral Argument at Home and Abroad*.[28] Readers may know of Walzer as one of the more articulate and careful defenders of the just war theory.[29] In this relatively small book he defends a view of justice whereby moral agents recognize a *thin* moral motivation even amongst people with whom they often disagree. This *thin* moral motivation enables agreement on many moral issues because it presupposes a moral awareness that transcends the tradition-based contingency of the moral arguments concerned.

---

26. Immanuel Kant, 'On a Supposed Right to Tell Lies from Benevolent Motives' (1797), in *Kant's Critique of Practical Reason and Other Works on the Theory of Ethics* (trans. Thomas K. Abbot; London: Longmans, Green and Co., 6th edn, 1954), p. 361.

27. See Robert W. Burth, 'Are There Moral Experts', *The Monist* 58.4 (1974), pp. 646-58; Martha Nussbaum, 'Moral Expertise? Constitutional Narrative and Philosophical Argument', *Metaphilosophy* 33 (2002), pp. 502-520.

28. Michael Walzer, *Thick and Thin: Moral Argument at Home and Abroad* (Notre Dame: University of Notre Dame Press, 1994), pp. 1-4.

29. Michael Walzer, *Just and Unjust Wars: A Moral Argument with Historical Illustrations* (New York: Basic Books, 4th edn, 2006; 1st edn, 1977); *Arguing about War* (New Haven: Yale University Press, 2004).

Walzer suggests that moral thinkers often agree on *thin* moral universals even when they interpret these universals through a *thick* historical narrative. He refers to this type of moral agreement as 'thin moral agreement' or 'moral minimalism'.[30] Moral minimalism is not foundational because a minimalist expression, such as 'slavery is wrong', is *grounded* in an already *thick* narrative understanding of human life which varies from one tradition to another.[31] A rational justification that explains why slavery is wrong is already a *thick* moral claim, either because slavery is inconsistent with broader religious concerns, or because it is inconsistent with the universalisable expression that all humans have rights, or because it is inconsistent with various forms of utilitarianism, or some other moral claim. Walzer argues that a *thin* agreement against slavery is predicated on a *thick* view of the moral life, a type of 'moral maximalism'.[32] He contends that a moral term, such as justice, is understood first as a *thick* description from within a particular tradition before it becomes a *thin* concept that is shared by people from different traditions. For Walzer, the concept of justice is *thick* from the beginning because it is 'culturally integrated, fully resonant, and it reveals itself thinly only on special occasions, when moral language is turned to specific purposes'.[33] This *thick* view of justice is referred to by Walzer as a form of moral maximalism because it is already *thick* with a narrative history of 'qualification, compromise, complexity and disagreement'.[34]

For Walzer, this *thick* view is not a better view of justice, simply the first view with which a moral agent is confronted. The *thin* view of justice is a second order concept, but it is more crucial for Walzer because it is as close as one can get to a moral universal. A *thin* or minimalist view of morality acknowledges that a common thread exists between different *thick* traditions. There are 'rules of engagement' for a principle like justice because 'minimalism leaves room for thickness elsewhere; indeed, it presupposes thickness elsewhere'.[35] Thus, in a pragmatist sense, a *thin* moral universal has greater cash value because it transcends the limitations of *thick* traditions so that people can agree on the practical application of a principle even if they disagree over its justification.

The example he uses to show the difference between *thick* and *thin* moral argument is the 1989 *Velvet Revolution* in Prague during which news coverage showed people carrying signs that simply said 'Truth' or 'Justice'. Walzer claims that a serious thinker who watched this revolution unfold via news

---

30. Walzer, *Thick and Thin*, p. 4.
31. Walzer, *Thick and Thin*, p. 4.
32. Walzer, *Thick and Thin*, pp. 4-6.
33. Walzer, *Thick and Thin*, p. 4.
34. Walzer, *Thick and Thin*, p. 6.
35. Walzer, *Thick and Thin*, p. 12.

coverage, as he did, would share a *thin* perception of what the marchers were appealing to with their signs.[36] The Prague marchers were entirely unfamiliar to Walzer, and he could neither speak their language nor know what they had experienced. Yet he could conceivably stand in solidarity with them and, had he been there, he too would have carried the same signs. The reason for this, according to Walzer, is that the march had nothing to do with epistemology. The marchers were not defending a correspondence or coherence theory of truth, and they were not marching in defence of one ethical theory rather than another.[37] Walzer claims that they were marching for mainly pragmatic reasons; they did not want to be lied to and they wanted their political leaders to end arbitrary arrests and to abolish the privileges of the few.[38]

Walzer is not suggesting that various moral agents accept, or even recognize, that the language they use has this *thin* aspect to it. Because this shared recognition is *thin* we might see injustice in one setting but fail to see a greater injustice in another. Thomas Jefferson, for instance, appealed to self-evident truths of God, equality and the rights of man when he wrote the *Declaration of Independence*. Yet he remained to his death the owner of many slaves, one of whom bore him several children. Walzer's point is that when moral maxims play themselves out in practice they have both a *thin* (minimalist) expression and a *thick* (maximalist) expression. For Walzer, moral *thinness* is the more vital aspect of moral discourse because it allows for an 'intense unity' between various moral agents, whereas moral *thickness* promotes 'qualification, complexity, and disagreement'.[39] Walzer is right about this because on many important ethical issues serious thinking people agree—consequentialists agree with non-consequentialists and theists agree with atheists—because they recognize in the opposing argument a conclusion that resonates with their own.

A contemporary Australian example of a *thin* moral consensus derived from diversely *thick* traditions was the Australia-wide rally against the second Gulf War, a month before conflict began in March 2003. At the Perth rally, approximately twenty thousand people gathered in the city square to voice disapproval at the decision of the Australian government to become involved in the conflict. The people who attended the rally came from diverse philosophical, religious and political traditions, but they shared a *thin* solidarity that something was wrong with the political justification for war being offered by the federal government. This 'garden variety' sense of wrongness, to use Walzer's term,[40] is all that is necessary for serious

---

36. Walzer, *Thick and Thin*, p. 4.
37. Walzer, *Thick and Thin*, p. 1.
38. Walzer, *Thick and Thin*, p. 2.
39. Walzer, *Thick and Thin*, p. 7.
40. Walzer, *Thick and Thin*, p. 3.

thinkers to stand together in a demonstration for a common purpose. No participant in a protest such as this is ever asked to give a *thick* justification for their presence because a *thin* solidarity has already been achieved and debate over epistemic issues would serve no useful purpose.

Examples like this show that a moral concept like justice has both a maximal moral value that is *thickly* contingent on a set of shared assumptions and a minimal moral value that is *thin* enough to be a shared universal principle. This *thin* universalisation provides the boundary conditions within which ethical discussion takes place in a pluralist society because it promotes the idea that there is something to be discussed about ethics that goes beyond both self-interest and the interests of a particular moral tradition. For example, a recent book by utilitarian atheist philosopher Peter Singer, *The Life You Can Save* (2009), bears strong resemblance in the practical suggestions it makes for overcoming global poverty (fairer distribution and a simplified life) to Mennonite theologian Ron Sider's earlier publication, *Rich Christians in an Age of Hunger* (1977).[41] When confronted by global poverty the utilitarian philosopher and the Mennonite theologian stand side-by-side because, independently of their respectively *thick* philosophical or theological justifications for alleviating poverty, they share a common *thin* perception that something is deeply wrong.

The lack of agreement among theologians, or among philosophers, or between theologians and philosophers over particular issues is precisely what one ought to expect from human beings in a liberal democracy. But the shared *thin* minimalist concept of justice transcends the contingencies of both philosophy and theology because it is the formal appreciation of an evolutionary reality for complex social primates like us. You scratch my back and I will scratch yours, you do this for me and I will do it for you, if you hurt my family I will hurt yours. Over time this practical survival necessity begins to take shape as a moral principle commonly known as the Golden Rule.

> Confucian
> *Is there one word which may serve as a rule of practice for all one's life...*
> *Do not to others what you do not want done to yourself.*
>
> Hindu
> *The whole Dharma (law) can be summed up thus: 'Do not to others what you do not wish done to yourself.'*
>
> Hebrew
> *You shall love your neighbor as yourself.*

---

41. Peter Singer, *The Life You Can Save: Acting Now to End World Poverty* (Melbourne: Text Publishing Company, 2009); Ronald J. Sider, *Rich Christians in an Age of Hunger* (Nashville: Thomas Nelson, 5th edn, 2005; 1st InterVarsity Press edn, 1977).

Christian
Do for others what you want them to do for you. This is the meaning of the Law of Moses and of the teaching of the prophets.

Immanuel Kant
Act only in accordance with that maxim through which you can at the same time will that it become a universal law.

John Stuart Mill
Laws and social arrangements should place the happiness of every individual in harmony with the interest of the whole, and education and opinion should establish in the mind of every individual an indissoluble association between his own happiness and the good of the whole.

Golden Rule principles cannot be used to solve particular cases but they can be used to set the boundary conditions under which particular cases are discussed. Natural justice in English law, for instance, is a Golden Rule type application to protect against bias and to ensure fair treatment. Cultural pluralism does not imply cultural relativism because Golden Rule maxims evolved independently in a manner that resonates beyond time and place.

One aspect of Aristotle's genius was to acknowledge limits associated with rational deliberation over ethics and politics. He seems disinclined to offer advice on specific moral issues because he does not think that rational enquiry lends itself to this level of precision. When Aristotle argues that 'every art and every inquiry, and similarly every action and pursuit, is thought to aim at some good' (1094^a), he uses medicine to illustrate how this teleological imperative ought to be understood.[42] He contends that there is general agreement about the *telos* of medicine because it is obvious to a rational agent that health is a necessary though not sufficient aspect of human flourishing (1101^b). In Book III of the *Nicomachean Ethics* (1113^a) Aristotle argues that a rational agent does not spend time deliberating about ends when he says, 'a doctor does not deliberate whether he should heal, nor an orator whether he shall persuade, nor a statesman whether he shall produce law and order'. For Aristotle, a rational agent ought to be more concerned with practical intelligence or prudence and thus the concentration of thought for doctors, orators, and statesmen is to 'assume the end' (health, persuasion, and law and order) and to spend time contemplating 'how and by what means' the end 'is to be attained' (1113^a).

Aristotle's concept of practical wisdom stands in stark contrast to the decision making models currently being advocated in applied ethics. For

---

42. Aristotle, *Nicomachean Ethics*, in Sarah Broadie and Christopher Rowe (eds.), *Aristotle: Nicomachean Ethics: Translation, Introduction, Commentary* (Oxford: Oxford University Press, 2002), p. 339. Hereafter references are provided using Bekker numbers (i.e., page and column numbers in the standard edition of Aristotle's works by Immanuel Bekker).

Aristotle, practical ethics is forged in a shared teleological activity of a specific practice (i.e., medicine→health; law→justice; politics→civil society), and the virtues of these practices are shaped by hands-on engagement of the practitioners concerned. Whatever the *telos* of the whole human life is—and this has proved difficult to define—Aristotle's cautious approach to unpacking human flourishing seems appropriate. Clearly there are survival needs that humans need to meet before they can flourish, and it is regrettable that two millennia after Aristotle a third of the human population still has to focus on 'flourishing' at this level. For Aristotle, human flourishing (*eudaimonia*) begins with a rough sketch of the good life that is filled in with more detail depending on what activity or practice a rational agent engages in. For this reason, a rational agent ought not to look for more precision than the activity or practice allows (1098^a). Aristotle seems to have in mind here that prudence or practical wisdom involves habituation acquired over time. Young men, for instance, can become 'geometricians and mathematicians', but Aristotle thinks that a 'young man of practical wisdom cannot be found' (1142^a). The reason for this is that intelligent young men can understand mathematics because mathematics requires knowledge, but not skill. Practical wisdom, on the other hand, requires both knowledge and skill and therefore young men have not had the time necessary to develop the skills associated with a complex social activity. Aristotle's engaged version of practical wisdom is very different from the most popular contemporary versions of practical ethics that argue for a disengaged process of decision making.

For Aristotle, practical wisdom is about means rather than ends. We take it for granted, for instance, that health is good for us and thus practical wisdom is devoted to achieving that end (1142^b). A rational agent acts 'for the right person, to the right extent, at the right time, with the right motive, and in the right way', depending on what one is aiming to achieve (1109^a). For Aristotle, the study of ethics and politics are linked because we are 'by nature social creatures' (1097^b). This natural human dependency is sufficient on its own to reject the idea the ethics is relative to culture. Given that we have several millennia of human social interaction to look back on, we can say with some confidence that human beings are wonderful co-operators. Further, human beings alive today are equally as good at living together as our ancient ancestors were.

Clearly, as stated before, philosophers can and do reach *thin* agreement on moral issues, but this type of agreement is also shared by many others who are not moral experts. Even if it were true that philosophers derive common conclusions from shared premises, this would still not help solve a significant practical problem associated with ethical decision making in a modern liberal democracy. A modern liberal democracy provides space for people from numerous cultural and religious persuasions. The inherent pluralism of a modern democracy allows people to hold to a variety of competing positions, and the search for an approach that ignores this diversity is misguided. Living in a large modern city involves social cooperation between numbers of people unimaginable for Aristotle. Living in a city with millions of other human beings involves a level of cooperation as significant as living in an aboriginal village or a small isolated community of families.[43] The social relationships are not as close, but the level of cooperation is as great, or even greater, due to the amount of human interaction that is necessary when vast numbers of humans live together. In large cities the capacity for human cooperation is often overlooked and is probably masked by media concentration on statistically small levels of violence and other forms of social conflict. Whether or not large human populations are sustainable long term is yet to be determined, but the perception that a larger population leads to more violence and dysfunction is routinely overstated.[44] People living in these mega-cities appeal to a plurality of moral traditions but they hold in common a *thin* sense of what justice means.

Given that Australia is a pluralist society in which no moral theory or tradition is held in common, we can build on the *thin* agreements that do exist by a process that Richard Rorty refers to as culture as conversation. He has in mind here a concept of culture that begins with conversation rather than with preconceived notions of moral truths that turn out to be illusory. He notes that this 'hermeneutical notion of knowledge' allows for conversation between strangers and the conversation itself becomes 'a new virtue or skill', so *phronēsis* (practical wisdom) in this context is more crucial for a liberal democracy than *epistēmē* (knowledge).[45] For Rorty, this type of consensus is not only the best that philosophical objectivity can hope for but also, and more significantly, all that is necessary for moral philosophy to progress. This pragmatic approach overcomes the illusion of foundationalism because it works within established social and political frameworks. These frameworks replace what Rorty calls the 'notion of knowledge as the assemblage of representations' with a pragmatist awareness of what people

---

43. Twenty cities have populations of more than 10 million and the top five have populations of 15 million or more: Tokyo, Japan (28,025,000); Mexico City, Mexico (18,131,000); Mumbai, India (18,042,000); Sáo Paulo, Brazil (17,711,000) and New York City, USA (16,626,000).

44. David Indermaur states that 'the popular understanding that violence in this country [Australia] has increased dramatically and consistently in recent years is unfounded'. See David Indermaur, 'Violent Crime in Australia: Interpreting the Trends', *Trends and Issues in Crime and Criminal Justice*, No. 61 (Canberra: Australian Institute of Criminology, 1996), pp. 1-6 (6). See also Stephen Pinker, *The Better Angels of our Nature: Why Violence Has Declined* (New York: Viking Books, 2011).

45. Richard Rorty, *Philosophy and the Mirror of Nature* (Princeton, NJ: Princeton University Press, 1979), p. 319.

actually do.[46] Practice-guided pragmatism of this type facilitates three different types of conversation that can be edifyingly employed in a pluralist society.

The first type of conversation focuses on *thin* agreements that people in a pluralist society share—and that most moral theories endorse—namely, a shared awareness of virtues that sustain a civil community: justice, kindness, peacefulness, civility, beneficence, integrity, respect, etc. This primary conversation unites human beings from different cultures because the discussion is about issues that impact on all people, in every culture. Because the conversation over *thin* universals transcends the boundaries of culture, it is pragmatically useful because it invites people who are generally different from one another to focus on a requirement they share in common, the flourishing of civil society.

The second type of conversation builds on the first by focusing on those practices within a pluralist society on which there is already substantial agreement. In a stable pluralist society, people disagree over many things: religion, party politics, sport and, perhaps most intractably of all, moral issues. In the midst of this disagreement, however, there is also considerable agreement that practices such as medicine, law, education and politics (in the Aristotelian sense) sustain a civil society. Rorty refers to this type of pragmatism as 'epistemological behaviorism' because it invokes knowledge gained from social practices.[47] He further argues that this social justification of belief is the normal conversational discourse that happens amongst knowledgeable peers in particular social practices.[48]

The third type of conversation involves a discussion about the internal goods that sustain practices such as medicine, law, education and politics. Conversation such as this is, first and foremost, a conversation among practitioners, but it engages others whenever the internal goods of a practice intersect or clash with those of another. In a liberal pluralist society, the concept of philosophy as conversation involves dialogue over the things that moral agents hold in common and also dialogue over things that are conceptually incommensurable. A liberal society supports diversity but not without constraints because liberty and social responsibility are two sides of the same civil harmony coin. The attempt to codify the relationship between individual liberty and the prevention of harm to others is not without practical difficulties. The motivation to codify practical ethics stems from a Cartesian anxiety that the space between conceptually incommensurable moral theories needs to be filled if we are to avoid moral chaos. The rationale for a conversational and practice-based focus for moral enquiry is that the moral

---

46. Rorty, *Philosophy and the Mirror of Nature*, p. 126.
47. Rorty, *Philosophy and the Mirror of Nature*, p. 176.
48. Rorty, *Philosophy and the Mirror of Nature*, p. 9.

space between rival theories of ethics in a pluralist society is not as problematic as is often portrayed. In the same way that cultural difference does not deny common human imperatives, moral difference ought not to deny common moral imperatives. The *thin* moral universals that human beings share are often lost in the intractability associated with the focus on divisive issues of practical ethics.

Acknowledging pluralism in a liberal society involves an acceptance that moral agents can rarely be separated by the legitimacy or otherwise of their respective moral arguments. Serious thinking moral agents hold opposing views on a range of complex moral issues but they also hold many things in common. Pluralism invokes conversation about shared common values because cultural and moral difference never completes the separation between one moral agent and another.

Public Theology Through Popular Culture

Stephen Garner

Public theology is sometimes described as the offering of something distinctive, and that is gospel, to the world for the welfare of human society. As an activity, it is rooted in the distinctive theological discourse of faith communities, which is then communicated appropriately into a particular public sphere. In doing this, one of the challenges that public theology faces is to articulate that gospel understanding in a language that is accessible, credible and intelligible to those inside and outside the church. This, in turn, is complicated by the situation that, in Western societies, the original biblical texts, both inside and outside of churches, may have been 'terminated' and replaced by alternative cultural memories. This is not to say that in a discussion about compassion, biblical narratives such as the Good Samaritan or Prodigal Son are not remembered in these communities, but rather that the original texts and narratives have been cut loose from their biblical context and exist alongside competing 'afterlives' of those texts as the shape of societal religious literacy changes. The implications of this for public theology are twofold.

First, if public theology is rooted in a distinctive theological discourse, to what extent is that a solid foundation within wider church contexts? To what extent does a deep religious literacy concerning Scripture, Tradition and their interplay with past and present contexts exist within church communities who seek to do public theology? Moreover, to what degree does a desire even to engage with the public sphere depend upon the depth of that religious literacy and awareness? Second, to what extent does a loss of religious or biblical literacy within wider society make the doing of public theology harder, where particular categories of understanding and common ground based upon well-known cultural resonances with biblical narratives and theological concepts might no longer exist? Does that relegate public theology's modes of communication to ones that are completely secular, or are there other ways of articulating that gospel understanding in a language that is accessible, credible and intelligible to those inside and outside the church?

Popular storytelling is a pervasive feature of contemporary media society, from reality television to period dramas and major sporting events, with varying levels of depth and profundity. However, if popular culture is also the raw material through which people communicate their values and enthusiasms, as well as maintain relationships, then it might provide a 'language' for engaging with religious literacy and also serve as a location for doing public theology. In this essay, examples from popular culture that connect particularly with the biblical afterlives of the Good Samaritan will serve as the starting point for contemplating how popular culture might be used constructively by public theology for educating about and engaging with the theme of compassion—where mercy and justice work together to provide paths for reconciliation and restoration of relationships, and towards the curbing of violence.

Public Theology

The 'classical' definition of public theology, if something as relatively young as the named discipline of 'public theology' can have such a definition, would be Duncan Forrester's understanding that public theology is

> theology which seeks the welfare of the city before protecting the interests of the Church, or its proper liberty to preach the Gospel and celebrate the sacraments. Accordingly, public theology often takes 'the world's agenda', or parts of it, as its own agenda, and seeks to offer distinctive and constructive insights from the treasury of faith to help in the building of a decent society, the restraint of evil, the curbing of violence, nation-building, and reconciliation in the public arena, and so forth. It strives to offer something that is distinctive, and that is gospel, rather than simply adding the voice of theology to what everyone is saying already. Thus it seeks to deploy theology in public debate, rather than a vague and optimistic idealism which tends to disintegrate in the face of radical evil.[1]

Here the agenda for public theology is set by the world, but this cannot be the only impetus for this kind of theological engagement, for within the world there are issues and concerns to which the world itself is blind. What is at the heart of public theology is a community of faith, informed by Scripture and Tradition, which is committed to reading the 'signs of the times' and acting for the common good for society.[2] Therefore, if we are thinking about compassion in the context of public theology, we are thinking about how our understanding of compassion might be offered in distinctive and constructive ways so as to enrich wider society, help restrain evil and violence, and promote the building of communities of reconciliation.

---

1. D.B. Forrester, 'The Scope of Public Theology', *SCE* 17.2 (2004), pp. 5-19 (6).
2. M.L. Stackhouse, 'Civil Religion, Political Theology and Public Theology: What's the Difference?', *PT* 5.3 (2004), pp. 275-93 (284).

This commitment to a common good by public theology is shared by other approaches such as civil religion and political theology, where each is concerned in their own way with what Max Stackhouse identifies as '[t]he goal of finding a more inclusive, genuinely ecumenical and catholic way of identifying a valid, viable inner convictional and ethical framework on which to build the moral and spiritual architecture of our increasingly common life'.[3] However, public theology should not be subsumed under either civil religion, which desires the creation of symbols or structures that express the core values of a community cultivated into a set of norms by which all must conform, or a political theology in which religion is infused by a particular political ideology, and theology becomes the servant of politics. Rather, argues Stackhouse, public theology seeks both to critique and to reform the values that underpin civil religion, while at the same time rejecting the utopianism of political theology. It does this because it is realistic about both the potential for reform as well as the abuse of power and the establishment of self-interest. Public theology may use political and social theories, but those should seek to serve society, not the other way around.[4]

Public theology, therefore, is in part a reformist movement, rejecting both the conservatism of civil religion and the revolutionary thrust of political theology because it is realistic about what might be achieved at any given time. But one must be careful that this is not an impotent realism, for as Elaine Graham, Heather Walton and Frances Ward assert:

> the task of living within a pluralistic and fallen world will generate questions, anxieties and challenges to which the gospel must be seen to respond; and that the credibility of Christian truths must be argued in ways that fulfil prevailing standards of intellectual coherence.[5]

The crucial question for public theology, then, is how to communicate in a credible and intelligible manner the riches and insight of the gospel of Jesus Christ to the variety of publics found within the contexts of church, state, civil society, the marketplace and the academy.

The Language of Public Theology

Whether a public theology has anything particular to offer to the world depends upon the theological foundation that underpins this task, which raises questions about the depth of theological understanding present in the community that is attempting that task. It may be that the first task of public theology is to address the public of the church, to seek to educate and

---

3. Stackhouse, 'Civil Religion', p. 277.
4. Stackhouse, 'Civil Religion', p. 284.
5. E.L. Graham, H. Walton and F. Ward, *Theological Reflection: Methods* (London: SCM Press, 2005), p. 139.

inform that community of faith as to the dimensions and features of their own theology, and to show the implications and trajectories of that faith.

This particular concern, of the need to educate the church in order to do robust public theology, is related to wider concern about notions of religious and biblical literacy. Religion scholar Stephen Prothero, writing in the context of the United States, argues that religious literacy is 'the ability to understand and use the religious terms, symbols, images, beliefs, practices, scriptures, heroes, themes, and stories that are employed in American public life' in such a way as to be able to participate in the ways religion functions in both private and public spheres.[6] This is not simply knowledge of the core doctrines and teachings of a particular religious faith such as Christianity or Islam but also of key characters, images and stories in their sacred texts, their rites and the history of the faith. This kind of knowledge allows people and communities to 'talk about religion in their homes, at work, in houses of worship, and in the rough-and-tumble of local and national politics'.[7]

While Prothero is concerned about the depth, or perceived lack thereof, of religious literacy within wider US society, biblical scholar Gary Burge raises similar concerns about a more narrow biblical literacy within the wider church community. In particular, Burge argues that while the Bible is still used as a starting point for personal piety and meditation, with an emphasis upon a thematic reading of the text, actual reading of the biblical text that engages with the narratives, metaphors and imagery of the Bible has been lost. This, he argues, leads to a faith that has been cut adrift from the foundational source of Christian life and faith, hence open to other influences that appear 'biblical'.[8]

This is further echoed by sociologist Christian Smith, who contends that there is a layer beneath religious belief and practice within the US context that looks similar to Judeo-Christian values and beliefs but in many ways undermines them. According to Smith,

> The language—and therefore the experience—of Trinity, holiness, sin, grace, justification, sanctification, church, Eucharist, and heaven and hell appear, among most Christian teenagers in the USA at the very least, to be being supplanted by the language of happiness, niceness, and an earned heavenly reward.[9]

---

6. S.R. Prothero, *Religious Literacy: What Every American Needs to Know—and Doesn't* (New York: HarperOne, 2008), pp. 17-18.

7. Prothero, *Religious Literacy*, p. 19.

8. G.M. Burge, 'The Greatest Story Never Read: Recovering Biblical Literacy in the Church', *Christianity Today* 43.9 (1999), pp. 45-49.

9. C. Smith, 'On "Moralistic Therapeutic Deism" as US Teenagers' Actual, Tacit, De Facto Religious Faith', in *Religion and Youth* (ed. S. Collins-Mayo and P. Dandelion; Farnham, Surrey: Ashgate, 2010), pp. 41-46 (46).

While some see Smith's description of this kind of religious life—*moralistic therapeutic deism*—as only part of the picture, it again stresses the disconnection of religious life from the biblical text and core Christian doctrine about which both Prothero and Burge are also concerned, and which is picked up in various surveys and research in other parts of the Western world.[10] This, in turn, connects back to the two earlier questions which asked, first, if public theology is rooted in a distinctive theological discourse, to what extent is that a solid foundation with wider church contexts and, second, to what extent does a loss of an understanding of religious or biblical literacy within wider society make the doing of public theology more difficult?

The former question is particularly pertinent for, as we have already noted, one of the things public theology does is to 'deploy theology in public debate, rather than a vague and optimistic idealism which tends to disintegrate in the face of radical evil'.[11] One struggles to see how a theology that looks like *moralistic therapeutic deism* might confront, resist and bring hope when faced with that situation. Similarly, approaches to public theology that seek to use distinctive 'God language' or 'God talk' in the public arena may struggle when not only is that language and imagery not part of the cultural background of society, but when perhaps religion is now seen as passé or irrelevant.

In his recent book, *Compassionate Justice*, Christopher Marshall's discussion of the Good Samaritan in Luke 10 attempts to address these kinds of questions.[12] Moving beyond a Sunday School telling of the story with a general moral ideal of being kind to people, Marshall highlights that compassion and justice are central to Jesus' teaching and hence an integral part of the good news. Moreover, this compassion is multifaceted, involving not only that initial emotional response to suffering (if suffering is even mentioned in the Sunday School account) but also short-term and long-term consequences of compassionate agency, where actions are situated in a reflective context of praxis. Faith leads to action, but that action also then

---

10. See S.C. Bachand, 'Living God or Cosmic Therapist? Implications of the National Survey of Youth and Religion for Christian Religious Education', *Religious Education* 105.2 (2010), pp. 140-56; P. Hughes and C. Pickering, *Bible Engagement among Young Australians: Patterns and Social Drivers* (Nunawading, Australia: Christian Research Association, 2010); S. Opie, *Bible Engagement in New Zealand: Survey of Attitudes and Behaviour* (Wellington, NZ: Bible Society New Zealand, 2008); N. Spencer and H. Weldin, *Post-religious Britain? The Faith of the Faithless* (London: Theos, 2012).

11. Forrester, 'The Scope of Public Theology', p. 6.

12. C.D. Marshall, *Compassionate Justice: An Interdisciplinary Dialogue with Two Gospel Parables on Law, Crime, and Restorative Justice* (Eugene, OR: Cascade Books, 2012).

leads back to reflection upon faith—a never-ending feedback loop between faith and agency.

This connects to Stackhouse's description of public theology as having a two-fold movement whereby the top-down source of revelation provides the norm, but that norm is realized through the personal convictions present in the community of faith.[13] The narratives and examples of compassion and justice found in parables such as the Good Samaritan and the Prodigal Son are received from their scriptural, revelatory source, but at the same time the norms found in those sources are impotent until worked out through the personal convictions of people in the contexts where they work, live, play and worship. What form should this dialogue between faith and agency take, and in particular how should this vision of compassion be communicated? Should one take a 'common-currency' approach in which the God-talk is muted in an attempt to find some common ground with other groups through the use of a common secular discourse, or should one attempt to 'out-narrate' other competing narratives within the public square by offering a 'distinctive discourse' rooted in the language of faith?[14]

Perhaps, as Marshall comments, following Robert Gascoigne, one should not introduce God too early into the conversation because it may act as a barrier to being heard, but at the same time not leave God out so much as to lose the Christian identity of one's message. The point is that 'Christians must be able to speak the language of political discourse effectively, albeit with a foreign accent'.[15] In a world within which popular storytelling is a pervasive feature of contemporary media society, might the ability to 'read' and 'write' popular culture be that accent?

Popular Culture

Trying to define popular culture is problematic because both academic and non-academic discourse about popular culture is often disconnected from any deep accounts of both culture and the popular.[16] One particularly helpful way of thinking about it, however, is that offered by practical theologian Gordon Lynch, who suggests that it might be better to think of popular

---

13. Stackhouse, 'Civil Religion', p. 291.
14. See C. Marshall, 'What Language Shall I Borrow? The Bilingual Dilemma of Public Theology', *Stimulus* 13.3 (2005), pp. 11-18 (14-16).
15. Robert Gascoigne, *The Public Forum and Christian Ethics* (Cambridge: Cambridge University Press, 2001); Marshall, 'What Language Shall I Borrow?', p. 17.
16. Simon Frith, 'Popular Culture', in *Dictionary of Cultural and Critical Theory* (ed. Michael Payne; Blackwell Publishing, 1997, eBook), http://www.blackwellreference.com/subscriber/tocnode.html?id=g9780631207535_chunk_g978063120753519_ ss1-29.

culture as 'the shared context, practices and resources of "everyday life"'.[17] This emphasis on the broad, everyday world means that an examination of popular culture deals not only with its 'texts' or cultural products such as films or music but also with the study of how these are produced and consumed in society, thereby giving insight into the wider structures, patterns and activities of meaning-making in everyday life. Media scholar Lelia Green captures this nicely when she argues that popular culture is 'that subsection of mass media which are appropriated by people in their daily lives and remodelled as the raw material through which they communicate their values and enthusiasms, and through which they connect to others'.[18]

If this is the case, then a language for doing public theology might be found within popular culture, including information not only about what compassion is but also about compassionate worldviews that orient, are imitated and serve to nurture the flourishing of life. This is especially pertinent in relation to Gospel parables because they offer particular perspectives on the reality of the world in which we find ourselves and the trajectory of the Kingdom of God, in a form embedded in the shared context, practices and resources of 'everyday life'.

Biblical Afterlives

The telling of biblical parables, particularly parables such as the Good Samaritan and the Prodigal Son, and their use as a starting point for thinking about compassionate agency in the world depends upon the currency of these stories and wider biblical material. Within the post-Christendom context, where increasingly knowledge of the Bible and theological concepts is waning in light of a declining religious literacy, echoes of the Good Samaritan or the Prodigal Son exist within popular storytelling, albeit not necessarily in a form that connects to the biblical story. For example, the idea that a 'Samaritan' is someone who helps another person is widespread, seen in references to the charity of the same name that provides emotional support to people through their telephone helpline while, on the other hand, the film *The Samaritan* (2012) starring Samuel L. Jackson with its tagline, 'Vengeance has a new name', plays ironically with that common understanding.[19]

Many of these narratives tap into what biblical scholar Yvonne Sherwood calls the 'afterlives' or memories of biblical texts that exist within wider culture. She notes that particular details of a biblical text are remembered,

---

17. G. Lynch, *Understanding Theology and Popular Culture* (Malden, MA: Blackwell, 2005), p. 13.
18. L. Green, *Technoculture: From Alphabet to Cybersex* (Crowsnest, NSW: Allen and Unwin, 2002), p. 156.
19. D. Weaver, *The Samaritan* (Canada: H2O Motion Pictures, 2012).

but they have come adrift from the wider biblical context within which they exist. In speaking of the biblical story of Jonah, for example, she observes: 'Biblical critics may deem the fish to be an interpretative minnow, but for most readers it is the veritable centre (or navel) of the text, the vortex into which our attention is sucked.'[20] Thus, people have some understanding of Adam and Eve (a garden, an apple, being naked, temptation and a snake) because of their representation in advertising or the title sequence of a television show like *Desperate Housewives*. Similarly, when considering the use of the biblical Samson and Delilah story within the science fiction television show, *Terminator: The Sarah Connor Chronicles* (2008–2009), Robert Myles, drawing upon Sherwood, comments that one must recognize that biblical texts are not the sole property of the religious and scholarly communities, but rather that they exist as cultural memories or 'afterlives' where the original text may have been 'terminated' but new versions and interpretations continue to exist and shape wider engagement with the biblical material.[21]

One particular intersection with biblical afterlives concerning love and compassion occurs in the family-friendly animated *Green Lantern* superhero television show (2011–13). In his recent retelling of the Green Lantern superhero mythos, set within the wider DC Comic universe in which Superman and Batman also exist, writer Geoff Johns introduces what he calls the 'emotional spectrum' of distinct powers. Traditionally the Green Lantern characters, effectively a space-based police force with green 'magic' rings controlled by the wearer's will-power, were unique, but in his retelling Johns introduces other groups focused around a particular 'emotional characteristic' such as fear (yellow), rage (red), hope (blue), love (violet), compassion (indigo) and avarice (orange). Johns then uses these categories to explore what these 'emotional characteristics' entail: What does true love look like? Can compassion be coerced? Is hope essential to the human spirit? Do fear, avarice and rage trump love, hope and compassion? For example, the emotional spectrum characteristic of love is modelled primarily in the actions and community of the female Amazon-like Zamarons. Here love is seen as connected to one's heart's true desire, typically in relation to a soul-mate. Love, which is represented as aggressively pursuing the beloved, is a mixture of *erōs* (sexual, sensual love) and *agapē* (self-giving love). There is little evidence of *philia* (friendship) and *storgē* (affection); rather, it's about the intensity of passion.

---

20. Y. Sherwood, *A Biblical Text and Its Afterlives: The Survival of Jonah in Western Culture* (Cambridge: Cambridge University Press, 2000), p. 141.
21. R.J. Myles, 'Terminating Samson: The *Sarah Connor Chronicles* and the Rise of New Biblical Meaning', *Relegere: Studies in Religion and Reception* 1.2 (2011), p. 331; J. Friedman, *Terminator: The Sarah Connor Chronicles* (Bartleby Company, 2008–2009).

In episode 22 of the television series, 'Love is a Battlefield', itself an intertextual reference to Pat Benatar's 1983 pop song, Carol Ferris, a human woman who sometimes manifests the violet power of love, is asked by the villain, Aya, to define love. Struggling to come up with an answer, Ferris starts with 'love is a battlefield' but then falls back to quoting parts of 1 Corinthians 13, including 'love is patient, love is kind…it is not proud. It is not easily angered', before ending with 'All I said is that love is about doing what's best for the one you love. It's as simple as putting his or her needs before your own, but I'm no expert. I'm just someone who fell in love'.[22] Here we see the cultural memory or biblical afterlife of 1 Corinthians 13, where love is patient, kind and not proud, and the selflessness of putting another's needs before one's own—perhaps a starting point for wider engagement with compassion and love and a theological exploration of such themes.

Compassion, Popular Culture and Public Theology

The identification of biblical afterlives and themes within popular culture may be a starting point for initiating a discussion about the true nature of love and compassion, and even to point back to the original biblical material being drawn upon, but by itself it is simply that—a starting point. What would be better is the development of a robust way to draw people, both within and outside of the church, into a dialectical relation between compassionate faith and compassionate agency lived out in the world.

Marshall's description of the parable of the Good Samaritan highlights the complete compassionate engagement of the Samaritan with the victim and the victim's past, present and future. As Marshall puts it, 'the Samaritan's love for the Jewish victim is depicted as engaging in all the powers of his personality: his sight, his heart, his hands, his strength, his time, his possessions, and his intelligence'.[23] How then might we find a way to put this parable into a contemporary form that shapes compassionate thought and action, where the eyes and ears of the public—their heart and feelings, their mind, their response, their willingness to act to change victims' circumstances—are engaged in such a way as to morally implicate them in the situations and generate an ongoing response of compassion?

In response to this question, I suggest that the concept of theological praxis, the interplay between critical reflection and agency, might be a vehicle for educating about and communicating compassion to various publics

---

22. J. Keene and R. Morales, *Love is a Battlefield*, *Green Lantern: The Animated Series* (Warner Bros., 2013).

23. Marshall, *Compassionate Justice*, p. 120.

inside and outside of the church. The particular model of contextual theology, in which Scripture and Tradition dialogue with the experience of the material reality of the everyday world, is also known as the pastoral cycle.[24] This cycle brings together orthodoxy and orthopraxy to generate a dialectical relation between the theological positions of faith seeking intelligent action and considered action leading to theological insight. The result is an iterative spiral between reflection and action, often initiated by the experience of individuals or communities seeking to make sense of their own or another's particular situation.[25] There are various implementations of this cycle, but the one used here has the following steps:

1. listening to the stories of individuals and communities;
2. locating those stories in their wider context;
3. bringing those stories and their context into dialogue with theological sources and other disciplines;
4. articulating a deep theological understanding of the situation;
5. planning appropriate action based upon that theological reflection; and
6. evaluating the efficacy of that action before returning to the first step of the process.

This is a kind of hermeneutical spiral, though the 'texts' being read and reflected upon tend to be people's lived experiences no less than traditional biblical texts. Marshall's identification of the breadth and depth of love exhibited by the Samaritan maps onto a similar model of action-reflection, with action making the praxis cycle an appropriate vehicle for our purposes here.

The first two steps of the praxis process above connect to Marshall's dimensions of sight and heart. In the first step, one 'sees' or 'hears' that there is a problem or issue through one's own personal experience, the personal narratives of other individuals or the experience of an affected community. This, in turn, engenders an affective response to the situation, of the heart and feelings, and together this attention to the local and personal narratives leads to the volitional choice to enter into the sufferer's world and become personally involved.[26]

---

24. Paul Ballard, 'Tools for Practical Theology: Introducing the Pastoral Cycle', in *Practical Theology in Action: Christian Thinking in the Service of Church and Society* (ed. Paul Ballard and John Pritchard; London: SPCK, 1996), pp. 73-86; L. Green, *Let's Do Theology: Resources for Contextual Theology* (London: Mowbray, 2009), pp. 17-38; Graham et al., *Theological Reflection: Methods*, pp. 170-99.

25. S.B. Bevans, *Models of Contextual Theology* (Maryknoll, NY: Orbis Books, 2002), pp. 70-87.

26. Marshall, *Compassionate Justice*, pp. 120-21.

This personal involvement, with its recognition of the sufferer as a person of worth and subject of love, leads to an understanding of the wider context within which the one who suffers and their experience are situated. In the parable, the Samaritan recognizes the one suffering as a person, but not as one dislocated from the context they both share personally, socially and institutionally. Thus, in this step we look to the wider social, political, economic and religious contexts within which the one suffering is located, in order to seek a deeper understanding of their context and to raise further critical questions with which to engage.

This is perhaps the most common way in which popular cultural narratives might be used in public theology, telling the story of others in a powerful, engaging way that bridges the gap between victims and observers. It might be a film that explores aspects of the human condition and injustice, such as *Romero* (1989) or *Of Gods and Men* (2010), or a song that articulates human experience such as a pop song like U2's *Walk On*, with its articulation of 'A singing bird in an open cage. Who will only fly for freedom',[27] a description of politician Aung San Suu Kyi's situation in Myanmar:

> [The children of prisoners] have known what it is like to be young birds fluttering helplessly outside the cages that shut the parents away from them. They know that there will be no security for their families as long as freedom of thought and freedom of political action are not guaranteed by the law of the land.[28]

It might also be a documentary film such as *Black Gold* (2006), which explores the plight of Ethiopian coffee growers and questions of fair trade, the book and film *Whale Rider* (1987; 2003) highlighting indigenous (in this case Māori) concerns about the preservation and future of cultural life and practice, or even one of the multitudes of television soap operas and dramas that draw upon and accentuate aspects of everyday human situations and relationships.[29]

The third step brings the dimension of 'intelligence' or 'mind' to faith seeking intelligent action. Here personal experience and wider context are brought into dialogue with theological and non-theological sources and disciplines. This is typically an area on which public theology is focused,

---

27. J. Duigan, *Romero* (United States: Paulist Pictures; Four Seasons Entertainment, 1989); X. Beauvois, *Of Gods and Men* (France: Why Not Productions; Armada Films; Mars Distribution, 2010); U2, *All that you can't leave behind* (CD; Island Records, 2001).

28. A.S. Suu Kyi, *Letters from Burma* (London: Penguin, 1997).

29. W. Ihimaera, *The Whale Rider* (Auckland, NZ: Heinemann, 1987); N. Caro, *Whale Rider* (Culver City, CA: Columbia TriStar Home Entertainment, 2003); M. Francis and N. Francis, *Black Gold* (UK: Speakit Films; Fulcrum Productions, 2006).

particularly with the 'middle axiom' approach whereby experts from theological and other disciplines work together toward an understanding of the issue and context at hand so as to integrate this expertise in faithful and constructive ways.

This approach echoes Australian theologian Terry Veling's idea of a practical theology that combines active reflection upon Scripture and Tradition with skill at 'reading the signs of the times', and in which the theological community pays attention to God's concern for the world while listening and responding to the questions and insights offered by our culture, society and human lives.[30] This also connects with Bevans' description of contextual theology as one that brings the experience of the past as recorded in Scripture and preserved and defended in Tradition into dialogue with the experience of the present represented in personal experience, social location and culture.[31] In the public theology context, Forrester sums up these kinds of approaches when he says:

> Public theology, it is held, is too important a matter to be left to the theologians. Theologians need to be involved, but only alongside other people with varied and relevant skills and experience for dealing with the specific matters under consideration. Along with theologians, we need to have people who have inside knowledge of the situation being considered.[32]

Forrester's comment about involving 'insiders' with knowledge of the actual situation is critical. It would be too easy to reduce this step to a collective of scholars and experts from various disciplines, with the consequence that those practitioners and participants embedded in the context being engaged find their voices marginalized. This is particularly pertinent with respect to indigenous voices, which bring with them a depth of history and tradition that can complement and critique existing structures and models of engagement and thinking. The final result of this step is the collection and generation of resources that can then be passed on to the next step of the process.

In this particular step, it may be that the narratives of popular culture serve as a vehicle for reconnecting those seeking to think theologically with the biblical narratives and themes with which they have consciously or unconsciously lost touch. The discussion around love, hope and compassion in the *Green Lantern* stories is one example, as might be the way that the film *Billy Elliot* (2000), set in the mid-1980s coalminers' strike in Northern England, becomes a kind of prodigal son story, complete with elder brother

---

30. T.A. Veling, *Practical Theology: On Earth as It Is in Heaven* (Maryknoll, NY: Orbis Books, 2005), p. 25.
31. Bevans, *Models of Contextual Theology*, pp. 3-9.
32. Forrester, 'The Scope of Public Theology', p. 12.

and father who are reconciled with the their brother/son, Billy.[33] The film, *The Blind Side* (2009), contains within it a powerful Good Samaritan narrative and extended reflection on compassion.[34] These stories do not replace biblical parables and texts, but they perhaps serve as contemporary parables that lead to deeper theological and biblical encounter.

The fourth step in the process brings the questions, stories and resources together in such a way as to develop a particular theological way of thinking about the issue at hand, which can then provide the basis for 'intelligent action'. This step, no less than the previous one, goes some way to addressing Marshall's observation that the emotive response to the suffering or sufferer may paralyse a person or community who are then unable to respond or to generate any concrete actions.[35] Not only that, but the aid that is being proposed is going to prove beneficial in the situation confronted and not going to disintegrate when faced by evil and resistance. It is a vision of what could be in light of the inaugurated Kingdom of God. And as Forrester observes,

> A concern with visions serves to remind Christians that theology is not exclusively engaged with 'academic' questions, or with particular problems and policies and ethical conundrums. It is at least as concerned with the visions which provide a horizon of meaning within which a society exists, policies are formulated, actions are taken and vocations are fulfilled. Visions generate and sustain utopias, if you prefer that language.[36]

If the first four steps of this theological praxis process bring the volitional, emotive and intellectual strands together, the next step is concerned to plan concrete agency in the situation and then enact that agency in the world. This brings another dimension of Marshall's Good Samaritan analysis into play: 'the interior experience of compassion was translated into the exterior deed of deliverance'.[37] Here the theological insight developed in previous steps is put into action, not in an unfocused or half-hearted way but rather with insight into the heart of the issue and its context, a strong underpinning justification for the action considered and a commitment to 'get one's hands dirty'. In effect, this is what we're going to do, this is why we're doing it and this is why we've chosen to do it this way. Popular culture can play a role here, too, by providing concrete imagery for the

---

33. S. Daldry and L. Hall, *Billy Elliot* (UK: BBC Films; StudioCanal; Tiger Aspect Pictures; WT2 Productions, 2000).

34. J.L. Hancock and M. Lewis, *The Blind Side* (Burbank, CA: Alcon Entertainment, 2009).

35. Marshall, *Compassionate Justice*, pp. 122-23.

36. Duncan B. Forrester, 'Politics and Vision', *The Bible in Transmission* (Autumn 1999), pp. 1-4.

37. Marshall, *Compassionate Justice*, p. 123.

theological visions developed that lift one's eyes to the horizon of future possibilities, as well as by offering an appropriate voice to do that. A biblical example of this can be found in the book of Revelation where its apocalyptic theological vision is expressed in a powerful critique of the empire and its emperor cult. Here (Revelation 4–5; 12) parody and the retelling of stories from contemporary popular culture and civil religion concerning the emperor and empire in a form that uses the cultural motifs of the day are used to show that Christ, not Caesar, is lord of all.[38]

Thus one form of engendering agency within the everyday world is to tell powerful and well-formed stories through music, art, writing, television and film that make people consider that another course of action, when the world is seen through a different lens, is possible. A good example of this is the novel and film *Pay it Forward* (2000), which articulates both the power and trials of beneficiaries of good deeds 'repaying' those deeds to others rather than the original benefactor with the aim of making the world a better place.[39] The story clearly articulates key principles and motivations combined with a course of action, the fifth praxis step, highlighting how rendering compassion to another caused enmeshment in the situation at hand, drawing people into further action and reflection. Other examples include New Zealander Mike Riddell's novel and film, *The Insatiable Moon* (1997; 2010), which deals particularly with the community housing of psychiatric patients within a community that is often hostile towards them or oblivious to their situation, as well as *The Blind Side* (2009), a film that re-enacts a cross-cultural Good Samaritan story within middle-class American society.[40] Similarly, satire in a form similar to that found in animated TV shows such as *bro'Town* and *The Simpsons* might also be a vehicle to speak effectively into the public square, mixing humour with pointed social commentary.[41]

In itself this might be enough, but the last step of the theological praxis process is critical reflection that ties into Marshall's argument that, by choosing to act and intervene in a situation, the benefactor remains morally implicated. There are consequences, both positive and negative, for the actions chosen, so there needs to be further reflection on whether the action

---

38. P. Trebilco, 'Gospel, Culture, and the Public Sphere: Perspectives from the New Testament', *Evangel* 24.2 (2006), pp. 39-42.

39. M. Leder and C.R. Hyde, *Pay it Forward* (Burbank, CA: Warner Bros.; Bel Air Entertainment; Tapestry Films, 2000).

40. M. Riddell, *The Insatiable Moon* (Auckland, NZ: Flamingo, 1997); R. Riddell and M. Riddell, *The Insatiable Moon* (New Zealand: Vendetta Films; Rialto Distribution, 2010).

41. The Naked Samoans and Firehorse Films, *bro'Town* (Auckland, NZ: Firehorse Films, 2004–2009). M. Groening, *The Simpsons* (Beverly Hills, CA: Gracie Films; 20th Century Fox, 1989–).

performed is effective, life-giving and persevering.[42] The Samaritan's concern for the continuing well-being of the victim through the ongoing provision of care and hospitality, which he will monitor at a later date, forms this kind of reflection and ongoing commitment to the victim. The implication of this reflective step is that it makes the process iterative. The insights and new personal stories gleaned from reflecting upon compassionate action enacted lead not to termination but rather to further engagement with the process in light of such insights. Again, the creation of resources such as films, novels and songs that highlight and document insights gleaned from this step of reflection can resource others engaging in related areas.

Following a series of steps such as those outlined in the process above has a number of distinct advantages. First, as noted earlier, it aids those who are struggling with how to respond to a situation so as to initiate some form of considered compassionate agency and to move beyond either being paralysed in their response or taking some form of ill-considered action. Moreover, the process pays particular attention to both the situation and its wider context, alerting those involved that the appropriate solution will need to address wider, underlying concerns in addition to the immediate concerns of those suffering. Another potential advantage is the possibility of collaboration throughout the different steps of the process in which individuals and groups with particular skill sets might focus on a particular step in the process. Finally, the iterative nature of the process recognizes that life goes on and hence that compassionate engagement is a long-term activity.

Against this, however, there are various dangers or pitfalls that such a process might introduce. The first of these is that the process itself can become oppressive, forcing people to serve the process rather than vice versa, and perhaps becoming idolatrous in some ways. Second, human life is inherently 'messy', and it may be the situation being encountered doesn't necessarily fit the steps of the model exactly, so some flexibility in implementation is needed. Third, it is possible for people to get stuck at a particular point in the process for both good and bad reasons. For example, the emotional effects of the personal narratives, the sheer enormity of the wider context and the desire to have more information before formulating a plan of action can all cause the process to break down, as can the struggle to find a starting point when multiple steps all demand attention simultaneously. Finally, it may be that either action or reflection is overemphasized rather than both being involved in a holistic way, leaving action without reflection or reflection without action.[43]

Furthermore, in many cases one simply does not have the time to go through a considered and sometimes lengthy process when called to act

---

42. Marshall, *Compassionate Justice*, pp. 126-27.
43. Green, *Let's Do Theology*, pp. 25-27.

compassionately; the need is urgent. However, the continual use of a process like this and a commitment to practise faith seeking intelligent action moves the practitioner towards unconsciously performing reflective action in much the same way that modelling virtues such as prudence, courage, faith and love leads to them becoming inherently part of the practitioner. Moreover, such a framework provides numerous occasions in which popular culture might be employed in the 'reading' of a situation, in educating about compassion and indeed as a vehicle for ongoing compassionate agency in the public sphere.

Conclusion

In conclusion, public theology is sometimes described as the offering of something distinctive, and that is gospel, to the world for the welfare of human society. Rooted in the distinctive theological discourse of faith communities, which is then communicated appropriately to a particular public sphere, public theology has much to learn from popular culture about communicating this theological discourse in the form of popular storytelling. It does this not only to communicate particular courses of action in the world but also to educate both church and non-church communities about the essence of compassionate living. The combination of public theology and popular culture through a process of theological praxis provides for a multi-level engagement with both theology and the issue or concern at hand.

On one level, this process provides a source for action-reflection as well as raw materials to enable people to engage with others' experiences and for exploring biblical afterlives of love, compassion and justice with a view to reconnecting with the original Gospel parables and wider biblical texts. On another level, it provides languages for speaking to the church and the world in ways that are credible and intelligible, much as Jesus did with his telling of everyday parables. In a post-biblically literate society, where the original texts and narratives have been cut loose from their biblical context and exist alongside competing 'afterlives' of those texts, the reframing of parables such as the Good Samaritan and the Prodigal Son in such a praxis process might serve to reconnect church communities with the texts and themes that underpin public theological engagement, while at the same time communicating particular categories of understanding and common ground from compassionate agency based upon well-known cultural resonances with biblical narratives and theological concepts in wider society. As the parables of first-century Palestine captured the heavenly and the everyday in stories that provoked response, so too might the retelling of the faith through contemporary stories and parables have a similar effect.

BIBLIOGRAPHY

Adam, A.K.M., *Faithful Interpretation: Reading the Bible in a Postmodern World* (Minneapolis: Fortress Press, 2006).
Allison, Dale C., Jr, *The Sermon on the Mount: Inspiring the Moral Imagination* (New York: Crossroad, 1999).
Anselm, *Why God Became Man*, in *A Scholastic Miscellany: Anselm to Ockham*, LCC (ed. Eugene R. Fairweather; Philadelphia: Westminster Press, 1956), pp. 100-183.
Astley, Jeff, and Leslie J. Francis (eds.), *Exploring Ordinary Theology* (Surrey: Ashgate, 2013).
Auerbach, Eric, *Mimesis: The Representation of Reality in Western Literature* (trans. Willard R. Trask; Princeton, NJ: Princeton University Press, fiftieth anniversary edn, 2003).
Bachand, Sarah Caffrey, 'Living God or Cosmic Therapist? Implications of the National Survey of Youth and Religion for Christian Religious Education', *Religious Education* 105.2 (2010), pp. 140-56.
Bailey, Kenneth E., *Poet & Peasant and Through Peasant Eyes: A Literary-Cultural Approach to the Parables of Luke* (Grand Rapids: Eerdmans, combined edn, 1983).
—*Finding the Lost: Cultural Keys to Luke 15* (St Louis: Concordia, 1992).
Ballard, Paul, 'Tools for Practical Theology: Introducing the Pastoral Cycle', in *Practical Theology in Action: Christian Thinking in the Service of Church and Society* (ed. Paul Ballard and John Pritchard; London: SPCK, 1996), pp. 73-86.
Balthasar, Hans Urs von, *Theo-drama: Theological Dramatic Theory* (trans. G. Harrison; San Francisco: Ignatius Press, 1988–1998 [1973–1983]).
Barth, Karl, *Church Dogmatics. III/2. The Doctrine of Creation* (trans. G.W. Bromiley *et al.*; Edinburgh: T. & T. Clark, 1960).
Bartholomew, C.G., and M.W. Goheen, *The Drama of Scripture: Finding our Place in the Biblical Story* (London: SPCK, 2006).
Beauvois, Xavier, *Of Gods and Men* (France: Why Not Productions; Armada Films; Mars Distribution, 2010).
Beavis, Mary Ann, 'The Power of Jesus' Parables: Were They Polemical or Irenic?', *JSNT* 82 (2001), pp. 3-30.
Bell, Daniel M., Jr, 'Deliberation: Justice and Liberation', in *The Blackwell Companion to Christian Ethics* (ed. Stanley Hauerwas and Samuel Wells; Oxford: Blackwell, 2004), pp. 182-95.
—'Jesus, the Jews, and the Politics of God's Justice', *Ex Auditu* 22 (2006), pp. 87-111.
Bell, Richard H., *Rethinking Justice: Restoring Our Humanity* (Lanham, MD: Lexington Books, 2007).
Bevans, Stephen B., *Models of Contextual Theology* (Maryknoll, NY: Orbis Books, 2002).
Birch, Bruce C., 'The Role of Scripture in Public Theology', *WW* 4.3 (1984), pp. 260-68.

Blass, F., and A. Debrunner, *A Greek Grammar of the New Testament and Other Early Christian Literature* (trans. and ed. Robert W. Funk; Chicago: University of Chicago Press, 1961).
Bock, Darrell L., *Luke 9:51–24:53* (Grand Rapids: Baker Books, 1996).
Borg, Marcus J., 'The Truth of Easter', in Marcus J. Borg and N.T. Wright, *The Meaning of Jesus: Two Visions* (London: SPCK, 1999), pp. 129-42.
Boyarin, Daniel, 'Midrash in Parables', *Association of Jewish Studies Review* 20.1 (1995), pp. 123-38.
Bradstock, Andrew, 'The Bible and Public Theology', in *The Bible: Culture, Community, Society* (ed. Angus Paddison and Neil Messer; London: Bloomsbury T. & T. Clark, 2013), pp. 171-88.
Braithwaite, John, *Crime, Shame and Reintegration* (Cambridge: Cambridge University Press, 1989).
Broadie, Sarah, and Christopher Rowe (eds.), *Aristotle: Nicomachean Ethics: Translation, Introduction, Commentary* (Oxford: Oxford University Press, 2002).
Broughton, Geoff, 'Reading the Bible through the Lens of the Street', in *Reflections on a Remarkable Church* (ed. Katharine Brisbane; Sydney: St John Foundation, 2008), pp. 103-105.
—'Restorative Justice and Jesus Christ: Why Restorative Justice Requires a Holistic Christology' (PhD dissertation, Charles Sturt University, 2011).
—*Restorative Christ: Jesus, Justice, and Discipleship* (Eugene, OR: Pickwick Publications, 2014).
Bruckner, James K., 'Justice in Scripture', *Ex Auditu* 22 (2006), pp. 1-9.
Brueggemann, Walter, *Interpretation and Obedience: From Faithful Reading to Faithful Living* (Minneapolis: Fortress Press, 1991).
—*Theology of the Old Testament: Testimony, Dispute, Advocacy* (Minneapolis: Fortress Press, 1997).
—*Disruptive Grace: Reflections on God, Scripture, and the Church* (ed. Carolyn J. Sharp; Minneapolis: Fortress Press, 2011).
Bruehler, Bart B., *A Public and Political Christ: The Social-Spatial Characteristics of Luke 18:35–19:43 and the Gospel as a Whole in Its Ancient Context* (Eugene, OR: Pickwick Publications, 2011).
Burge, Gary M., 'The Greatest Story Never Read: Recovering Biblical Literacy in the Church', *Christianity Today* 43.9 (1999), pp. 45-49.
Burth, Robert W., 'Are There Moral Experts', *The Monist* 58.4 (1974), pp. 646-58.
Byrne, Brendan, *The Hospitality of God: A Reading of Luke's Gospel* (Strathfield, NSW: St Pauls Publications, 2000).
Carlson, M., *Performance: A Critical Introduction* (New York: Routledge, 2nd edn, 2004).
Caro, Niki, *Whale Rider* (Culver City, CA: Columbia TriStar Home Entertainment, 2003).
Carroll, John T., *Response to the End of History: Eschatology and Situation in Luke–Acts* (Atlanta: Scholars Press, 1988).
—'Welcoming Grace, Costly Commitment: An Approach to the Gospel of Luke', *Interpretation* 57.1 (January 2003), pp. 16-23.
—*Luke: A Commentary* (Louisville, KY: Westminster/John Knox Press, 2012).
Carroll, M.D., 'A Passion for Justice and the Conflicted Self: Lessons from the Book of Micah', *Journal of Psychology and Christianity* 25.2 (2006), pp. 169-76.
Carroll, R.P., *Jeremiah* (London: SCM Press, 1986).

Carter, Warren, *Matthew and the Margins: A Socio-Political and Religious Reading* (Sheffield: Sheffield Academic Press, 2000).
—'Resisting and Imitating the Empire: Imperial Paradigms in Two Matthean Parables', *Interpretation* 56.3 (July 2002), pp. 260-72.
Cavanaugh, William T. '"A Fire Strong Enough to Consume the House": The Wars of Religion and the Rise of the State', in *Radical Orthodoxy* (ed. Graham Ward, Catherine Pickstock and John Milbank; London: Routledge, 1999), pp. 397-419.
—*The Myth of Religious Violence: Secular Ideology and the Roots of Modern Conflict* (Oxford: Oxford University Press, 2009).
—*Migrations of the Holy: God, State, and the Political Meaning of the Church* (Grand Rapids: Eerdmans, 2011).
Cavanaugh, William T., Jeffrey W. Bailey and Craig Hovey (eds.), *An Eerdmans Reader in Contemporary Political Theology* (Grand Rapids: Eerdmans, 2012).
Chaplin, Jonathan, 'Beyond Liberal Restraint: Defending Religiously-based Arguments in Law and Public Policy', *UBC Law Review* 33 (2000), pp. 617-46.
—'The Future of Theological Ethics: A Response to Robin Lovin and Nigel Biggar', *SCE* 25.2 (2012), pp. 148-52.
—'Law, Religion and Public Reasoning', *Oxford Journal of Law and Religion* 1.2 (2013), 1-21.
Chilton, Bruce, and J.I.H. McDonald, *Jesus and the Ethics of the Kingdom* (London: SPCK, 1987).
Conquergood, D., 'Of Caravans and Carnivals: Performance Studies in Motion', *The Drama Review* 39.4 (1995), pp. 137-41.
Conzelmann, Hans, *The Theology of St. Luke* (trans. Geoffrey Buswell; Philadelphia: Fortress Press, 1961).
Coomber, Matthew J.M. (ed.), *Bible and Justice: Ancient Texts, Modern Challenges* (London: Equinox, 2011).
Cronin, Kieran, *Rights and Christian Ethics* (Cambridge: Cambridge University Press, 1992).
Crossan, John Dominic, 'Historical Jesus as Risen Lord', in John Dominic Crossan, Luke Timothy Johnson and Werner H. Kelber, *The Jesus Controversy: Perspectives in Conflict* (Harrisburg, PA: Trinity Press International, 1999), pp. 1-47.
—*God and Empire: Jesus Against Rome, Then and Now* (San Francisco: HarperCollins, 2007).
—'Divine Violence in the Christian Bible', in *The Bible and the American Future* (ed. Robert L. Jewett with Wayne L. Alloway Jr and John G. Lacey; Eugene, OR: Cascade Books, 2009), pp. 208-236.
Daldry, Stephen, and Lee Hall, *Billy Elliot* (UK: BBC Films; StudioCanal; Tiger Aspect Pictures; WT2 Productions, 1989).
Davis, T.C., 'Introduction: The Pirouette, Detour, Revolution, Deflection, Deviation, Tack, and Yaw of the Performative Turn', in *The Cambridge Companion to Performance Studies* (ed. T.C. Davis; Cambridge: Cambridge University Press, 2008), pp. 1-8.
Davis, T.C. (ed.), *The Cambridge Companion to Performance Studies* (Cambridge: Cambridge University Press, 2008).
De Gruchy, John W., 'Public Theology as Christian Witness: Exploring the Genre', *IJPT* 1 (2007), pp. 26-41.
DeLoughrey, Elizabeth M., *Routes and Roots: Navigating Caribbean and Pacific Island Literatures* (Honolulu: University of Hawai'i Press, 2007).

Dempsey, Carol J., *Justice: A Biblical Perspective* (St Louis: Chalice Press, 2008).
Doan, W., and T. Giles, *Prophets, Performance, and Power* (New York: T. & T. Clark, 2005).
—'The Song of Asaph: A Performance-critical Analysis of 1 Chronicles 16.8-36', *CBQ* 70 (2008), pp. 29-43.
Donahue, John R., 'Biblical Perspectives on Justice', in *The Faith that Does Justice: Examining the Christian Sources for Social Change* (ed. John C. Haughey; New York: Paulist Press, 1977), pp. 68-112.
Dowling, Elizabeth V., *Taking Away the Pound: Women, Theology and the Parable of the Pounds in the Gospel of Luke* (London: T. & T. Clark, 2007).
—'Slave Parables in the Gospel of Luke—Gospel "Texts of Terror"?', *AusBR* 56 (2008), pp. 61-68.
Duigan, John, *Romero* (United States: Paulist Pictures; Four Seasons Entertainment, 1989).
Dyer, Keith D., 'Paul and Embodied Resurrection: Rethinking 1 Corinthians 15', in *Resurrection and Responsibility: Essays on Theology, Scripture, and Ethics in Honor of Thorwald Lorenzen* (ed. Keith D. Dyer and David J. Neville; Eugene, OR: Pickwick Publications, 2009), pp. 136-61.
Dykstra, Laurel, 'The Top One Hundred Books on the Bible and Social Justice', in *Liberating Biblical Study: Scholarship, Art, and Action in Honor of the Center and Library for the Bible and Social Justice* (ed. Laurel Dykstra and Ched Myers; Eugene, OR: Cascade Books, 2011), pp. 223-45.
Dykstra, Laurel, and Ched Myers (eds.), *Liberating Biblical Study: Scholarship, Art, and Action in Honor of the Center and Library for the Bible and Social Justice* (Eugene, OR: Cascade Books, 2011).
Ekblad, Bob, *Reading the Bible with the Damned* (Louisville, KY: Westminster/John Knox Press, 2005).
Elliott, John H., 'The Jewish Messianic Movement: From Faction to Sect', in *Modelling Early Christianity: Social-Scientific Studies of the New Testament in Its Context* (ed. Philip F. Esler; London: Routledge, 1995), pp. 75-95.
Elvey, Anne, 'Legacies of Violence toward the Other: Toward a Consideration of the Outsider within the Lukan Narrative', *Colloquium* 34.1 (2002), pp. 21-34.
—'Love and Justice in the Gospel of Luke—Ecology, the Neighbour and Hope', *AusBR* 60 (2012), pp. 1-17.
Esler, Philip F., *New Testament Theology: Communion and Community* (London: SPCK, 2005).
Eubank, Nathan, 'What does Matthew Say about Divine Recompense? On the Misuse of the Parable of the Workers in the Vineyard (20.1-16)', *JSNT* 35.3 (2013), pp. 242-62.
Fiddes, P.S., 'Story and Possibility: Reflections on the Last Scenes of the Fourth Gospel and Shakespeare's The Tempest', in *Revelation and Story: Narrative Theology and the Centrality of Story* (ed. G. Sauter and J. Barton; Aldershot: Ashgate, 2000), pp. 29-51.
Fitzmyer, Joseph A., *The Gospel according to Luke I–IX* (Garden City, NY: Doubleday, 1981).
—*The Gospel according to Luke X–XXIV* (Garden City, NY: Doubleday, 1985).
Floyd, M.H., 'Prophecy and Writing in Habakkuk 2.1-5', *ZAW* 105.3 (1993), pp. 462-81.
Ford, David F., and C.C. Pecknold (eds.), *The Promise of Scriptural Reasoning* (Oxford: Blackwell, 2006).

Forrester, Duncan B., *Christian Justice and Public Policy* (Cambridge: Cambridge University Press, 1997).
—'Politics and Vision', *The Bible in Transmission* (Autumn 1999), pp. 1-4.
—'The Scope of Public Theology', *SCE* 17.2 (2004), pp. 5-19.
Foucault, Michel, *Discipline and Punish: The Birth of the Prison* (trans. Alan Sheridan; New York: Vintage, 1995).
Fowl, Stephen E., *Theological Interpretation of Scripture* (Eugene, OR: Cascade Books, 2009).
Francis, Marc, and Nick Francis, *Black Gold* (UK: Speakit Films; Fulcrum Productions, 2006).
Freyne, Sean, 'Herodian Economics in Galilee: Searching for a Suitable Model,' in *Modelling Early Christianity: Social-Scientific Studies of the New Testament in Its Context* (ed. Philip F. Esler; London: Routledge, 1995), pp. 23-46.
Friedman, Josh, *Terminator: The Sarah Connor Chronicles* (Bartleby Company, 2008–2009).
Frith, Simon, 'Popular Culture', in *Dictionary of Cultural and Critical Theory* (ed. Michael Payne; Blackwell Publishing, 1997): http://www.blackwellreference.com/subscriber/tocnode.html?id=g9780631207535_chunk_g978063120753519_ss1-29.
Gascoigne, Robert, *The Public Forum and Christian Ethics* (Cambridge: Cambridge University Press, 2001).
Giesen, B., 'Performance Art', in *Social Performance: Symbolic Action, Cultural Pragmatics, and Ritual* (ed. J.C. Alexander, B. Giesen and J.L. Mast; Cambridge: Cambridge University Press, 2006), pp. 315-24.
Gill, Athol, 'Good News to the Poor', in Harold Pidwell, *A Gentle Bunyip: The Athol Gill Story* (Westlake, SA: Seaview Press, 2007), pp. 180-275.
Gill, Robin, 'Public Theology and Health Care Ethics', *St Mark's Review: A Journal of Christian Thought and Opinion*, No. 203 (November 2007), pp. 9-22.
Girard, René, *Things Hidden since the Foundation of the World* (trans. Stephen Bann and Michael Metteer; Stanford: Stanford University Press, 1987).
Glavin, J., *After Dickens: Reading, Adaptation and Performance* (Cambridge: Cambridge University Press, 2004).
Goffman, E., *The Presentation of Self in Everyday Life* (Harmondsworth: Penguin Books, 1959).
Goodacre, Mark, 'Criticizing the Criterion of Multiple Attestation: The Historical Jesus and the Question of Sources', in *Jesus, Criteria, and the Demise of Authenticity* (ed. Chris Keith and Anthony Le Donne; London: T. & T. Clark International, 2012).
Gorringe, Tim, 'Political Readings of Scripture', in *The Cambridge Companion to Biblical Interpretation* (ed. John Barton; Cambridge: Cambridge University Press, 1998), pp. 67-80.
—'Political Theology', *ExpTim* 122.9 (2011), pp. 417-24.
Gottwald, Norman T., *The Tribes of Yahweh: A Sociology of the Religion of Liberated Israel, 1250–1050 BCE* (Maryknoll, NY: Orbis Books, rev. edn, 1999).
Gowler, David B., *What Are They Saying About the Parables?* (New York/Mahwah, NJ: Paulist Press, 2000).
Graham, Elaine L., Heather Walton and Frances Ward, *Theological Reflection: Methods* (London: SCM Press, 2005).
Graves, Mike, 'Luke 10:25-37: The Moral of the "Good Samaritan" Story?', *RevExp* 94 (1997), pp. 269-75.

Green, Joel B., *The Gospel of Luke* (Grand Rapids: Eerdmans, 1997).
Green, Laurie, *Let's Do Theology: Resources for Contextual Theology* (London: Mowbray, 2009).
Green, Lelia, *Technoculture: From Alphabet to Cybersex* (Crowsnest, NSW: Allen and Unwin, 2002).
Grey, Mary, 'To Struggle with a Reconciled Heart: Reconciliation and Justice', *New Blackfriars* 85.995 (2004), pp. 56-73.
—'It all began with Miriam... Feminist Theology's Journey from Liberation to Reconciliation', *FemTh* 20.3 (2012), pp. 222-29.
Groening, Matt, *The Simpsons* (Beverly Hills, CA: Gracie Films; 20th Century Fox, 1989).
Hancock, John Lee, and Michael Lewis, *The Blind Side* (Burbank, CA: Alcon Entertainment, 2009).
Hanson, Paul D., *Political Engagement as Biblical Mandate* (Eugene, OR: Cascade Books, 2010).
Hart, David Bentley, *Atheist Delusions: The Christian Revolution and Its Fashionable Enemies* (New Haven: Yale University Press, 2009).
Hauerwas, Stanley, *The Peaceable Kingdom: A Primer in Christian Ethics* (Notre Dame: University of Notre Dame Press, 1983).
—*After Christendom? How the Church Is to Behave if Freedom, Justice, and a Christian Nation Are Bad Ideas* (Nashville: Abingdon Press, 1991).
—*Performing the Faith: Bonhoeffer and the Practice of Nonviolence* (Grand Rapids: Brazos Press, 2004).
—'Punishing Christians', in *Public Theology for the 21st Century: Essays in Honour of Duncan B. Forrester* (ed. William F. Storrar and Andrew R. Morton; London: T. & T. Clark, 2004), pp. 285-301.
—*Matthew* (Brazos Theological Commentary on the Bible; Grand Rapids: Brazos Press, 2006).
—*Hannah's Child: A Theologian's Memoir* (Grand Rapids: Eerdmans, 2010).
—*War and the American Difference: Theological Reflections on Violence and National Identity* (Grand Rapids: Baker Academic, 2011).
—'Jesus: The Justice of God', in *Bible and Justice: Ancient Texts, Modern Challenges* (ed. Matthew J.M. Coomber; London: Equinox, 2011), pp. 70-90.
—'Remembering How and What I Think: A Response to the *JRE* Articles on Hauerwas', *JRE* 40.2 (2012), pp. 296-306.
Havea, Jione, "Unu'unu ki he loloto, shuffle over into the deep, into island-spaced reading', in *Still at the Margins: Biblical Scholarship Fifteen Years after Voices from the Margin* (ed. R.S. Sugirtharajah; New York: T. & T. Clark, 2008), pp. 88-97.
—'Welcome to Talanoa', in *Talanoa Ripples: Across Borders, Cultures, Disciplines...* (ed. Jione Havea; Auckland: Masilamea Press and Massey University, 2010), pp. 11-22.
—'Cons of contextuality...Kontextuality', in *Contextual Theology for the Twenty-First Century* (ed. Stephen Bevans and Katalina Tahaafe-Williams; Eugene, OR: Pickwick Publications, 2011), pp. 38-52.
—'Diaspora Contexted: Talanoa, Reading, and Theologizing, as Migrants', *Black Theology* 11.2 (2013), pp. 185-200.
Hengel, Martin, *The Cross of the Son of God* (trans. John Bowden; London: SCM Press, 1986).

Herzog, William R., II, *Parables as Subversive Speech: Jesus as Pedagogue of the Oppressed* (Louisville, KY: Westminster/John Knox Press, 1994).
—'Jesus and the Justice of the Reign of God', in *Prophecy and Passion: Essays in Honour of Athol Gill* (ed. David Neville; Adelaide: Australian Theological Forum, 2002), pp. 31-64.
Holladay, W.L., *Jeremiah 1–25* (Philadelphia: Fortress Press, 1986).
Houston, Walter J., *Contending for Justice: Ideologies and Theologies of Social Justice in the Old Testament* (London: T. & T. Clark, 2nd edn, 2008).
—*Justice—The Biblical Challenge* (London: Equinox, 2010).
Hughes, Philip, and Claire Pickering, *Bible Engagement among Young Australians: Patterns and Social Drivers* (Nunawading, Australia: Christian Research Association, 2010).
Ihimaera, Witi, *The Whale Rider* (Auckland, NZ: Heinemann, 1987).
Indermaur, David, 'Violent Crime in Australia: Interpreting the Trends', *Trends and Issues in Crime and Criminal Justice*, No. 61 (Canberra: Australian Institute of Criminology, 1996), pp. 1-6.
Isasi-Díaz, Ada María, 'A *Mujerista* Hermeneutic of Justice and Human Flourishing', in *The Bible and the Hermeneutics of Liberation* (ed. Alejandro F. Botta and Pablo R. Andiñach; Atlanta: SBL, 2009), pp. 181-95.
Jacobs, Alan, *Looking Before and After: Testimony and the Christian Life* (Grand Rapids: Eerdmans, 2008).
Jenkins, Philip, *The Next Christendom: The Coming of Global Christianity* (New York: Oxford University Press, 2002).
—*The New Faces of Christianity: Believing the Bible in the Global South* (New York: Oxford University Press, 2006).
Jeremias, Joachim, *The Parables of Jesus* (trans. S.H. Hooke; London: SCM Press, 3rd rev. edn, 1972).
Johnson, Luke Timothy, 'The Lukan Kingship Parable (Lk. 19:11-27)', *NovT* 24 (1982), pp. 139-59.
—*The Gospel of Luke* (Collegeville: Liturgical Press, 1991).
Johnstone, Brian V., CSsR, 'Transformation Ethics: The Moral Implications of the Resurrection', in *The Resurrection: An Interdisciplinary Symposium on the Resurrection of Jesus* (ed. Stephen Davis, Daniel Kendall, SJ, and Gerald O'Collins, SJ; Oxford: Oxford University Press, 1997), pp. 339-60.
Johnstone, Gerry, and Daniel W. Van Ness, 'The Meaning of Restorative Justice', in *Handbook of Restorative Justice* (ed. Gerry Johnstone and Daniel W. Van Ness; Cullompton, Devon: Willan Publishing, 2007), pp. 5-23.
Jonsen, Albert R., and Stephen Toulmin, *The Abuse of Casuistry: A History of Moral Reasoning* (Berkeley: University of California Press, 1988).
Joyce, Paul, 'Reading the Bible within the Public Domain', in *Dare We Speak of God in Public?* (ed. Frances Young; London: Mowbray, 1995), pp. 67-79.
Kant, Immanuel, 'On a Supposed Right to Tell Lies from Benevolent Motives' (1797), in *Kant's Critique of Practical Reason and Other Works on the Theory of Ethics* (trans. Thomas K. Abbot; London: Longmans, Green and Co., 6th edn, 1954).
Keene, Jennifer, and Rick Morales, *Love Is a Battlefield, Green Lantern: The Animated Series* (Warner Bros., 2013).
Keller, Timothy, *The Prodigal God: Recovering the Heart of the Christian Faith* (London: Hodder & Stoughton, 2008).
Kim, Sebastian C.H., *Theology in the Public Sphere* (London: SCM Press, 2011).

Kinman, Brent, 'Parousia, Jesus' "A-Triumphal" Entry, and the Fate of Jerusalem (Luke 19:28-44)', *JBL* 118 (1999), pp. 279-94.
Kitchen, Merrill, 'Rereading the Parable of the Pounds: A Social and Narrative Analysis of Luke 19:11-28', in *Prophecy and Passion: Essays in Honour of Athol Gill* (ed. David Neville; Adelaide: Australian Theological Forum, 2002), pp. 227-46.
—'The Good News of Restoration: Reading Luke–Acts Then and Now', *Pacifica* 23.2 (2010), pp. 157-72.
Knight, Philip, 'Pragmatism, Postmodernism and the Bible as a Meaningful Public Resource in a Pluralistic Age', in *Biblical Interpretation: The Meanings of Scripture—Past and Present* (ed. John M. Court; London: T. & T. Clark International, 2003), pp. 310-25.
Kreider, Alan, *The Change of Conversion and the Origin of Christendom* (Harrisburg, PA: Trinity Press International, 1999).
—'Beyond Bosch: The Early Church and the Christendom Shift', *International Bulletin* 29.2 (2005), pp. 59-68.
Lebacqz, Karen, *Six Theories of Justice: Perspectives from Philosophical and Theological Ethics* (Minneapolis: Augsburg Publishing House, 1986).
—*Justice in an Unjust World: Foundations for a Christian Approach to Justice* (Minneapolis: Augsburg Publishing House, 1987).
Leder, Mimi, and Catherine Ryan Hyde, *Pay It Forward* (Burbank, CA: Warner Bros.; Bel Air Entertainment; Tapestry Films, 2000).
Lehner, Ulrich L., *Monastic Prisons and Torture Chambers: Crime and Punishment in Central European Monasteries, 1600–1800* (Eugene, OR: Cascade Books, 2013).
Lenski, Gerhard, *Privilege and Power: A Theory of Social Stratification* (Chapel Hill, SC: University of South Carolina Press, 2nd edn, 1984).
Lerner, Berel Dov, 'Oppressive Metaphor and the Liberating Literal Sense', in *Metaphor, Canon and Community: Jewish, Christian and Islamic Approaches* (ed. Ralph Bisschops and James Francis; New York: Peter Lang, 1999), pp. 233-41.
Lévinas, Emmanuel, *Ethics and Infinity: Conversations with Philippe Nemo* (trans. Richard A. Cohen; Pittsburgh: Duquesne University Press, 1985).
Levy, S., *The Bible as Theatre* (Brighton: Sussex Academic Press, 2000).
Litwak, Kenneth Duncan, *Echoes of Scripture in Luke–Acts: Telling the History of God's People Intertextually* (London: T. & T. Clark, 2005).
Longenecker, Bruce C., 'The Story of the Samaritan and the Innkeeper (Luke 10:30-35): A Study in Character Rehabilitation', *BibInt* 17 (2009), pp. 422-47.
Lorenzen, Thorwald, *Resurrection and Discipleship: Interpretive Models, Biblical Reflections, Theological Consequences* (Maryknoll, NY: Orbis Books, 1995; Eugene, OR: Wipf & Stock, 2004).
—'The Crucified Christ as Lord of the Church: Theological Reflections on 1 Corinthians 11–14', in *Prophecy and Passion: Essays in Honour of Athol Gill* (ed. David Neville; Adelaide: Australian Theological Forum, 2002), pp. 83-125.
—*Resurrection – Discipleship – Justice: Affirming the Resurrection of Jesus Christ Today* (Macon, GA: Smyth & Helwys, 2003).
Lynch, Gordon, *Understanding Theology and Popular Culture* (Malden, MA: Blackwell, 2005).
MacIntyre, Alasdair, 'Why is the search for the foundations of ethics so frustrating?', *Hastings Center Report* 9.4 (1979), pp. 16-22.
—*After Virtue: A Study in Moral Theory* (Notre Dame: University of Notre Dame Press, 1981; 3rd edn, 2007).

—*Whose Justice? Which Rationality?* (Notre Dame: University of Notre Dame Press, 1988).
—*Three Rival Versions of Moral Enquiry: Encyclopaedia, Genealogy, and Tradition* (Notre Dame: University of Notre Dame Press, 1990).
—'Précis of *Whose Justice? Which Rationality?*', *Philosophy and Phenomenological Research* 51.1 (March 1991), pp. 149-52.
Macquarrie, John, *The Concept of Peace* (London: SCM Press, 1973).
Malina, Bruce J., and Richard L. Rohrbaugh, *Social-Science Commentary on the Synoptic Gospels* (Minneapolis: Fortress Press, 1992).
Mandela, Nelson, *Long Walk to Freedom: The Autobiography of Nelson Mandela* (London: Abacus, 1994).
Manlove, Colin, 'The Bible in Fantasy', *Semeia* 60 (1992), pp. 91-110.
Marsh, Charles, *Wayward Christian Soldiers: Freeing the Gospel from Political Captivity* (Oxford: Oxford University Press, 2007).
Marshall, Christopher D., *Faith as a Theme in Mark's Narrative* (Cambridge: Cambridge University Press, 1989).
—*Kingdom Come: The Kingdom of God in the Teaching of Jesus* (Auckland: Impetus Publications, rev. edn, 1993).
—*Beyond Retribution: A New Testament Vision for Justice, Crime, and Punishment* (Grand Rapids: Eerdmans, 2001).
—'Atonement, Violence and the Will of God: A Sympathetic Response to J. Denny Weaver's *The Nonviolent Atonement*', *MQR* 77 (2003), pp. 69-92.
—'The Moral Vision of the Beatitudes: The Blessings of Revolution', in *Faith and Freedom: Christian Ethics in a Pluralist Culture* (ed. David Neville and Philip Matthews; Adelaide: ATF Press, 2003), pp. 11-33.
—*The Little Book of Biblical Justice: A Fresh Approach to the Bible's Teachings on Justice* (Intercourse, PA: Good Books, 2005).
—'What Language Shall I Borrow? The Bilingual Dilemma of Public Theology', *Stimulus* 13.3 (2005), pp. 11-18.
—'A Prophet of God's Justice: Reclaiming the Political Jesus', *Stimulus* 14.3 (2006), pp. 28-41.
—'Offending, Restoration, and the Law-Abiding Community: Restorative Justice in the New Testament and in the New Zealand Experience', *JSCE* 27.2 (2007), pp. 3-30.
—'Reflections on the Spirit of Justice', in *Restorative Justice and Practices in New Zealand: Towards a Restorative Society* (ed. Gabrielle Maxwell and James H. Lui; Wellington, NZ: Victoria University Institute of Policy Studies, 2007), pp. 311-19.
—'Terrorism, Religious Violence and Restorative Justice', in *Handbook of Restorative Justice* (ed. Gerry Johnstone and Daniel W. Van Ness; Cullompton, Devon: Willan Publishing, 2007), pp. 372-94.
—*Compassionate Justice: An Interdisciplinary Dialogue with Two Gospel Parables on Law, Crime, and Restorative Justice* (Eugene, OR: Cascade Books, 2012).
Marshall, I. Howard, 'Biblical Patterns for Public Theology', *EJT* 14.1 (2005), pp. 73-86.
Marty, Martin E., 'Reinhold Niebuhr: Public Theology and the American Experience', *JR* 54 (1974), pp. 332-59.
Mathews, Jeanette, *Performing Habakkuk* (Eugene, OR: Pickwick Publications, 2012).
Mays, James L., 'Justice: Perspectives from the Prophetic Tradition', *Interpretation* 37.1 (1983), pp. 5-17.

McKenzie, Alyce M., *The Parables for Today* (Louisville, KY: Westminster/John Knox Press, 2007).
Milbank, John, *Theology and Social Theory: Beyond Secular Reason* (Oxford: Blackwell, 1990).
Moltmann, Jürgen, *Theology of Hope: On the Ground and the Implications of a Christian Eschatology* (trans. James W. Leitch; London: SCM Press, 1967).
—*The Crucified God: The Cross of Christ as the Foundation and Criticism of Christian Theology* (trans. R.A. Wilson and John Bowden; London: SCM Press, 1974).
—*The Way of Jesus Christ: Christology in Messianic Dimensions* (trans. Margaret Kohl; London: SCM Press, 1990).
—*Ethics of Hope* (trans. Margaret Kohl; Minneapolis: Fortress Press, 2012).
Moltmann, Jürgen, Nicholas Wolterstorff and Ellen T. Charry, *A Passion for God's Reign: Theology, Christian Learning, and the Christian Self* (ed. Miroslav Volf; Grand Rapids: Eerdmans, 1998).
Morgan, Robert, 'Sachkritik in Reception History', *JSNT* 33.2 (2010), pp. 175-90.
Moule, C.F.D., *Essays in New Testament Interpretation* (Cambridge: Cambridge University Press, 1982).
—*Forgiveness and Reconciliation and Other New Testament Themes* (London: SPCK, 1998).
Myers, Ched, 'Introduction', in *Liberating Biblical Study: Scholarship, Art, and Action in Honor of the Center and Library for the Bible and Social Justice* (ed. Laurel Dykstra and Ched Myers; Eugene, OR: Cascade Books, 2011), pp. xxiii-xxvii.
Myers, Ched, and Elaine Enns, *Ambassadors of Reconciliation, Vol. I: New Testament Reflections on Restorative Justice and Peacemaking* (Maryknoll, NY: Orbis Books, 2009).
Myles, Robert J., 'Terminating Samson: The Sarah Connor Chronicles and the Rise of New Biblical Meaning', *Relegere: Studies in Religion and Reception* 1.2 (2011), pp. 329-50.
Nadar, Sarojini, 'Beyond the "Ordinary Reader" and the "Invisible Intellectual": Pushing the Boundaries of Contextual Bible Study Discourses', in *The Future of the Biblical Past: Envisioning Biblical Studies on a Global Key* (ed. Roland Boer and Fernando F. Segovia; Atlanta: SBL, 2013), pp. 13-28.
Neville, David J., 'The Bible as a Public Document: A Perspective on the Contribution of Anglicanism', *St Mark's Review: A Journal of Christian Thought and Opinion*, No. 203 (November 2007), pp. 35-45.
—'Dialectic as Method in Public Theology: Recalling Jacques Ellul', *IJPT* 2.2 (2008), pp. 163-81.
—'Justice and Divine Judgement: Scriptural Perspectives for Public Theology', *IJPT* 3.3 (2009), pp. 339-56.
—'Christian Scripture and Public Theology: Ruminations on their Ambiguous Relationship', *IJPT* 7.1 (2013), pp. 5-23.
—*A Peaceable Hope: Contesting Violent Eschatology in New Testament Narratives* (Grand Rapids: Baker Academic, 2013).
Northcott, Michael S., 'Reading Hauerwas in the Cornbelt: The Demise of the American Dream and the Return of Liturgical Politics', *JRE* 40.2 (2012), pp. 262-80.
Nussbaum, Martha, 'Moral Expertise? Constitutional Narrative and Philosophical Argument', *Metaphilosophy* 33 (2002), pp. 502-520.
Oakman, Douglas E., *Jesus and the Economic Questions of His Day* (Lewiston: Edwin Mellen Press, 1986).

—'The Ancient Economy in the Bible', *BTB* 21 (1991), pp. 34-39.
—*Jesus and the Peasants* (Eugene, OR: Cascade Books, 2008).
O'Connell, Terry, Ben Wachtel and Ted Wachtel, *Conferencing Handbook: The New Real Justice Training Manual* (Pipersville: Pipers Press, 1999).
Opie, Stephen, *Bible Engagement in New Zealand: Survey of Attitudes and Behaviour* (Wellington, NZ: Bible Society New Zealand, 2008).
Paddison, Angus, and Darren Sarisky, 'A Comprehensive Bibliography of the Writings of Stanley Hauerwas', *MQR* 84 (2010), pp. 311-55.
Paddison, Angus, and Neil Messer (eds.), *The Bible: Culture, Community, Society* (London: Bloomsbury T. & T. Clark, 2013).
Pelias, R.J., *Performance Studies: The Interpretation of Aesthetic Texts* (Dubuque: Kendall/Hunt Publishing Company, 1992).
Pidwell, Harold, *A Gentle Bunyip: The Athol Gill Story* (Westlake, SA: Seaview Press, 2007).
Pinker, Stephen, *The Better Angels of our Nature: Why Violence Has Declined* (New York: Viking Books, 2011).
Pitts, Jamie, *Principalities and Powers: Revising John Howard Yoder's Sociological Theology* (Eugene, OR: Pickwick Publications, 2013).
Pounder, Sadie, 'Prison Theology: A Theology of Liberation, Hope and Justice', *Dialog* 47 (2008), pp. 278-91.
Prothero, Stephen R., *Religious Literacy: What Every American Needs to Know—and Doesn't* (New York: HarperOne, 2008).
Punt, J., 'Popularising the Prophet Isaiah in Parliament: The Bible in Post-apartheid, South African Public Discourse', *Religion and Theology* 14 (2007), pp. 206-223.
Punt, Jeremy, 'Violence in the New Testament and the Roman Empire: Ambivalence, Othering, Agency', in *Coping with Violence in the New Testament* (ed. P.G.R. de Villiers and J.W. van Henten; Leiden: Brill, 2012), pp. 29-41.
Putnam, Nathanael, 'Annotated Bibliography on Justice', *Ex Auditu* 22 (2006), pp. 222-32.
Redditt, P.L., *Introduction to the Prophets* (Grand Rapids: Eerdmans, 2008).
Reid, Barbara E., 'Beyond Petty Pursuits and Wearisome Widows: Three Lukan Parables', *Interpretation* 56.3 (July 2002), pp. 284-94.
Riddell, Michael, *The Insatiable Moon* (Auckland, NZ: Flamingo, 1997).
—*Sacred Journey: Spiritual Wisdom for Times of Transition* (London: SPCK, 2nd edn, 2010).
Riddell, Rosemary, and Michael Riddell, *The Insatiable Moon* (New Zealand: Vendetta Films; Rialto Distribution, 2010).
Rindge, Matthew S., *Jesus' Parable of the Rich Fool: Luke 12:13–34 among Ancient Conversations on Death and Possession* (Early Christianity and Its Literature, 6; Atlanta: Society of Biblical Literature, 2011).
Robinette, Brian D., *Grammars of Resurrection: A Christian Theology of Presence and Absence* (New York: Crossroad, 2009).
Rojtman, Betty, *Black Fire on White Fire: An Essay on Jewish Hermeneutics, from Midrash to Kabbalah* (trans. Steven Randall; Berkeley: University of California Press, 1998).
Rorty, Richard, *Philosophy and the Mirror of Nature* (Princeton, NJ: Princeton University Press, 1979).
Ryken, Leland, *Words of Life: A Literary Introduction to the New Testament* (Grand Rapids: Baker House, 1987).

Saldarini, Anthony J., *Pharisees, Scribes, and Sadducees in Palestinian Society* (Grand Rapids: Eerdmans, 1988).
Saunders, Stanley P., and Charles L. Campbell, *The Word on the Street: Performing the Scriptures in the Urban Context* (Grand Rapids: Eerdmans, 2000).
Schaberg, Jane, 'Luke', in *Women's Bible Commentary: Expanded edition, with Apocrypha* (ed. Carol A. Newsom and Sharon H. Ringe; Louisville, KY: Westminster/John Knox Press, 1998), pp. 363-80.
Schottroff, Luise, *The Parables of Jesus* (trans. Linda M. Maloney; Minneapolis: Fortress Press, 2006).
Schüssler Fiorenza, Elisabeth, *Jesus and the Politics of Interpretation* (New York: Continuum, 2001).
—*Transforming Vision: Explorations in Feminist Theology* (Minneapolis: Fortress Press, 2011).
Schwartz, Regina M., *The Curse of Cain: The Violent Legacy of Monotheism* (Chicago: University of Chicago Press, 1997).
Schweizer, Eduard, *Jesus The Parable of God: What Do We Really Know about Jesus?* (Allison Park, PA: Pickwick Publications, 1994).
Seccombe, David, 'Incongruity in the Gospel Parables', *TynBul* 62.2 (2011), pp. 161-72.
Segovia, Fernando F., 'Toward a Hermeneutics of the Diaspora: A Hermeneutics of Otherness and Engagement', in *Reading from this Place: Social Location and Biblical Interpretation in the United States*, Vol. 1 (ed. Fernando F. Segovia and Mary Ann Tolbert; Minneapolis: Augsburg Fortress, 1995), pp. 57-74.
Sherwood, Yvonne, 'Prophetic Scatology: Prophecy and the Art of Sensation', *Semeia* 82 (1998), pp. 183-224.
—*A Biblical Text and Its Afterlives: The Survival of Jonah in Western Culture* (Cambridge: Cambridge University Press, 2000).
—'Prophetic Performance Art (Editorial)', *The Bible and Critical Theory* 2.1 (2006), pp. 1.1-1.4. http://novaojs.newcastle.edu.au/ojsbct/index.php/bct/article/view/70
Sider, Ronald J., *Rich Christians in an Age of Hunger* (Downers Grove: InterVarsity Press, 1977; Nashville: Thomas Nelson, 5th edn, 2005).
Singer, Peter, *Practical Ethics* (New York: Cambridge University Press, 1979; 2nd edn, 1993).
—*The Expanding Circle* (New York: Farrar, Straus & Giroux, 1981).
—*The Life You Can Save: Acting Now to End World Poverty* (Melbourne: Text Publishing Company, 2009).
Smith, Christian, 'On "Moralistic Therapeutic Deism" as US Teenagers' Actual, Tacit, De Facto Religious Faith', in *Religion and Youth* (ed. S. Collins-Mayo and P. Dandelion; Farnham, Surrey, England; Burlington, VT: Ashgate, 2010), pp. 41-46.
Snodgrass, Klyne, *Stories with Intent: A Comprehensive Guide to the Parables of Jesus* (Grand Rapids: Eerdmans, 2008).
Snyder Belousek, Darrin W., *Atonement, Justice, and Peace: The Message of the Cross and the Mission of the Church* (Grand Rapids: Eerdmans, 2012).
Soskice, Janet Martin, 'Can a Feminist call God "Father"?', in *Speaking the Christian God: The Holy Trinity and the Challenge of Feminism* (ed. A.F. Kimel, Jr; Grand Rapids: Eerdmans, 1992), pp. 81-94.
Spencer, Nick, and Holly Weldin, *Post-Religious Britain? The Faith of the Faithless* (London: Theos, 2012).
Sprinkle, Preston M., 'The Use of Genesis 42:8 (not Leviticus 18:5) in Luke 10:28: Joseph and the Good Samaritan', *Bulletin for Biblical Research* 17.2 (2007), pp. 193-205.

Stacey, D., *Prophetic Drama in the Old Testament* (London: Epworth Press, 1990).
Stackhouse, Max L., 'Public Theology and Political Economy in a Globalizing Era', *SCE* 14.2 (2001), pp. 63-86.
—'Civil Religion, Political Theology and Public Theology: What's the Difference?', *PT* 5.3 (2004), pp. 275-93.
Stendahl, Krister, 'The Bible as a Classic and the Bible as Holy Scripture', *JBL* 103 (1984), pp. 3-10.
Stern, David, *Parables in Midrash: Narrative and Exegesis in Rabbinic Literature* (Cambridge: Harvard University Press, 1991).
Stewart, Robert B. (ed.), *The Resurrection of Jesus: John Dominic Crossan and N.T. Wright in Dialogue* (Minneapolis: Fortress Press, 2006).
Stewart, W., 'Crown of Thorns: Ancient Prophecy and the (Post)modern Spectacle', *The Bible and Critical Theory* 2.1 (2006), pp. 4.1-4.24. http://novaojs.newcastle.edu.au/ojsbct/index.php/bct/article/view/73
Stout, Jeffrey, *Democracy and Tradition* (Princeton, NJ: Princeton University Press, 2004).
Suu Kyi, Aung San, *Letters from Burma* (London: Penguin, 1997).
Swartley, Willard M., *Covenant of Peace: The Missing Peace in New Testament Theology and Ethics* (Grand Rapids: Eerdmans, 2006).
—'The Relation of Justice/Righteousness to *Shalom/Eirēnē*', *Ex Auditu* 22 (2006), pp. 29-53.
Talbert, Charles H., *Reading Luke: A Literary and Theological Commentary on the Third Gospel* (New York: Crossroad, 1987).
Tannehill, Robert, *The Narrative Unity of Luke–Acts: A Literary Interpretation*, Vol. 2: *The Acts of the Apostles* (Minneapolis: Fortress Press, 1990).
The Naked Samoans and Firehorse Films, *bro'Town* (Auckland, NZ: Firehorse Films, 2004–2009).
Theissen, Gerd, *The Bible and Contemporary Culture* (trans. David E. Green; Minneapolis: Fortress Press, 2007).
Theissen, Gerd, and Annette Merz, *The Historical Jesus: A Comprehensive Guide* (London: SCM Press, 1996).
Thomson, Heather, 'Stars and Compasses: Hermeneutical Guidelines for Public Theology', *IJPT* 2.3 (2008), pp. 258-76.
—*The Things That Make for Peace* (Canberra: Barton Books, 2009).
Toulmin, Stephen, *Cosmopolis: The Hidden Agenda of Modernity* (Chicago: University of Chicago Press, 1990).
—'Theology in the Context of the University', *Theological Education* 26.2 (Spring 1990), pp. 51-65.
Tracy, David, *The Analogical Imagination: Christian Theology and the Culture of Pluralism* (New York: Crossroad, 1981).
Trebilco, Paul, 'Gospel, Culture, and the Public Sphere: Perspectives from the New Testament', *Evangel* 24.2 (2006), pp. 37-45.
Turner, V., 'Are there Universals of Performance in Myth, Ritual and Drama?', in *By Means of Performance* (ed. R. Schechner and W. Appel; Cambridge: Cambridge University Press, 1990), pp. 8-19.
U2, *All That You Can't Leave Behind* (Island Records, 2001).
Van Ness, Daniel W., and Karen H. Strong, *Restorative Justice* (Cincinnati: Anderson, 3rd edn, 2006).

Veling, Terry A., *Practical Theology: On Earth as It Is in Heaven* (Maryknoll, NY: Orbis Books, 2005).
Volf, Miroslav, *Exclusion and Embrace: A Theological Exploration of Identity, Otherness, and Reconciliation* (Nashville: Abingdon Press, 1996).
—'Original Crime, Primal Care', in *God and the Victim: Theological Reflections on Evil, Victimization, Justice, and Forgiveness* (ed. Lisa Barnes Lampman; Grand Rapids: Eerdmans, 1999), pp. 17-35.
—*Free of Charge: Giving and Forgiving in a Culture Stripped of Grace* (Grand Rapids: Zondervan, 2005).
—*The End of Memory: Remembering Rightly in a Violent World* (Grand Rapids: Eerdmans, 2006).
—*Captive to the Word of God: Engaging the Scriptures for Contemporary Theological Reflection* (Grand Rapids: Eerdmans, 2010).
Walzer, Michael, *Just and Unjust Wars: A Moral Argument with Historical Illustrations* (New York: Basic Books, 1977; 4th edn, 2006).
—*Thick and Thin: Moral Argument at Home and Abroad* (Notre Dame: University of Notre Dame Press, 1994).
—*Arguing about War* (New Haven: Yale University Press, 2004).
Watson, Francis, 'Hermeneutics and the Doctrine of Scripture: Why They Need Each Other', *IJST* 12.2 (2010), pp. 118-43.
Weaver, Alain Epp, 'Parables of the Kingdom and Religious Plurality: With Barth and Yoder toward a Nonresistant Public Theology', *MQR* 72 (1998), pp. 411-40.
Weaver, David, *The Samaritan* (Canada: H2O Motion Pictures, 2012).
Weaver, J. Denny, *The Nonviolent Atonement* (Grand Rapids: Eerdmans, 2001).
Whiston, William (trans.), *The Works of Josephus, Complete and Unabridged* (Peabody, MA: Hendrickson, 1987).
Wierzbicka, Anna, 'What did Jesus Mean? The Lord's Prayer Translated into Universal Human Concepts', in *Metaphor, Canon and Community: Jewish, Christian and Islamic Approaches* (ed. Ralph Bisschops and James Francis; New York: Peter Lang, 1999), pp. 180-216.
Williams, Bernard, *Morality: An Introduction to Ethics* (Cambridge: Cambridge University Press, 1972).
—*Moral Luck* (Cambridge: Cambridge University Press, 1981).
—*Ethics and the Limits of Philosophy* (London: Fontana Press, 1985, 1993).
Williams, Rowan, *Writing in the Dust: After September 11* (Grand Rapids: Eerdmans, 2002).
—*Grace and Necessity: Reflections on Art and Love* (London: Continuum, 2005).
Wilmot, Brett T. 'Defending Democracy Against its "Cultured Despisers": A Critical Consideration of Some Recent Approaches', *JSCE* 26.1 (2006), pp. 37-59.
Wolterstorff, Nicholas, *Justice: Rights and Wrongs* (Princeton, NJ: Princeton University Press, 2008).
—*Justice in Love* (Grand Rapids: Eerdmans, 2011).
Wright, N.T., *Jesus and the Victory of God* (Minneapolis: Fortress Press, 1996).
—*The Resurrection of the Son of God* (Minneapolis: Fortress Press, 2003).
—*Surprised by Hope* (London: SPCK, 2007).
Zehr, Howard, 'Evaluation and Restorative Justice Principles', in *New Directions in Restorative Justice: Issues, Practice, Evaluation* (ed. Elizabeth Elliott and Robert M. Gordon; Cullompton, Devon: Willan Publishing, 2005), pp. 296-303.

INDEXES

INDEX OF REFERENCES

OLD TESTAMENT

Genesis		2 Samuel		106.3	93
1.1-2	67	5.14	47	110	98
4.2-16	72	15	62		
18.25	90	17.25	62	Proverbs	
25.8	119	19.3	62	22.7	54
35.29	119	20	62-63	25.11	107
42.8	70	20.2	62	28.5	93
		20.9-10	62		
Exodus		20.12-13	63	Isaiah	
22.25-27	54			1.11-17	122
		1 Kings		1.17	93
Leviticus		11.26-40	106	2.4	112
18.5	70			5.8	54
19.15	93	2 Kings		6	107
19.18	96	4.1	54	20.4	106-107
24.16	120			28.17	7
25	54	1 Chronicles		30.18	93, 122
25.39-46	126	14.4	47	49.6-9	50
		16.8-36	103	52.10	50
Deuteronomy		29.28	119	61.2	50
13	120			61.8	122
15	54	Nehemiah			
15.1-7	52	5.1-5	54	Jeremiah	
15.12-17	126			3.19	139
16.20	93	Job		7.21-28	122
17	120	37.23	93	9.23-24	7
23.15-16	126	42.17	119	19	105
23.19-20	54			22	7
24.19-22	7	Psalms		22.3	7
27.19	93	7.11	91	22.15-16	7
30.11-20	122	10.17-18	91	32.1-15	105
		24.1	115, 131		
Judges		33.5	93	Ezekiel	
2.17-19	91	50.7-15	122	3.12-15	107
		76.9	91	4.9-15	106
1 Samuel		82.1-8	91	24.1-14	105-106
15.22	122	99.4	90	34.15-16	93
22.2	54				

Hosea		*Amos*		*Habakkuk*	
1	104-105	5.12	56	2.1-5	108
1.4-5	105	5.15	56	2.6	54
1.6	105	5.21-24	122	3.16	107
1.9	105	5.24	7, 91, 93		
1.11	105			*Zechariah*	
2.23	105	*Micah*		12.1–13.1	47
3	104	4.3	112		
6.6	122	6.6-8	122		
8.13	122	6.8	7, 91, 93		

INTERTESTAMENTAL WRITINGS

Damascus Document		10.4	159	*Testament of Judah*	
1.7-11	159	11.6	159	23.5	159
		15.12	159		
1 Maccabees				*Testament of Asher*	
2.1-70	47	*Testament of Levi*		7.3	159
		4.4	159		
Psalms of Solomon				*Wisdom of Solomon*	
3.11	159			3.7	159

NEW TESTAMENT

Matthew		18.35	150	4.10-12	38
5.6	123	19.16-30	151	4.13	37
5.9	38	19.30	151	4.22-25	37
5.10	123	20.1-16	151-53	4.23-24	37
5.38-48	38	20.16	151	4.33-34	36
6.33	90	20.34	149	5.21-24	115
7.12	96	21.12	51	5.35-43	115
9.17	53	22.15-22	51	6.8-9	50
9.36	149	25.14-30	153	6.34	149
10.9	50	25.31-46	20, 39, 91, 124	7.18	37
10.26-33	51			8.2	149
10.37-39	51	26.14	51	8.17-20	37
10.38-39	57	27.52-53	116	8.34–9.1	51, 57
11.2-6	7	28.1-8	128	9.22	149
12.18	93	28.9-10	128	9.36-37	124
13.10-16	38	28.18-20	130	11.15	51
13.34	36			12.13-17	51
14.14	149	*Mark*		12.40	51
15.32	149	1.41	149	14.10-11	51
16.17-19	127	2.22	53	15.39	119
16.24-28	51	2.27-28	119	15.40	128
18.23-35	149-51	4.3	37	16.9	128
18.27	149	4.3-20	37	16.19	130
18.33	149	4.9	37		

Luke		7.13	149, 158, 159, 160		55, 72-87, 95-96, 99
1.5	46, 47				
1.32-33	47	7.16	159	15.12	77, 78
1.36	47	7.23	49	15.16	56
1.46-55	47	8.9-10	38	15.17-19	77
1.49-53	124	9.3	50	15.20	149, 158, 160
1.50	158	9.7	57		
1.51-53	56	9.9	46	16.1-9	55
1.52-53	91	9.23-24	51	16.10-13	55
1.54	158	9.23-27	57	16.19-31	39, 56
1.67-79	159	9.46-48	155	16.21	56
1.68	159	9.51	153	17.20	57
1.68-79	47	9.51-52	130	17.22-37	156
1.78	149, 158, 159, 160	9.51–19.46	153	17.33	57
		10	179	18.9-14	38
1.78-79	159	10.4	50	18.18-30	57
2.1-7	46	10.11	57	18.22-25	51
2.4	47	10.25-28	53	18.31-34	51
2.30-32	50	10.25-29	2	19.1-10	51, 57, 124
2.40-47	47	10.25-37	1-3, 58, 59-71, 95, 99, 156	19.11	153, 154-55
3.1-2	46				
3.10-14	50			19.11-27	56-57
3.18	57	10.28	70	19.11-28	153-57
3.20	46	10.30-35	64, 68	19.20	56-57
3.21	50	10.31	61	19.22	56
3.22-38	49	10.32	61	19.28	153
3.24	47	10.33	63, 149, 158, 160	19.28-44	153
3.29	47			19.29-40	153
3.31	47	10.34	70	19.38	48
4.1-13	48	10.35	68	19.41-44	153, 159
4.16-19	50	10.36	68	19.44	159
4.16-21	7	10.37	68	19.45	153
4.16-30	49	11.37-44	55	19.45-46	51
4.18-19	91, 124, 129	11.37-52	55	19.45-48	153
		11.42	93	20.20-26	48, 51
4.19	50	12.4	51	20.45–21.4	51
5.1-6	127	12.13-34	55	21.5-6	48
5.8	127	12.16-21	39	21.20	48
5.11	50	12.33	51	21.20-24	48
5.27-28	50	13.33-34	48	22.3-6	51
5.33-39	53	14.25-27	57	22.24-26	155
5.36-39	58	14.27	51	22.31-32	127
5.39	53	14.35	37	22.39–24.49	48
6.20	51	15.3-10	54	22.71	56
6.20-21	124, 129	15.3-32	58	23.1-25	46
6.27-36	51, 156	15.4-6	73	23.2	51
6.46-49	58	15.8-9	73	23.2-3	48
7.11-15	115	15.11-32	1, 3-4, 54,	23.11	57
				23.13-25	57

Luke (cont.)

23.28	48	7.54-60	57	15.23	116
23.36-38	48	7.58–9.22	57	15.43-44	114
23.47	119	10.44-48	160		
23.49	128	12.12	128	*2 Corinthians*	
23.53	56-57	13.32-33	130	4.10	118, 121
24.12	128	15.1-29	33	5.17-21	132
24.26	130	15.8	160	10–13	121
24.33-50	48	15.14	159-60	13.11	125
24.34	127, 128	16.14-15	128		
24.36-53	125	16.40	128	*Galatians*	
24.40	118	17.30-32	93	3.28	126-28
		18.18	128	6.17	118, 121
		18.26	128		
John				*Ephesians*	
1.1-18	118	*Romans*		1.19-22	130
3.14	130	1.3-4	130, 131	1.20-23	130
3.16	132	1.4	123	2.6	130
8.2-11	99	2.15	28	4.8-10	130
10.10	122	6.9	115		
11.38-44	115	8.11	123, 131-32	*Philippians*	
12.32	130			2.6-11	130
12.34	130	8.29	116	3.4-10	125
12.39-40	38	8.34	130	4.9	125
19.26-27	128	12.1	122		
20.1-10	128	14.1–15.13	33	*Colossians*	
20.14-18	128	14.9	130	1.15-20	130
20.19-23	125	15.33	125	1.18	116
20.20	118	16.1	128	2.8	130
20.26	125	16.3	128	2.10	130
21.1-14	127	16.5	128	3.1	130
21.15-17	127	16.7	128	4.15	128
21.18-22	127	16.20	125		
				1 Thessalonians	
Acts		*1 Corinthians*		1.10	130
1.1-2	130	2.2	118	5.23	125
1.1-8	160	3.9	115, 123		
1.4-26	48	11–14	118	*2 Thessalonians*	
1.16-20	51	11.20	118	3.16	125
1.18	149	11.23	118		
1.21-22	130	12.10	117	*1 Timothy*	
2.1-4	48	13	183	2.9-10	52
2.1-42	57	14.33	125	2.11-15	128
2.32-33	160	14.34-35	128	3.3	52
2.32-35	130	15	116	3.16	130
2.44-45	51	15.3-5	116	5.7-8	52
3.19-21	130	15.3-7	128	6.10	52
4.32-37	51	15.5	127		
5.1-11	52	15.5-7	128	*2 Timothy*	
5.30-32	130	15.20	116	3.2	52
				4.19	128

Titus
1.7-8	52

Hebrews
1.3	130
4.14	130
5.5	130
7.26	130
8.1	130
10.12	130
12.2	130
13.12-13	122
13.20	125

James
1.27	93
2.12-17	92

1 Peter
1.20-21	130
2.12	159
3.18-22	130
3.22	130

1 John
4.1	117

Revelation
1.5	116
4–5	188
12	188

INDEX OF AUTHORS

Adam, A.K.M. 97
Allison, D.C. 151
Andrews, D. 109-10
Anselm 86
Aristotle 27, 51, 165, 170-72
Astley, J. 89
Auerbach, E. 89

Bachand, S.C. 179
Bailey, K.E. 78-79, 86
Ballard, P. 184
Barth, K. 115, 116, 148
Bartholomew, C.G. 102
Beauvois, X. 185
Beavis, M.A. 40
Bell, D.M. 19-20
Bell, R.H. 8, 82, 131
Benatar, P. 183
Bentham, J. 166
Bevans, S.B. 184, 186
Birch, B.C. 11, 12
Bock, D.L. 153
Borg, M. 114-15, 131
Boyarin, D. 98-99
Bradstock, A. 8
Braithwaite, J. 76
Brueggemann, W. 47, 48, 50, 58, 97
Bruehler, B.B. 47
Bultmann, R. 114-15
Burge, G.M. 178-79
Burth, R.W. 166
Byrne, B. 50, 54, 55, 56

Campbell, C.L. 76
Carlson, M. 106
Caro, N. 185
Carroll, J.T. 152, 154
Carroll, M.D. 107
Carroll, R.P. 105
Carter, W. 150
Cavanaugh, W.T. 30, 33-34

Chaplin, J. 31
Chilton, B. 39-40, 42
Cicero 27
Conquergood, D. 104
Conzelmann, H. 51
Coomber, M.J.M. 6
Cronin, K. 23-24
Crossan, J.D. 6, 42, 99, 131

Daldry, S. 186-87
Daly, M. 138
Davis, T.C. 101
De Gruchy, J.W. 25
DeLoughrey, E.M. 67
Dempsey, C.J. 8
Descartes, R. 162
Dewey, J. 162
Dickinson, E. 99-100
Doan, W. 103, 108
Donahue, J.R. 7
Dowling, E.V. 57, 154
Duigan, J. 185
Dyer, K.D. 116
Dykstra, L. 6

Ebeling, G. 114-15
Ekblad, B. 59
Elliott, J.H. 45
Elvey, A. 54, 158
Esler, P.F. 89
Eubank, N. 152
Eusebius 27

Fiddes, P.S. 103
Fitzmyer, J.A. 47, 56
Floyd, M. 108
Forrester, D.B. 25, 34, 43, 176, 179, 186, 187
Foucault, M. 59, 60
Fowl, S.E. 75
Francis, L.J. 89

Index of Authors

Francis, M. 185
Francis, N. 185
Freyne, S. 46
Friedman, J. 182
Frith, S. 180

Gascoigne, R. 180
Giesen, B. 107
Giles, T. 103, 108
Gill, A. 129
Gill, R. 14
Girard, R. 72
Glavin, J. 103
Goffman, E. 102
Goheen, M.W. 102
Goodacre, M. 148-49
Gorringe, T. 11, 13
Gottwald, N.T. 48
Gowler, D.B. 52
Graham, E.L. 177, 184
Graves, M. 69
Green, J.B. 55, 56
Green, Laurie, 184, 189
Green, Lelia, 181
Grey, M. 134, 135, 141-42
Groening, M. 188

Hall, L. 186-87
Hancock, J.L. 187
Hanson, P.D. 13
Hart, D.B. 146
Hauerwas, S. 16-21
Heidegger, M. 162
Hengel, M. 118
Henry, C.F.H. 114
Herzog, W.R. 37, 45, 52-53, 151
Heyward, C. 141
Holladay, W.L. 105
Houston, W.J. 5-8
Hughes, P. 179
Hyde, C.R. 188

Ihimaera, W. 185
Indermaur, D. 172
Isasi-Díaz, A.M. 151

Jacobs, A. 94
Jefferson, T. 168
Jenkins, P. 9
Jeremias, J. 77-78, 156

Johns, G. 182
Johnson, L.T. 154
Johnstone, B.V. 125, 126
Jonsen, A. 162-63
Josephus 54-55, 56, 154
Joyce, P. 9

Kant, I. 165-66, 170
Keene, J. 183
Keller, T. 73, 78
Kim, S.C.H. 9, 13
Kinman, B. 153
Kitchen, M. 154, 155
Knight, P. 9
Kreider, A. 33

Lebacqz, K. 14-16
Leder, M. 188
Lehner, U.L. 60-61
Lenski, G. 50
Lerner, B.D. 92-93
Levinas, E. 72
Levy, S. 104
Lewis, M. 187
Litwak, K.D. 49
Longenecker, B.C. 68, 69
Lynch, G. 180-81

MacIntyre, A. 13, 15, 18, 163-64
Macquarrie, J. 125
Malina, B.J. 95-96
Mandela, N. 124
Manlove, C. 39
Maritain, J. 99
Marsh, C. 25-26
Marshall, C.D. vii-viii, 1-5, 7-8, 10, 13-14, 20-21, 45-46, 53-54, 57, 59, 60, 68, 69, 70, 73-77, 80-87, 88, 94, 95, 100, 135, 137, 139, 142-43, 145-60, 179-80, 183-84, 187, 188-89
Marshall, I.H. 11
Marty, M.E. 24
Mays, J.L. 7
McDonald, J.I.H. 39-40, 42
McKenzie, A.M. 63, 69
Menken, M.J.J. 158
Merz, A. 39
Milbank, J. 125
Mill, J.S. 166, 170

Moltmann, J. 26, 115, 116, 117, 121, 124, 129, 130-31
Morales, R. 183
Morgan, R. 9
Moule, C.F.D. 86-87
Myers, C. 75, 76
Myles, R.J. 182

Nadar, S. 59
Naked Samoans 188
Neville, D.J. 60, 62, 125
Niebuhr, R. 18
Northcott, M.S. 17
Nussbaum, M. 166

Oakman, D.E. 50, 55
O'Connell, T. 76
Opie, S. 179

Paddison, A. 17
Pannenberg, W. 114
Pearson, C. 13
Pelias, R.J. 102-103
Petersen, D.L. 104
Pickering, C. 179
Pidwell, H. 129
Pinker, S. 172
Pitts, J. 30
Pounder, S. 59-60, 63, 70
Prothero, S.R. 178-79
Punt, J. 45, 111
Putnam, N. 6

Redditt, P. 108
Reid, B.E. 137
Riddell, M. 108-109, 188
Riddell, R. 188
Rindge, M.S. 55
Robinette, B. 115, 121, 125, 131
Rohrbaugh, R.L. 95-96
Rojtman, B. 98
Rorty, R. 162, 172-74
Rousseau, J.-J. 27
Ryken, L. 39

Saldarini, A.J. 49
Sarisky, D. 17
Saunders, S.P. 76
Schaberg, J. 138

Schottroff, L. 151
Schüssler Fiorenza, E. 134, 135-37
Schwartz, R.M. 72
Schweizer, E. 86
Seccombe, D. 156
Segovia, F.F. 94-95
Sherwood, Y. 106, 107, 110, 113, 181-82
Sider, R.J. 169
Singer, P. 163-64, 166, 169
Smith, C. 178-79
Snodgrass, K. 36, 66, 69, 150, 151, 154, 156
Snyder Belousek, D.W. 151-52
Soskice, J.M. 138-39
Spencer, N. 179
Sprinkle, P.M. 70
Stacey, D. 106, 108
Stackhouse, M.L. 25, 26-30, 73-74, 176-77, 180
Stendahl, K. 10
Stern, D. 98
Stewart, W. 112
Stout, J. 17-18
Strong, K.H. 81
Suu Kyi, A.S. 185
Swartley, W.M. 8, 119, 152

Talbert, C.H. 47
Theissen, G. 12, 39
Thomson, H. 11, 24
Toulmin, S. 161-63
Tracy, D. 10
Trebilco, P. 188
Turner, V. 104

U2 185

Van Ness, D.W. 81
Veling, T.A. 186
Volf, M. 72, 75, 79-80, 85-86, 134, 140-41, 143-44
Von Balthasar, H.U. 102
Von Kalm, N. 112

Wachtel, B. 76
Wachtel, T. 76
Wallis, J. 26
Walton, H. 177, 184
Walzer, M. 166-69

Ward, F. 177, 184
Watson, F. 10
Weaver, A.E. 148
Weaver, D. 181
Weaver, J.D. 73
Weil, S. 131
Weldin, H. 179
Wierzbicka, A. 90
Williams, B. 164-65

Williams, R. 99
Wilmot, B.T. 31
Wittgenstein, L. 162
Wolterstorff, N. 17, 19-20, 123, 124
Wright, N.T. 114, 115, 121, 129, 131, 154

Yoder, J.H. 18, 30, 148

Zehr, H. 76